survive
&thri

MW01274958

The Seniors Guide to
Digital Photos, Music, Movies, and More!

Gateway™

Notices

The Seniors Guide to Digital Photos, Music, Movies, and More!

is published by
Gateway, Inc.
14303 Gateway Place
Poway, CA 92064

In the interest of continued product development, Gateway reserves the right to make improvements in this book at any time, without notice or obligation.

Microsoft screen shot(s) reprinted by permission from Microsoft Corporation.

Trademark Acknowledgments

Version 1.0

ISBN: 1-57729-300-2

DATE: 10-20-03

Printed in the United States of America

Distributed in the United States by Gateway, Inc.

Welcome

From the introduction to digital media in Chapter 1 through a look at future digital technology in Chapter 11, *The Seniors Guide to Digital Photos, Music, Movies, and More!* provides you with what you need to know to experience and enjoy today's digital environment. This product is designed to accommodate your learning style, and to make learning easy, interesting, and fun. You can stick to just the bare essentials or learn in greater depth by practicing key skills and applying your new knowledge. Our goal is to show you how technology can enhance your life, provide some fun, and open up new opportunities.

Classroom Learning

A hands-on training course on this subject is offered to enhance and improve your skills. Classes are held at Gateway® stores nationwide and additional fees may apply. Our classes are ideal solutions for people who want to become knowledgeable and get up and running in just three hours. They provide the opportunity to learn from one of our experienced and friendly instructors and practice important skills with other students. Call 888-852-4821 for enrollment information. One of our representatives will assist you in selecting a time and location that is convenient for you. If applicable, please have your Gateway customer ID and order number ready when you call. Please refer to your Gateway paperwork for this information.

More Than a Book

The Seniors Guide to Digital Photos, Music, Movies, and More! is more than a book; it is a blended learning system that also includes a CD-ROM and Internet presentations and activities. These tools all work together to provide a truly unique learning experience. The book presents technical information in visual, practical, and understandable ways. The CD-ROM extends the book by providing additional material on the subject. Continue learning online by logging on to www.LearnwithGateway.com. The enrollment key provided with this book gives you access to additional content and interactive exercises. This Web site allows us to keep you updated on rapidly changing information and new software releases.

Contents

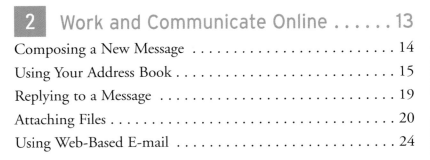

Contents

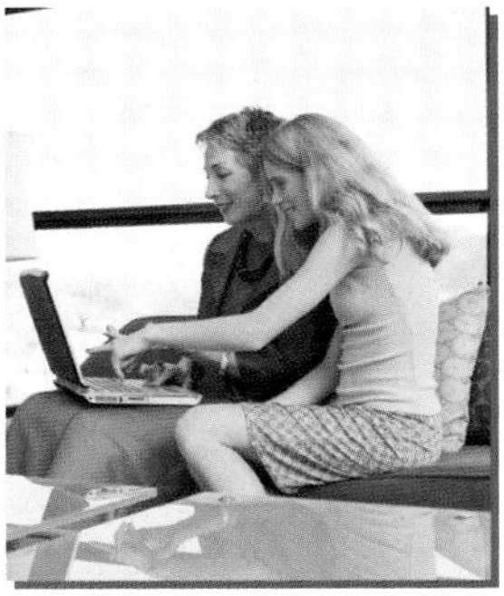

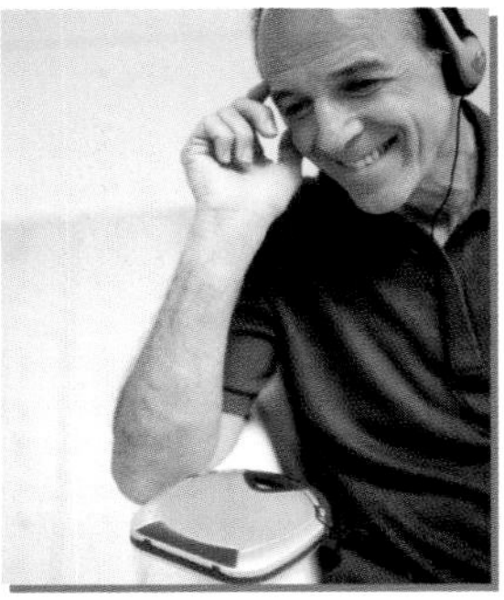

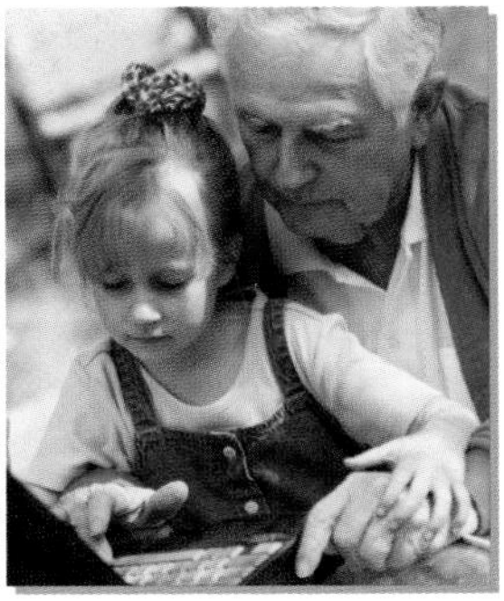

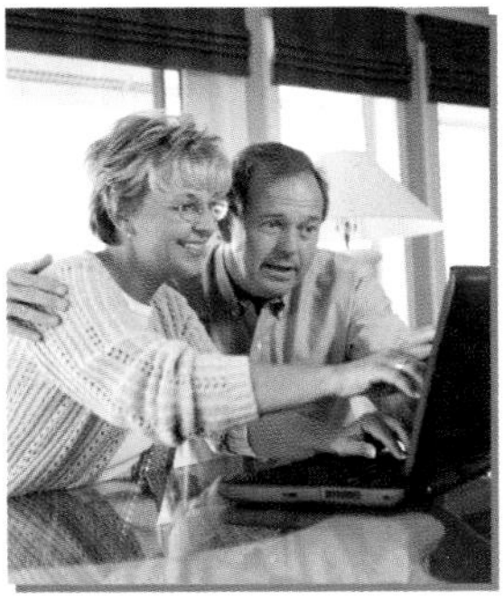

Contents

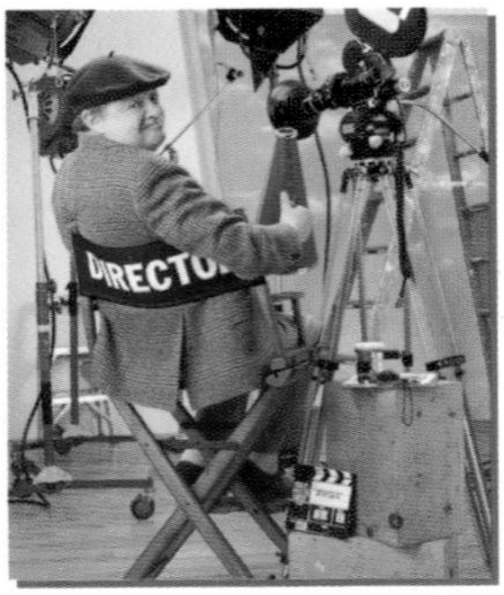
DIRECTO

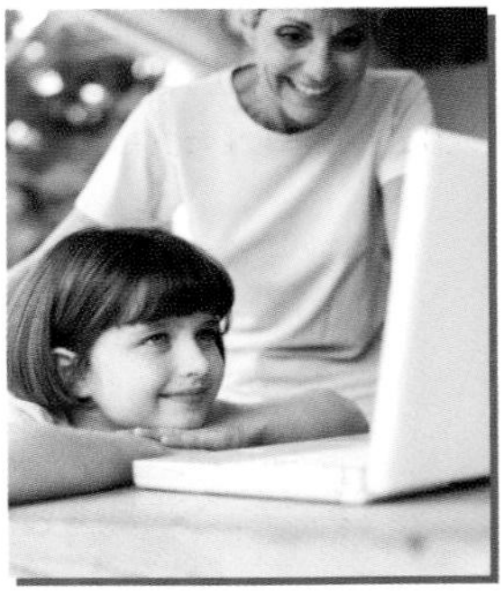

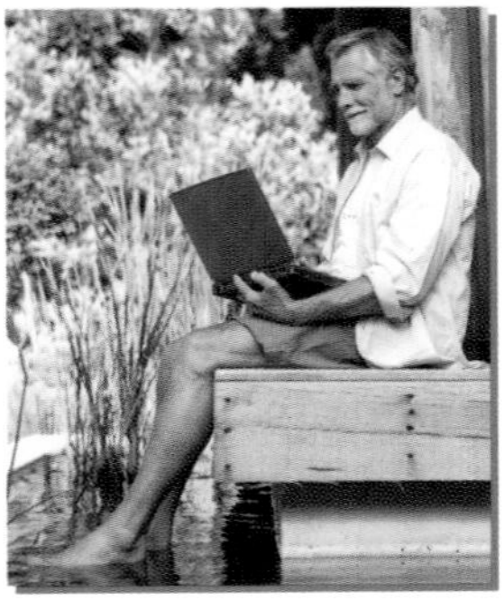

How to Use This Book

As you read the chapters in this book, you'll find pictures, figures, and diagrams to help reinforce key ideas and concepts. You'll also find pictures or icons that serve as cues to flag important information or provide directions. Here is a guide to help you understand the icons you'll encounter in this book:

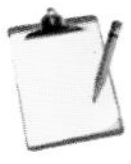

A Note identifies a relatively important piece of information that will make things easier or faster for you to accomplish on your PC. Most notes are worth reading, if only for the time and effort they can save you.

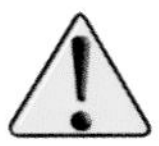

A Warning gives notice that an action on your PC can have serious consequences and could lead to loss of work, delays, or other problems. Our goal is not to scare you, but to steer you clear of potential sources of trouble.

You'll find sidebar information spread throughout the chapters, as follows:

More About . . .

The More About . . . information is supplementary, and is provided so you can learn more about making technology work for you. Feel free to skip this material during your first pass through the book, but please return to it later.

You can use each part of our innovative Survive & Thrive™ learning system by itself, or combine them for the ultimate learning experience.

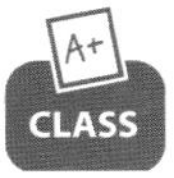
A+
CLASS

Come to a class at your local Gateway® store and enjoy a face-to-face learning experience with one of our expert instructors. Our state-of-the-art facilities and interactive approach are designed to build your new skills quickly – and let you have fun at the same time.

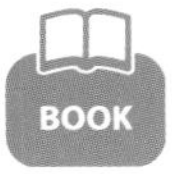
BOOK

Learn at your own pace using the enclosed full-color book. It combines high-tech images and concise overviews with simple instructions to create an ideal guide and ongoing reference.

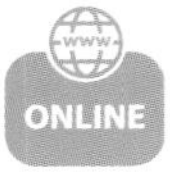
WWW
ONLINE

Enter the exciting world of online learning at www.LearnwithGateway.com, the Web site that delivers high-quality instruction the way you want it, when you want it.

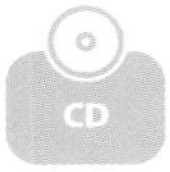
CD

Immerse yourself in the enclosed CD bonus materials. Simply insert the CD into your PC, and go. That's all it takes to launch the innovative extras we've included.

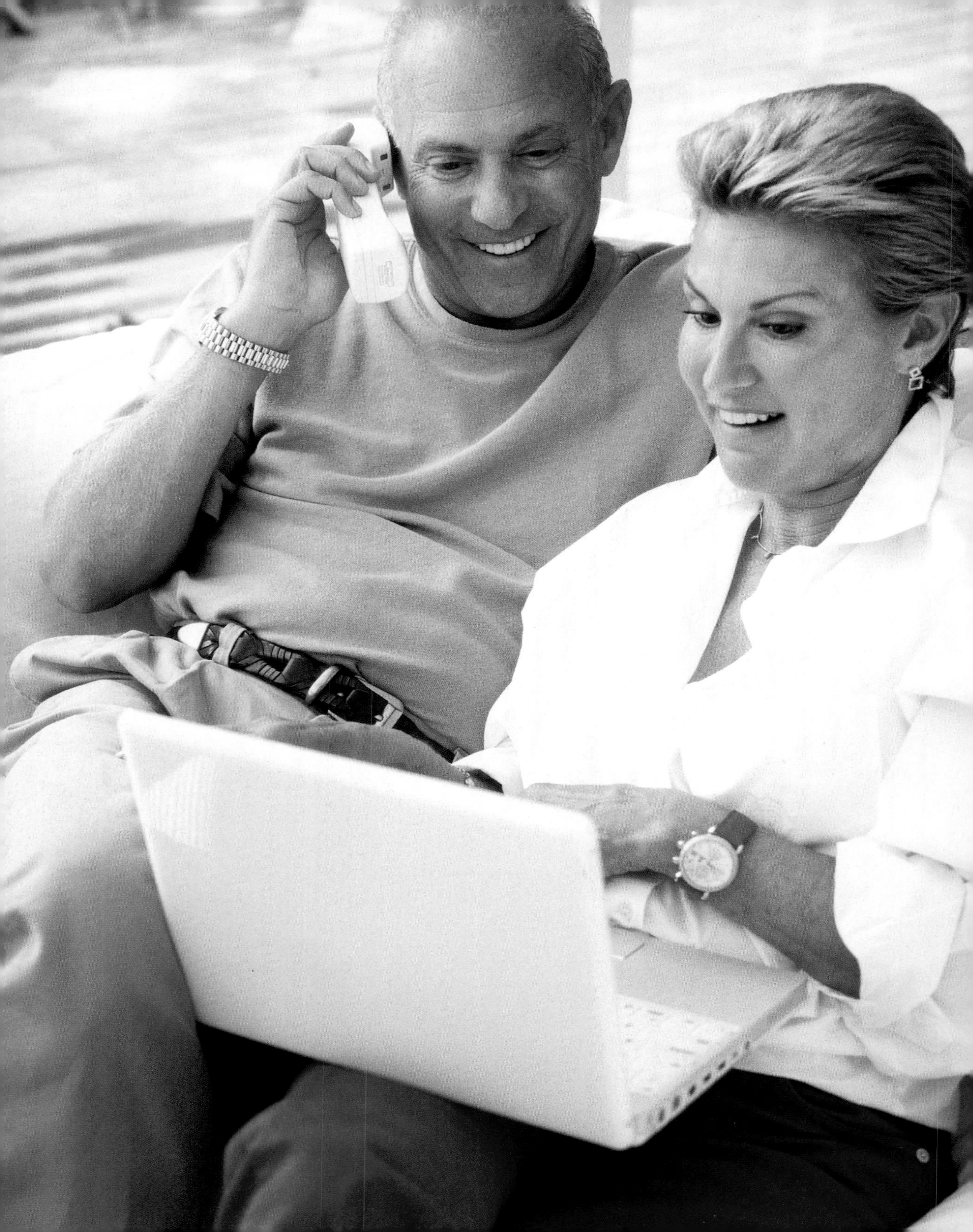

Welcome to Digital Media

The Digital Revolution

Here, at the beginning of the twenty-first century, the most dynamic cultural trend is the digital revolution. For many people, this simply means that there are a lot more computers in our lives; computers from which we shop to computers that use three-dimensional medical scanning techniques. We are living through an extraordinary moment in human history, and digital technology is expanding and evolving at an incredible rate.

Historians will look back on our times, the 40-year span between 1980 and 2020, and classify it among the handful of historical moments when humans reorganized their entire civilization around a new tool, a new idea.

What Does Digital Mean?

Many people think digital simply means using a computer; however, if you have ever listened to a CD, watched a DVD, talked on a cell phone, or used an ATM machine, you have experienced digital technology.

A digital device is any device that has at least one microprocessor in it. A microprocessor is a tiny electronic circuit that has a single job—to process simple mathematical or numerical calculations. Before sounds, pictures, or text can be stored and managed on a digital device, the object must first be converted to numbers called binary numbers, a process called digitization. The numbers, combinations of 0s and 1s that represent the text, sound, or image, are encoded as electronic pulses. These pulses are read by the various electronic components and then reassembled into a form the human senses can process, such as video, photographs, or sound.

What Does Analog Mean?

Prior to digital technology, electronic transmission was limited to analog technology, which conveys data as electronic signals of varying frequency or amplitude that are added to other waves of a given frequency. Virtually every audio recording before the advent of CDs was created using analog technology. Every sound you hear—be it music, words, or bumps in the night—travels to your ears in analog format. That is, the sounds are created in continuous waves, without any breaks. In fact, if you analyze a typical sound of any type using an oscilloscope (a tool used to measure sound and electronic waves), you can see the unbroken sound wave, like the one in Figure 1-1. The fluctuations in the wave correspond to the frequency and amplitude of the sound.

SAMPLES PER SECOND
GRADATIONS

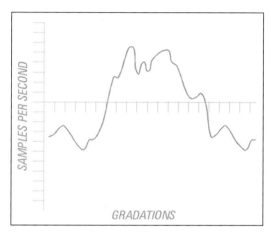

Figure 1-1 An analog sound wave, as measured with an oscilloscope, is continuous with no breaks and represents the fluctuations in air pressure that create sound.

Changes in light intensity and brightness and sound wave intensity and frequency are recorded along a band. Even subtle fluctuations are converted to changes in electrical voltage and recorded on tape or other analog medium. Similarly to sound, our eyes perceive light through waves. These waves are different sizes and vibrate at different speeds, or frequencies. Our eyes process changes in color and brightness very quickly; thus, we are able to see millions of color shades, and our brains process a huge array of combinations, distinguishing subtle changes in quality and character (see Figure 1-2).

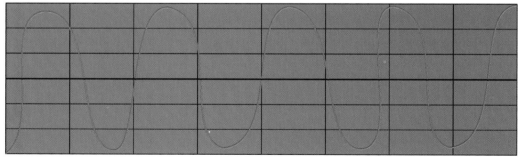

Figure 1-2 The world we perceive through our eyes is analog.

This book is designed to help you discover three popular digital elements: photography, music, and video.

Digital Photography

How many of us still have our old Brownie or Polaroid Swinger camera stuck away in a closet somewhere? Since Eastman Kodak popularized photography in February 1900 with its $1 Brownie camera, it was film that captured family stories, filling albums with glimpses of cherished moments that were passed lap to lap at reunions and parties. Even famed photographer Ansel Adams discovered his love for photography using a Kodak Brownie camera. My, how times have changed!

Today we use digital cameras, which are no longer an exotic toy only for computer enthusiasts, since 1 in every 4 American homes has a digital camera, and the number is quickly accelerating. Digital cameras far outsell their film counterparts.

The digital photography revolution goes way beyond capturing images on electronic sensors instead of a film's chemical mix. Digital photography provides new ways of keeping and sharing photos, and that is changing the business of photography and the role of photos in family ties and friendships.

Where photographs used to be relatively rare, we now take pictures by the thousands! We take fewer posed shots and capture more candid moments and pass those moments around more freely and faster than ever. Instead of developing prints and pasting them into albums, digital users often send their pictures by e-mail or even cell phone and display them onscreen.

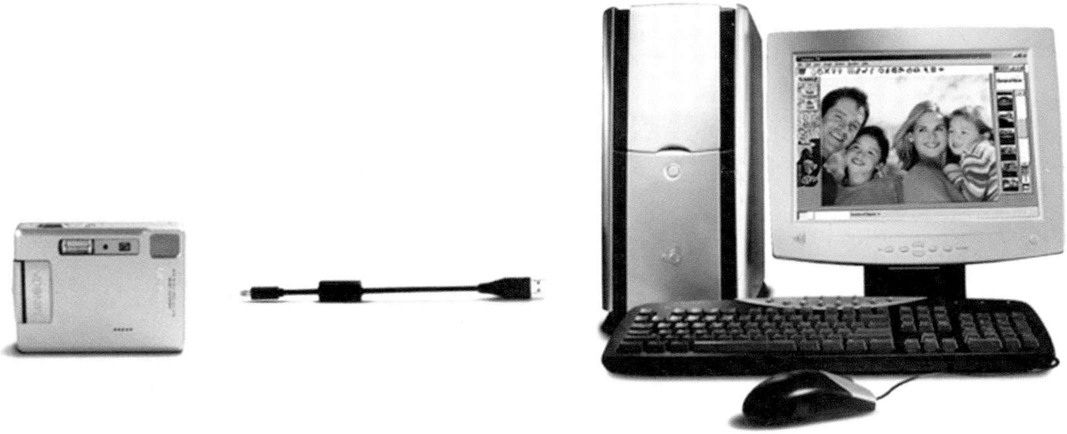

Additionally, those shots don't have to come from a high-end, expensive camera. Anyone can take a good picture with a digital camera. The difference is in you, the photographer, as you put your heart into taking the picture. But for those less-than-perfect shots, the computer provides assistance with image-editing software, such as Adobe® Photoshop® Elements or Microsoft® Picture It!®, which can help you edit and enhance the pictures you took.

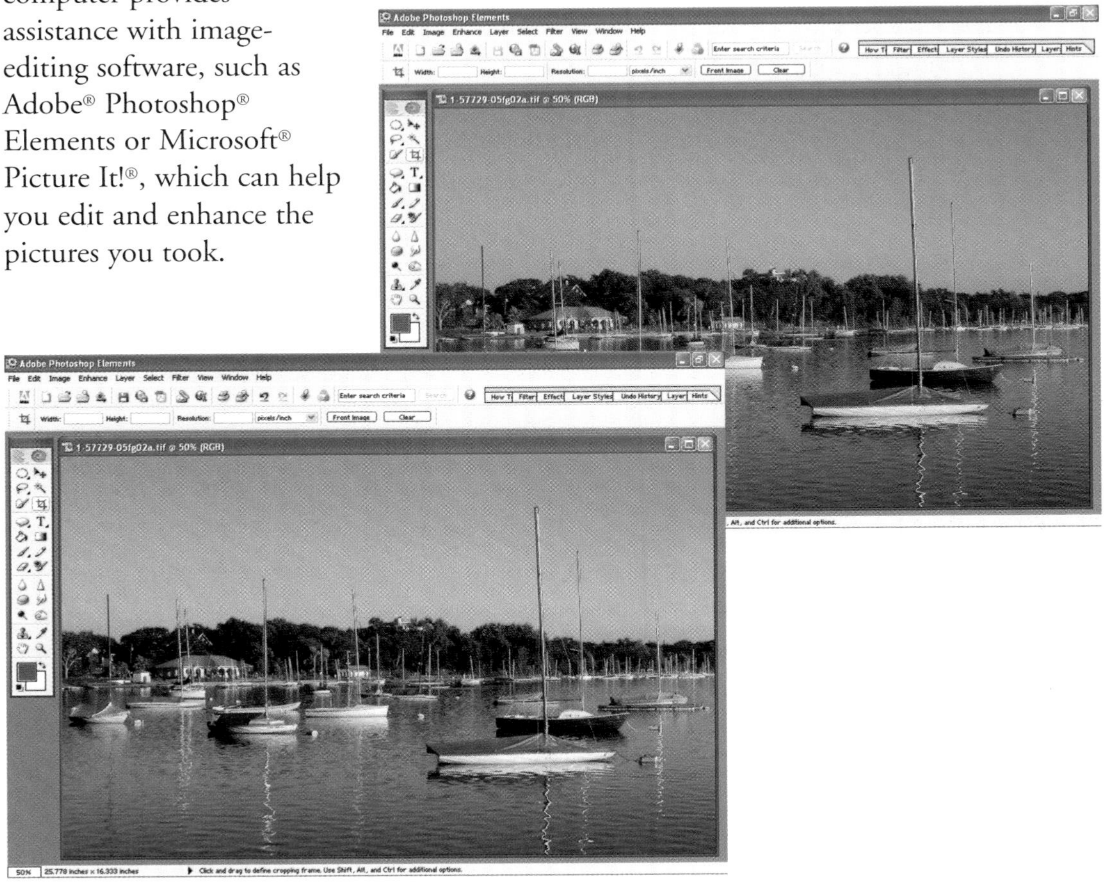
Adobe Photoshop Elements
1-57729-05fg02a.tif @ 50% (RGB)
Adobe Photoshop Elements
1-57729-05fg02a.tif @ 50% (RGB)

Digital Music

With the advent of digital music, your music experience is revolutionized. In recent years, innovations in hardware and software have brought the crystal-clear quality of digital music from your computer to your home or car stereo, or to anywhere you can bring a wallet-sized portable MP3 player. With searchable online resources boasting collections of hundreds of thousands of titles, all of your favorite music is only a few mouse clicks away. These days, you can even connect your PC to your home stereo for ultimate control of your music library, listen to digital music in the car, or even go jogging with your entire music collection. And if that doesn't get your blood pumping a little faster—if you recently bought a computer, much of this potential is already at your fingertips.

To fully appreciate the many advantages of digital music, let's take a brief journey through the history of sound recording, from early innovations in analog technology to the latest digital gadgets.

The Road to Digital Music

Listening to music wasn't always easy—like when the court musician charged a hefty fee to perform your favorite stuff, with no guarantees on sound quality. Broken lute strings and performance anxiety plagued the music industry for thousands of years. Sure, your banjo-wielding uncle would swing by now and then for an evening of knee-slappin' bluegrass, but for the most part, music was a scarce luxury.

It's not surprising that the introduction of Thomas Edison's phonograph in 1877 (see Figure 1-3) had a profound and widespread cultural impact. Capturing sound and playing it back was now reality, and soon we waltzed to phonographs in our parlors, huddled around radios for news and shows, and even slapped down our 45s and jived in leisure suits to disco renditions of classical symphonies. No, the revolution in sound recording was not without ailments. Along the way, we suffered through the incessant hissing and popping of vinyl records, the muddled sounds of our thrice-dubbed-over cassette tapes, and the annoying static of our favorite radio stations. Then, the digital music revolution erupts. Worn from abused ears, the haggard masses revolt and oust the evils of LPs and cassette tapes to behold the glory of near-perfect quality digital recording that's portable,

Figure 1-3 The earliest recordings were of very poor sound quality.

downloadable, and transferable. Our car radios now deliver digital-quality music from across the globe to the rural Midwest, and extensive music collections sit neatly organized in our back pockets.

In the last hundred years or so, recording technology's latest gizmos and media formats have brought vast improvements in sound quality and convenience, as well as a menagerie of new problems that needed to be resolved by the next generation of advancements in music technology.

A Timeline of Recorded Music

In 1877, Thomas Edison's phonograph used a horn, a sharp needle, and a rotating tin-foil cylinder to record sound. The horn collected the sound, whose waves caused the needle to vibrate up and down according to the pitch and volume of the sound, which in turn scratched grooves into the surface of the rotating foil cylinder. To play back a recorded sound, this process is simply reversed. Despite the impact of this revolutionary new technology, it had a long way to go. Not only were the recordings of poor sound quality, they could not be duplicated.

The use of tinfoil cylinders to record sound gave way to vinyl records that were mass-produced and distributed, but the essentials of Edison's sound-recording techniques remained the same: a vibrating needle is still used to cut patterns into a rotating medium. For decades, vinyl records remained the key medium for analog sound recordings, despite the developments of other analog sound-recording technologies.

In 1931, Fritz Pfleumer developed the tape recorder. This device used a microphone to convert sound waves into magnetic signals, which were then encoded on analog tape. This magnetic field on the tape could be "read" by a playback head, which generated electric energy that could be boosted in an amplifier and converted into sound by a speaker. Reel-to-reel analog tape averted the cracking and popping of a needle on vinyl, but players were expensive and still cumbersome to haul around.

On their 1966 model cars, Ford offered 8-track players as an option. Because of their ease of use and cleaner sound, this compact and portable medium became the format for portable and car audio recordings throughout most of the 1970s. Eight-track tapes became a popular item at truck stops and gas stations, but lugging your collection with you still took a couple of suitcases.

In the early 1980s, the era of digital audio began with the introduction of the CD player. Finally, supreme-quality recordings were available on 74-minute compact discs. Suddenly, vinyl and magnetic tape were abandoned as CD players appeared in home stereos and cars. Soon, digital quality sound followed wherever you could tote a small, battery-powered Sony® Discman. You could carry plenty of music in a case the size of this book, but recording your own compilations still required analog cassette tape.

Though developed at about the same time as the 8-track, cassette tapes began to appeal to consumers for their low price and smaller size, and they outsold the 8-track tape format by the late 1970s. Portable cassette tape players (or "boomboxes") and the smaller Walkman gave consumers the freedom to listen to music on-the-go. Now, the average hipster could record semi-respectable-sounding compilations of his favorite tunes to convenient analog cassettes.

In the late '90s and into the 21st century, digital music came into its own with astonishing growth in computer technology. CD-RW drives brought the power to record your own CDs and store entire music collections on a hard drive. Through the Internet, subscription services offered all your favorite music for download, and radio stations from around the world offered live streaming broadcasts, all of which can be connected and played through your home stereo. The PC became a complete digital audio entertainment system. The same music from your PC now is also played in your car stereo with transferable media, and pocket-sized portable devices are capable of storing thousands of songs. Digital technology also brings satellite radio, with broadcasts from around the world to anywhere you can drive your car.

PLAY/STOP
3-IN-1 DIGITAL
MUSIC PLAYER
Gateway

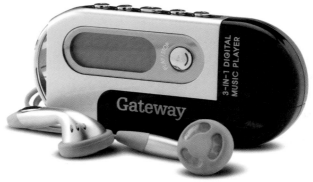

Digital Video

A third digital technology, digital video, combines the magic of moviemaking with the power and convenience of digital design. The entire world of movie creation is at your fingertips. With a digital camera, you can put your favorite uncle on top of Mount Everest, but with digital video, you can show him climbing to the top.

Consider that much of what you see on TV or at the movies, you can now do yourself. With a digital camcorder, a fairly powerful computer, and video-editing software like Pinnacle Studio or Ulead VideoStudio, you can create just about any visual effect or film you can imagine.

LTPS MONITOR
DV-S20
2.1 MEGA PIXELS

First you learn the basics of building a video project—from still images to using audio, using digital video creative tools, and how to transfer video from your camera to your computer. Then you learn what is involved when creating titles, transitions, voiceovers, and special effects like a pro. Let's take a moment to understand how your camcorder works, and how it differs from VHS and other predecessors.

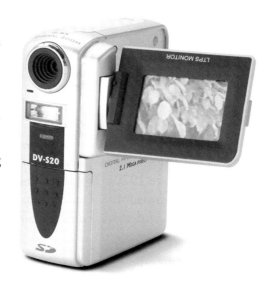

Why Digital Is Better

Fundamentally, a digital camcorder operates on similar principles as its predecessors. Light is focused through a lens and processes sound through a microphone. The main difference is how clear the footage looks, and how it is saved. Thus, digital video exceeds analog by producing a better image, facilitating easier storage, and also offers a few more advantages.

Your digital camcorder can use the same principles to create images that your computer does. Because of how they are made, digital images are generally clearer and have more definition than televised images.

Digital images are created using pixels, which are digital bits of color information combined to form a single "dot" in your computer image. On your PC, the greater the number of pixels per square inch, the higher-quality the image. This is called screen resolution, and a higher screen resolution (for example, 1024×768) translates into a better-looking image on your computer screen. Your digital camcorder, then, can produce movies with enough pixel data to look good on your computer screen or on DVD—not just on TV or saved onto old-fashioned analog VHS tape.

When it comes to storing your video, digital is a vast improvement over analog. Your movies are saved as binary code onto a digital medium, such as MiniDV tape or MiniDVD. As such, your movies can be transferred, edited, and copied without quality loss. Let's take a quick look at a variety of advantages of digital video over analog:

- Digital camcorders are much smaller than analog camcorders, such as VHS or 8mm.
- Digital videocassette tapes are smaller than their analog counterparts. (see Figure 1-4)

Canon
60
DVM-E60
Digital Videocassette
Mini DV
ME

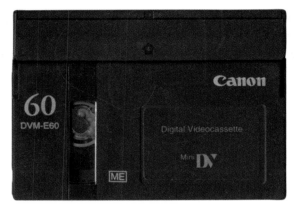

Figure 1-4 MiniDV cassettes are smaller than VHS or 8mm cassettes.

- Digital video is easy to transfer and edit on a PC and then transfer back to your camcorder on digital tape.
- Digital video incorporates CD and higher-than-CD-quality audio.
- Digital images are sharper and richer. Digital video uses color component information that transmits each primary color as a separate (component) value, rather than blending the color data into a single composite (combined) signal. Thus, colors are often more accurate than an analog video shot under similar conditions.
- It's very easy to save a "sync code" onto digital tape. Sync codes link the video to a soundtrack, other digital recorders, or professional time code devices that make it easy to correct frame errors.
- A digital video copy is as high-quality as the original. A digital copy of a digital copy also preserves original quality.

Your goal is not merely to shoot video, but to move it to your computer for customized editing and distribution. Video footage from your camcorder is like clay in your hands, ready to be shaped into a finished product.

Depending on how elaborate your plans are, shooting video footage may be only step one in the creative process. You can change and rearrange scene sequences as you like and eliminate parts you don't like. Movie segments can also be reused in your project. You can add titles or text to your footage, tighten your movie by cutting some of the boring or uninteresting frames, or even color-correct your movie, like brightening some of the dark parts and adding color depth to the segments that look washed out.

Now that you have learned some background about the evolution of some different types of digital media, it's time to explore each one more in-depth. This new digital media age is a very exciting time, and this book will show you how to take advantage of the benefits it offers.

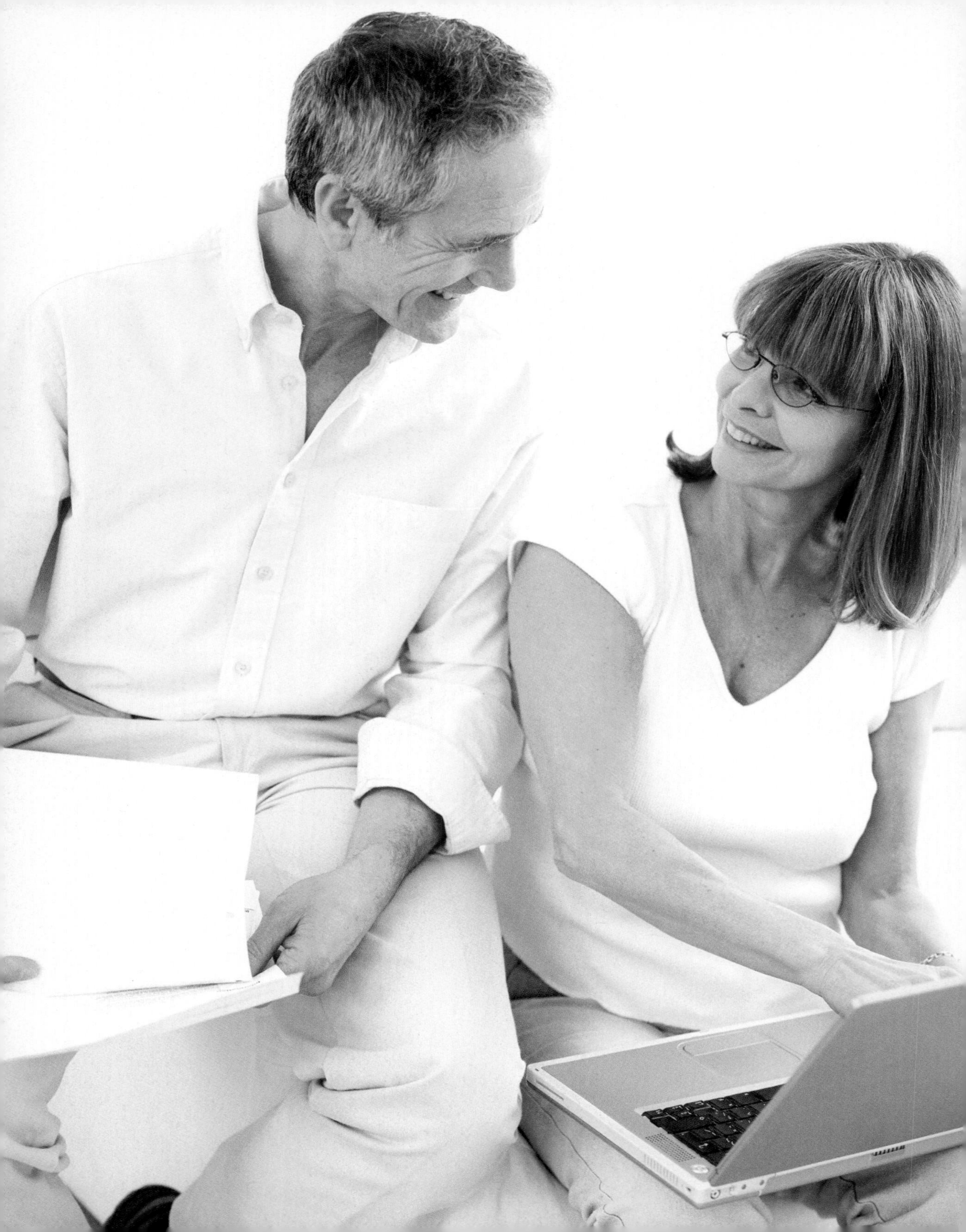

Work and Communicate Online

The intention of this book is to show you how to work with digital files such as music, photos, and video. As you accumulate some of these files, you'll probably want to share them with others. One easy method to share files is by using e-mail.

While e-mail doesn't allow us to really reach out and touch someone or hear the sound of their voice, it still provides a great avenue for exchanging messages with your family, friends, and business associates. One advantage of e-mail is you can send it anytime you want to, and the recipient can read and reply to it anytime they want to.

This chapter provides you with the basics you need to communicate via your e-mail. Although there are many e-mail client programs available, each program shares a set of common functions. We will use Outlook Express as an example, although the e-mail client program you use may require slightly different steps.

Composing a New Message

To create and send a message in Outlook Express, perform the following steps:

 If this is your first time using e-mail, compose and send a message to yourself by typing your own e-mail address in the To field in step 2. That way, you'll have an e-mail message you can use when you learn how to reply to and forward messages in the sections that follow.

1 In the Outlook Express window, click Create Mail. The New Message window opens.
2 In the To field, type the recipient's e-mail address. If the message is intended for multiple recipients, type each recipient's e-mail address, using commas or semicolons to separate them.

 In the section "Using Your Address Book" later in this chapter, you'll learn how to use your address book to enter the recipient's address in the To field, as well as how to use the Cc field.

3. In the Subject field, type a meaningful subject. For example, if you're writing to a friend to invite her to dinner, you might type **Dinner** in the Subject field.

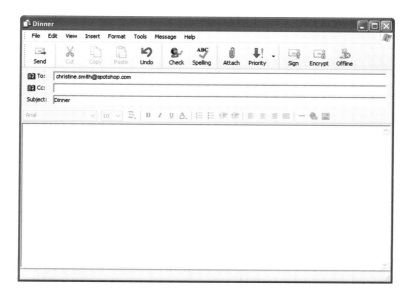

Dinner
File Edit View Insert Format Tools Message Help
Send Cut Copy Paste Undo Check Spelling Attach Priority Sign Encrypt Offline
To: christine.smith@spotshop.com
Cc:
Subject: Dinner
Arial
10

4. Type a salutation or greeting in the workspace, and then type your message and name.
5. Click the **Send** toolbar button in the New Message window. This will either send the message immediately (if you're online) or place it in your Outbox folder.

If you're connected to the Internet, you can click the **Send** button to send the message to your outgoing e-mail server. If you're not connected, the message is placed in the Outbox folder. Messages in this folder will be sent to your outgoing e-mail server the next time you connect to that server.

Using Your Address Book

You probably have an address book that you use to store friends' and family members' street addresses and telephone numbers. You'll want to do the same with their e-mail addresses. You can use your e-mail client's address book as your own personal contact list. Your address book retains all e-mail addresses you add to it, as well as other personal contact information you choose to add.

Addresses

There are several ways to add contacts to your address book, but the easiest is to do the following:

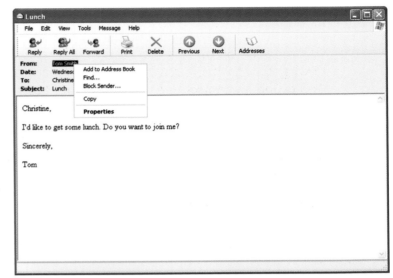

1. In the message list, right-click a message you've received from the person you want to add to your list of contacts. Alternatively, if the message is displayed in its own window, right-click the person's e-mail address in the From field.
2. A shortcut menu appears. Choose **Add Sender to Address Book** or **Add to Address Book**.

Lunch
File Edit View Tools Message Help
Reply
Reply All
Forward
Print
Delete
Previous
Next
Addresses
From:
Date:
To:
Subject:
Lunch
Add to Address Book
Find...
Block Sender...
Copy
Properties
Christine,
I'd like to get some lunch. Do you want to join me?
Sincerely,
Tom

Once an e-mail address is in your address book, you can quickly and easily add it to the To line of an outgoing e-mail message. Here's how:

1. Click the **To** button in the message window. The Select Recipients dialog box opens.

Select Recipients
Type name or select from list:
Find...
Main Identity's Contacts
Name
E-Mail A
Christine Smith
Debbie
Tom Smith
To: ->
Cc: ->
Bcc: ->
Message recipients:
Tom Smith
New Contact
Properties
OK
Cancel

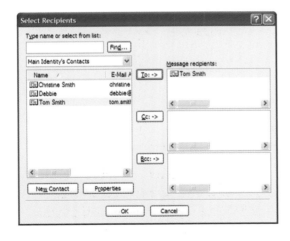

2. Click the recipient's name in the left column.
3. Click the **To:** button. The name now appears in the To field in the Message recipients column.
4. Click **OK**.

In step 3 you clicked the To: -> button, but notice that there are actually three buttons to choose from:

- **To:**. Click this button if the person you chose in step 2 is the message's primary recipient.
- **Cc:**. Click this button if the person you chose in step 2 should also receive the message but is not a primary recipient. For example, if you're e-mailing a co-worker about a project, you might add your boss's name to the Cc line of the e-mail message. (Cc stands for carbon copy.)
- **Bcc:**. Click this button if you want the person you selected in step 2 to receive the message but you don't want other recipients to know. (Bcc stands for blind carbon copy.)

2

To manage the contacts stored in your address book, click the **Addresses** button in the Outlook Express window or double-click a contact in the Contacts pane in the lower-left corner of the window. From the Address Book window that opens, you can create, edit, and delete contacts.

Address Book - Main Identity
File Edit View Tools Help
New Properties Delete Find People Print Action
Shared Contacts
Main Identity's Conta
Type name or select from list:
Name
E-Mail Address
Busin
Christine Smith
christine.smith@spotshop.com
Debbie
debbie@spotshop.com
Tom Smith
tom.smith@spotshop.com
3 items

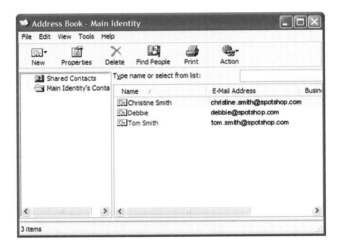

If you find yourself sending e-mail to the same group of people often, you may want to create an e-mail group to simplify the task. Instead of having to type in or select each person's e-mail address individually, you could just select the appropriate e-mail group. An e-mail group is a named collection of e-mail addresses, such as your co-workers or your softball team. After you define an e-mail group, you just type the group name in the To field to send the message to everyone in the group.

To create an e-mail group, perform the following steps:

1. Click the **Addresses** button in the main Outlook Express window.
2. The Address Book window opens. Click **File** and then choose **New Group**.
3. The Properties dialog box opens. On the Groups tab, type a name for this e-mail group, such as Softball or Friends.
4. Click **Select Members**. The Select Group Members dialog box opens.
5. Select each name and click **Select** to add it to the group. Continue to select people and click Select until you've chosen all the members for this group.

   Alternatively, you can hold down **CTRL** key while you click the names to select multiple names and then click the **Select** button.

6. Click **OK**. You're returned to the Properties window.

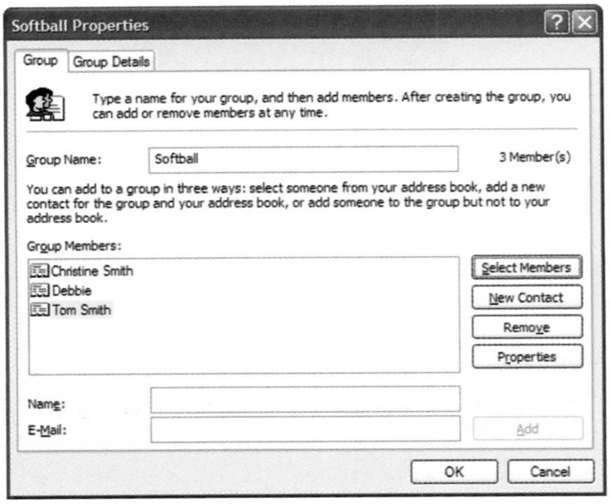

Softball Properties
Group
Group Details
Type a name for your group, and then add members. After creating the group, you can add or remove members at any time.
Group Name:
Softball
3 Member(s)
You can add to a group in three ways: select someone from your address book, add a new contact for the group and your address book, or add someone to the group but not to your address book.
Group Members:
Christine Smith
Debbie
Tom Smith
Select Members
New Contact
Remove
Properties
Name:
E-Mail:
Add
OK
Cancel

7. Review the list of group members. If you added someone's name by accident, select it and click **Remove**. If someone's name if missing, either use the Select Members button again or type the name and e-mail address in the fields at the bottom of the window and click **Add**. Click **OK**.

Now your group is listed as a separate contact in your address book.

Outlook Express, by default, automatically adds to your contact list (address book) the addresses of people you reply to. In other words, if you get a message from someone and click the **Reply** button, Outlook Express places that person's e-mail address into your contact list. This can be an excellent way to get e-mail addresses, but you may not always want an e-mail address in your contact list. You must either manually remove the unwanted contacts from your address book or disable this feature. To disable this feature, follow these steps:

1. Click **Tools**, and then choose **Options**.

Options
Spelling
Security
Connection
Maintenance
General
Read
Receipts
Send
Compose
Signatures
Sending
Save copy of sent messages in the 'Sent Items' folder
Send messages immediately
Automatically put people I reply to in my Address Book
Automatically complete e-mail addresses when composing
Include message in reply
Reply to messages using the format in which they were sent
International Settings...
Mail Sending Format
HTML
Plain Text
HTML Settings...
Plain Text Settings...
News Sending Format
HTML
Plain Text
HTML Settings...
Plain Text Settings...
OK
Cancel
Apply

2. The Options dialog box opens. Select the **Send** tab.
3. Clear the check box labeled **Automatically put people I reply to in my Address book**.
4. Click **OK**.

Replying to a Message

If someone sends a message to which you want to reply, you can easily do so. Click either

Reply

the **Reply** toolbar button (to respond only to the sender) or the **Reply All** toolbar button (to respond to the sender and any other people who received the original message). Your reply message will include the original message and any additional text you type.

To reply to a message from either the Outlook Express window or the message-display window, perform the following steps:

1. Select or open the message in your Inbox to which you want to reply. (We reply to the Welcome to Outlook Express 6 message in this exercise.)

To: Microsoft Outlook Express Team
Cc:
Subject: Re: Welcome to Outlook Express 6
Arial
10
----- Original Message -----
From: Microsoft Outlook Express Team
To: New Outlook Express User
Sent: Monday, February 25, 2002 10:21 AM
Subject: Welcome to Outlook Express 6
Outlook
Express
The solution for all your messaging needs

2. Click either the **Reply** button or the **Reply All** button. A new message window opens; notice that the To line lists all intended recipients and the original Subject line is prefixed with Re:. The message body includes a copy of the original message.

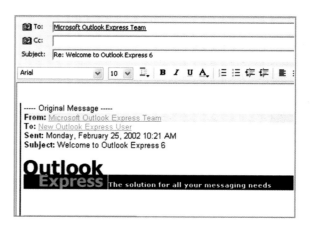

3. The blinking insertion point should already be in the upper-left corner of the message body area. If not, use your mouse to place it there, and then type your reply.
4. Click the **Send** toolbar button to send the message or place it in your Outbox.

Attaching Files

An attachment can be any type of file—such as a document, a picture, a music file, a compressed archive, or another e-mail message—that you send over the Internet along with your e-mail message. When the recipient receives the e-mail message with the attachment, a paper clip icon appears beside the message in the message list. This indicates that one or more attachments accompany the message.

To send an attachment, perform the following:

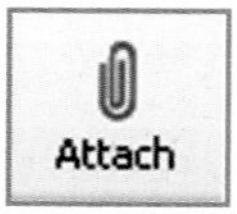

Attach

1. Click the paper clip button labeled **Attach** while creating a new e-mail message.
2. The Insert Attachment dialog box opens. Use this dialog box to locate and select the file you want to attach.
3. Click **Attach**. A new line labeled Attach appears just below the Subject line in the header. This field lists the name of the file attached to the message.

New Message
File Edit View Insert Format Tools Message Help
Send Cut Copy Paste Undo Check Spelling Attach Priority Sign Encrypt Offline
To:
Cc:
Subject:
Attach: My Trip to France.rtf (1.59 KB)
Arial 10
Christine Smith
christine.smith@spotshop.com

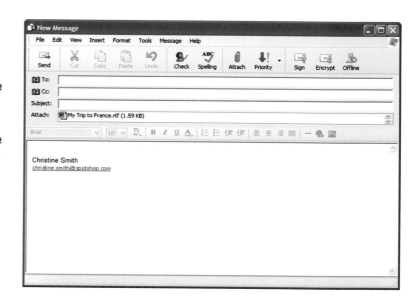

After the file is attached, you can either add other files as attachments or send the message (assuming you've added the recipient's e-mail address, the subject, and the body text).

Another way to add an attachment to an e-mail message is to drag and drop a file from the desktop, My Computer, or Windows Explorer onto the open New Message window. To make sure the file is attached to the message, drop it over the Attach line or the message body.

If you want to send someone an e-mail message as an attachment instead of just forwarding it, drag and drop the e-mail message from the Inbox to the open new e-mail message window. When the message you want to send is attached to the new outgoing message, it becomes a file with a .eml extension.

If you want to send someone a URL from your Favorites list, just drag and drop the Favorite from the Favorites list onto the open new e-mail message window. The URL will become a file with a .lnk extension.

When you receive e-mail with an attachment, you must first determine whether it's safe to open. You should always have anti-virus software installed and actively scanning your computer. Anti-virus software scans all incoming attachments for known viruses. With anti-virus software, most virus threats are automatically quarantined or deleted.

Here are some suggestions for determining whether an attachment is safe:

- ✦ If the message is from someone you don't know, delete it without opening the attachment.

- ✦ If the message is from someone you know but the message text is strange, includes bad grammar, or is otherwise not typical of text from that person, delete it without opening the attachment.

- ✦ If you receive multiple copies of the same e-mail from the same or different people, delete them without opening their attachments.

- ✦ If the subject line or the body text is blank, delete the message without opening the attachment.

- ✦ If you know the sender but were not expecting an attachment, contact the sender by e-mail or by phone to ask whether the attachment was intentional. If the sender doesn't know what you're talking about, delete it without opening the attachment.

If you think an attachment is safe because you were expecting it or because you verified that someone trustworthy sent it, go ahead and open it.

To open an attachment, follow these steps:

1. Double-click on the message to open it.

My trip to France
File Edit View Tools Message Help
Reply
Reply All
Forward
Print
Delete
Previous
Next
Addresses
From: Christine Smith
Date: Wednesday, April 03, 2002 8:51 PM
To: Christine Smith
Subject: My trip to France
Attach: My Trip to France.rtf (1.19 KB)
Christine Smith
christine.smith@spotshop.com

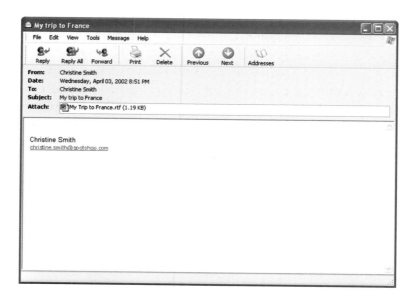

2. Double-click on the name of an item in the Attach field to open the item.

If you don't want to open an attachment, but you want to save it to your computer, do this:

1. Double-click on the message to open it.
2. Right-click over the name of an item in the Attach field and then choose **Save As**. The Save Attachment As dialog box opens.
3. Use this dialog box to indicate the folder in which you want to save the attachment, such as My Documents or Desktop. You can also change the file name to something more descriptive. Click **Save**.

The attachment is now a file on your computer. To locate the saved file, open My Computer or Windows Explorer to navigate to the file. If you saved it to the My Documents folder, click **My Documents** on the start menu. If you saved it to the Desktop, double-click its name on the Desktop.

If the attachment is an e-mail message, just double-click it to open and view the message. If the attachment is an Internet link, double-click it to open it in your Web browser.

Sharing Photos Online

Not since the development of the point-and-shoot camera has there been the interest in photography that we're witnessing today, and the Internet has played a huge part in its popularity. Whether you have a digital camera or a traditional film camera and a scanner (or you get your film printed onto photo CDs), you can now send photos to other people through e-mail or upload them to a photo-sharing Web site. Sending photos through e-mail is as easy as attaching the photo file to the e-mail message before you send it.

Several companies, such as MSN Photo (shown in Figure 2-1), offer digital picture sharing communities that you can use to share your favorite pictures with friends, family, or the whole world. You can usually define who you want to have access to your photos on these sites, making them ideal online photo albums.

MSN Photos - More Useful Everyday - Microsoft Internet Explorer
File Edit View Favorites Tools Help
Back Search Favorites Media
Address http://photos8.msn.com/home.aspx
Go Links
MSN Home | My MSN | Hotmail | Search | Shopping | Money | People & Chat | Sign In
msn
MSNBC HOT LIST Shop for your next barbeque now.
MSN Photos
by Picture It!
Home | My Photos | Gifts & Prints | Tips & Tricks
Help
Welcome
What would you like to do?
View my photos
Add photos
Share photos
Order prints
Edit, share, and get organized with MSN Photos Plus
Subscribe Now!
Gifts & Prints
Great back to school ideas
Mouse pads
T-shirts
Tote bags
Posters
Sponsored by:
Prints by Fuji
4x6 and more...
Tips & Tricks
Gear Tests & More
Feeling Like a Rookie Photographer
What I learned about myself using the new Nikon D2H.
Canon PowerShot ELPH SD10
Done
Internet

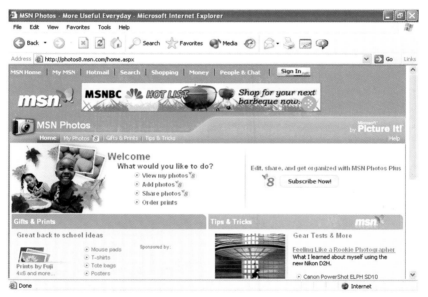

Figure 2-1 Share your photos with others through MSN Photo.

Each online photo sharing service works differently, so read the tutorial and help information to learn exactly how to upload pictures and share them with others using that specific service.

Using Web-Based E-mail

Having a local e-mail client installed on your computer isn't the only way to send and receive e-mail. Web-based e-mail is another popular tool. Web-based e-mail is accessed from a Web site instead of from software installed on your computer. When you use Web-based e-mail, you don't have to use the same computer all the time to send and receive e-mail. Instead, you can use any computer with Internet access and a Web browser.

Several companies offer Web-based e-mail, including Yahoo! Mail and MSN Hotmail. It's very easy to sign up for a Web-based e-mail account, and they're usually free, although if you want more storage space or access to additional features, additional fees may apply.

Yahoo! Mail - The best free web-based email! - Microsoft Internet Explorer
File Edit View Favorites Tools Help
Back Search Favorites Media
Address http://mail.yahoo.com/
Go Links
YAHOO! Mail
Yahoo! - Help
Welcome to Yahoo! Mail
You must sign in to read or send mail.
New to Yahoo!?
Get Yahoo! Mail with new more powerful SpamGuard, some of the best spam protection available.
And it's just one of the many great features of Yahoo! Mail:
Free email
Free 4MB storage - up to twice as much as other free email providers!
Access from virtually anywhere, anytime
Address Book, Calendar, and much more!
Sign up now
Learn more...
New and Improved!
Existing Yahoo! users
Enter your ID and password to sign in
Yahoo! ID:
Password:
Remember my ID on this computer
Sign In
Mode: Standard | Secure
Sign-in help Forgot your password?
Get the email address you've always wanted with Personal Address
Done
Internet

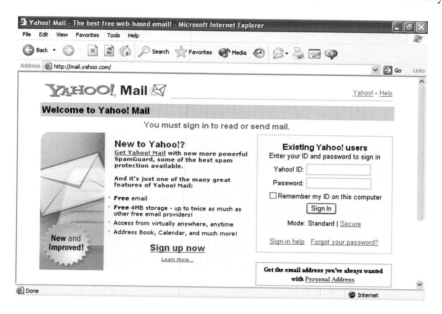

Your Web-based e-mail account will have a different e-mail address than the one assigned to you by your original ISP or online service. Each Web-based e-mail system has a unique e-mail address. For example, a Yahoo! e-mail address ends in @yahoo.com and an MSN Hotmail e-mail address ends in @hotmail.com.

Web-based e-mail gives you access to all the same functions you can perform with locally installed e-mail client software. This includes composing and sending new messages, reading messages, replying to and forwarding messages, filing messages, and sending and receiving attachments.

If you travel often or are always using different computers to connect to the Internet, Web-based e-mail may be the solution for you. Your e-mail is always accessible to you, no matter where you log on.

2

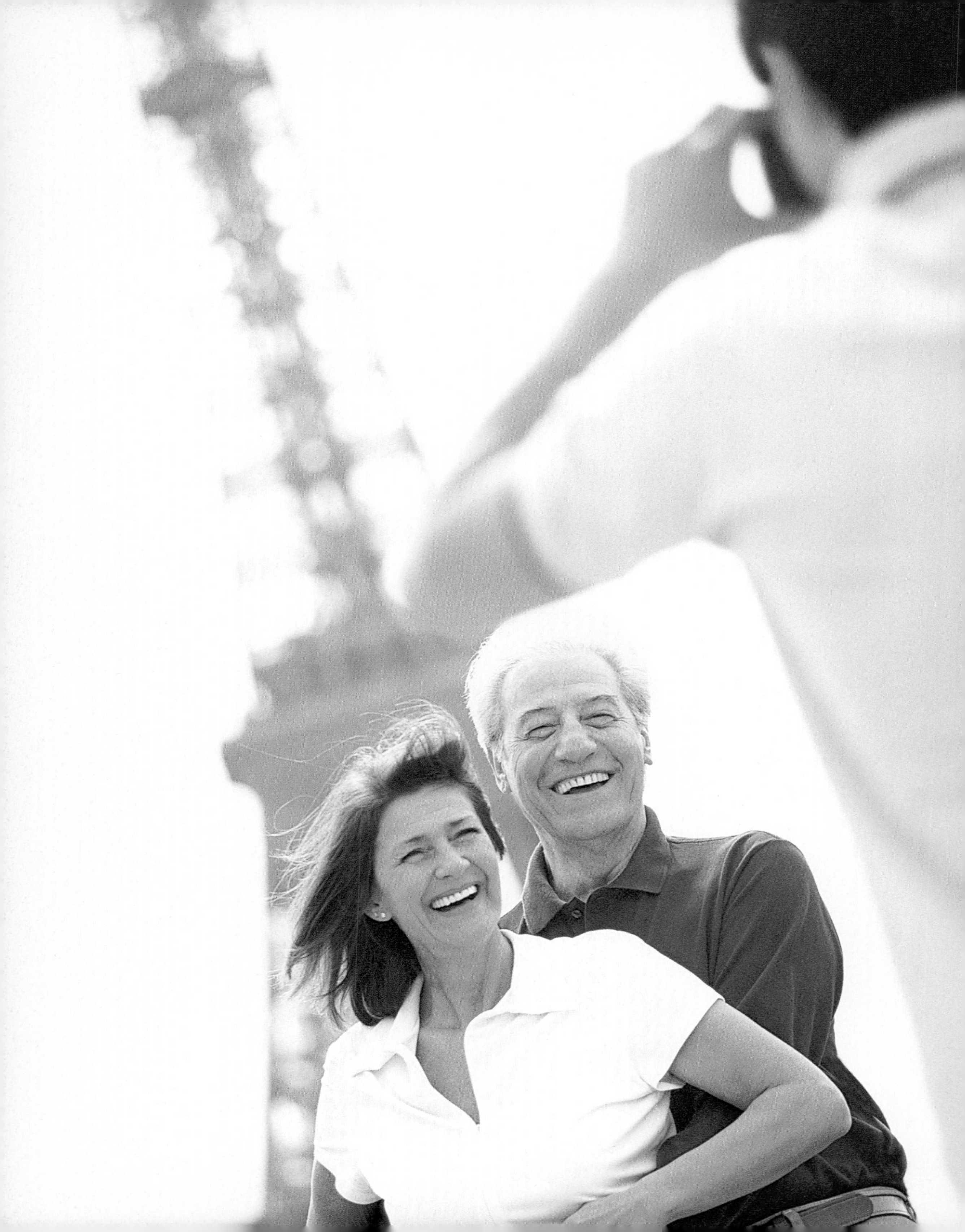

CHAPTER **3**

Discover Digital Photography

Welcome to the exciting world of digital photography! You are about to learn how the digital age has revolutionized the way you capture, view, organize, edit, and share images. Rolls of film, boxes full of negatives, and a stack of photo albums are no longer required to create memories, and that is just the beginning. Improved personal computer technology, the Internet, scanning devices, and digital cameras enable you to stretch the boundaries of traditional photography and do remarkable things that were impossible just a few years ago. Today you can view pictures on your camera's built-in monitor, remove pesky red-eye, print snapshots at home, and do much more. Many software packages provide simple tools that turn static photographic images into exciting works of art. In fact, after you realize the convenience provided by digital cameras and the incredible versatility of digital images, you might even decide to put away your film-based camera for good!

This chapter introduces you to the fundamentals of digital photography. In addition to learning what the phrase "digital photography" means, you'll discover all the fun things you can do with your digital images. You'll learn about the many sources of digital images, including pictures taken with a digital camera, scanned images, and other sources. You'll also discover the many advantages of working with digital images. With digital photography, you can e-mail photos, create a snapshot book, order prints online, and more. You'll also explore the various controls and buttons on your digital camera and discover what each one does while you gain an understanding of basic photography principles.

Traditional vs. Digital Photography: What's the Difference?

The easiest way to describe digital photography is to compare a digital camera to a traditional camera. In fact, digital cameras are quite similar to their film-based counterparts, given that they include such familiar features as lenses, flashes, and shutters. So what's the difference? The obvious one is that digital cameras don't use film to record the scene you are photographing. Instead, they use sensors or arrays called CCDs (Charge-Coupled Devices) that convert light information from the photographed scene into a digital image.

Digital images are made up of individual picture elements called pixels. A pixel is a tiny dot of light that is the basic unit of images on a computer screen or in a digital image.

These pixels combine to make the picture, and they are stored together as a digital file. Digital images can come from many sources, one of which is from digital cameras.

A digital camera works a lot like your computer; it converts the image you are photographing into a digital file. You can then use this digital file in many ways. (See "Taking Advantage of Digital Images" later in this chapter.)

The digital image is stored as a file in your camera's memory or on a memory card (a removable disk that is similar to a computer floppy disk, but smaller). Then you can transfer the image to your computer. The number of pictures you can store will vary depending on the amount of available memory in your camera or on a memory card, as well as the resolution of the images and the level of compression. Since higher-resolution images contain more pixels, the files containing the images are larger and thus consume more space in your camera's memory or on your memory card.

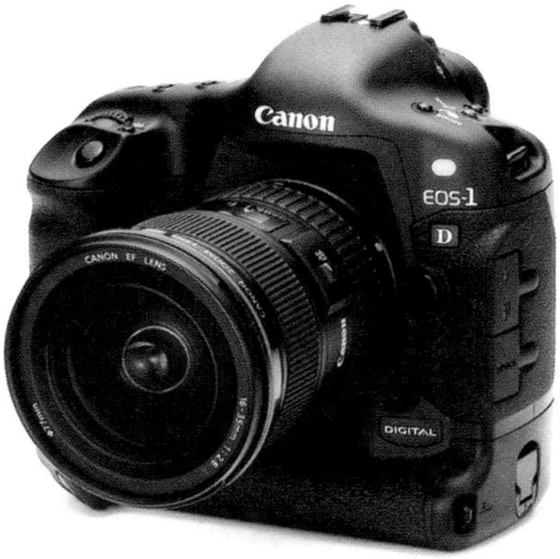
Canon
EOS-1
D
DIGITAL

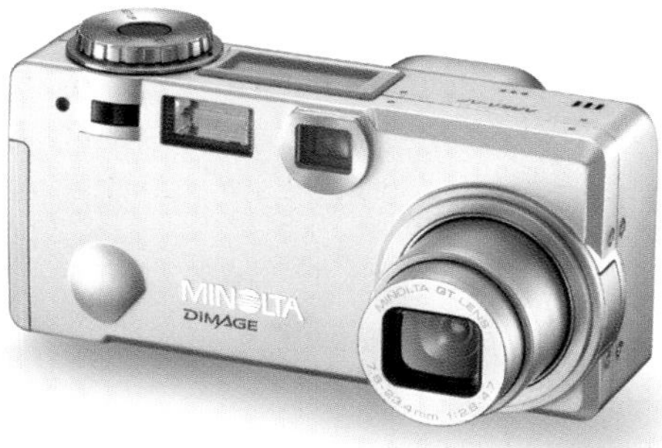
MINOLTA
DiMAGE

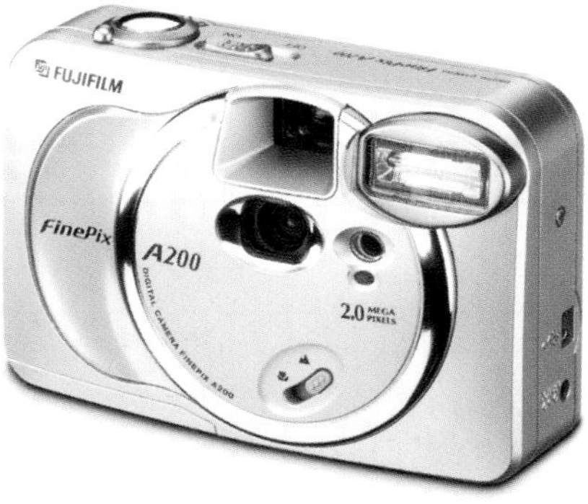
FUJIFILM
FinePix
A200
2.0 MEGA PIXELS

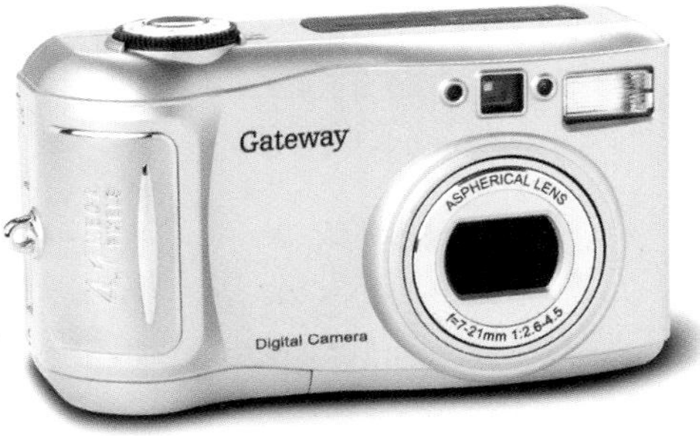
Gateway
ASPHERICAL LENS
f=7-21mm 1:2.6-4.5
Digital Camera

The quality of a picture, called its resolution, is a measure of the number of pixels per inch. The more pixels per inch an image contains, the better the image quality. Minimizing the file size is called compression. Electronic images are compressed automatically so more will fit into the camera's storage device. The higher the compression, the smaller the file sizes; however, at higher compression rates detail is lost from the image.

Once you've filled the memory in your digital camera or on your memory card, you simply copy the images from your camera to your computer in a process called downloading. Then you can delete the images from the camera's memory or memory card, and voila, you're ready to take more pictures. You never need to pay for film again!

 Throughout this book, when you see the phrase "digital image," it refers to pictures or illustrations from any one of these sources, not just pictures taken with a digital camera. Pictures taken with a digital camera are also referred to as digital pictures or photographs.

Why Go Digital?

Now that you have a good idea of what digital photography is, you can add up all the advantages. Doing so can help you evaluate whether it's worth purchasing a digital camera. If you already have one, you can get a better understanding of how this new piece of equipment, and the electronic images it produces, can make photography easier and more versatile. The following list details some key advantages of using a digital camera, and the benefits of working with electronic image files instead of traditional prints.

◆ **Preview pictures immediately.** On a digital camera, you can preview your pictures immediately after you take them. If you've ever picked up a set of pictures at your photo shop, eagerly anticipating your capture of that once-in-a-lifetime moment on film, only to discover blurry prints of what might be your daughter dancing at her wedding, you'll appreciate this feature. Most digital cameras feature a color LCD (Liquid Crystal Display) monitor on the back that displays each picture immediately after you take it. If the picture isn't good, you can discard it and take it again.

◆ **No film or negatives required.** Take as many pictures as you want. You can also use your digital camera's controls to delete unwanted pictures at any time. Because your pictures are stored in a digital format in the camera's memory or on the camera's memory card, you can copy the pictures to your computer, clear them from memory, and take new shots. Because you can store and organize all of your images on your computer, you never have to hunt through negatives to produce additional prints.

◆ **Organize photos on your computer.** You can use a simple connection to transfer digital images from your camera directly to your computer. Then, you can take advantage of all the helpful benefits your computer provides to manage them. You can organize images in folders, delete or rename them, or search for image files using the Microsoft® Windows® search function. You can also use other software programs to create albums and slideshows easily.

✦ **Share digital images online.** You can e-mail photos of your new puppy to your sister in Antarctica, or you can include photos on your Web page or in a document. Professional photographers especially benefit from this feature because they can quickly broadcast their work to their customers.

✦ **Edit your own photographs.** If you find some minor flaws in a photograph or you need to resize it, it's no problem. You can choose from a variety of software programs, such as Adobe® Photoshop® Elements or Microsoft Picture It!®, that are designed specifically to edit and enhance digital images. Crop images to a smaller size, remove red-eye, apply color effects, and perform other functions to improve your photos. In addition, you can use the software tools to repair traditional photographs after you have scanned and saved them on your computer, and you can use a variety of effects to generate interesting manipulations of the original image.

✦ **Choose from additional printing options.** Because you have the ability to preview an image, you can print only the desired images using your own printer or a special photo-quality printer. Alternatively, you can order prints online. If you are loyal to your local photo shop, you can take your images there and have them create the prints. More options ensure that you get what you want when you want it. Also, the ability to generate traditional prints from digital images gives you additional control over your photographs. If you commonly order double prints when you develop film from your traditional camera, you inevitably end up with 20 extra pictures you don't really need. With a digital camera, you can select not just the quantity of each print, but also the size, including 5×7s, wallets, and others.

✦ **Scan existing photographs.** Have a collection of photos that you want to store on your computer? You can scan these photos and convert them into digital images. Your old photos can now benefit from all of the same advantages as photos taken with a digital camera.

✦ **It's easy to learn and economical.** Once you learn the features of your digital camera and the basics for managing images, you have the ability to do almost anything you can do with a conventional camera. Because you never have to purchase film, the more pictures you take, the more you benefit from going digital. In addition, prices for digital cameras and scanners have gotten so low that buying one of these devices is more affordable than ever.

3

Discovering Many Sources of Digital Images

Using today's technology, there are many ways to acquire, store, and transfer digital images. Therefore, you can find them everywhere. Just do a quick Internet search, and you'll find thousands of images of just about anything imaginable. Of course, most important is that creating your own digital images is easier than ever before. Using a digital camera is the most common way to produce original digital photos. You'll learn more about taking good pictures using a digital camera later in this chapter.

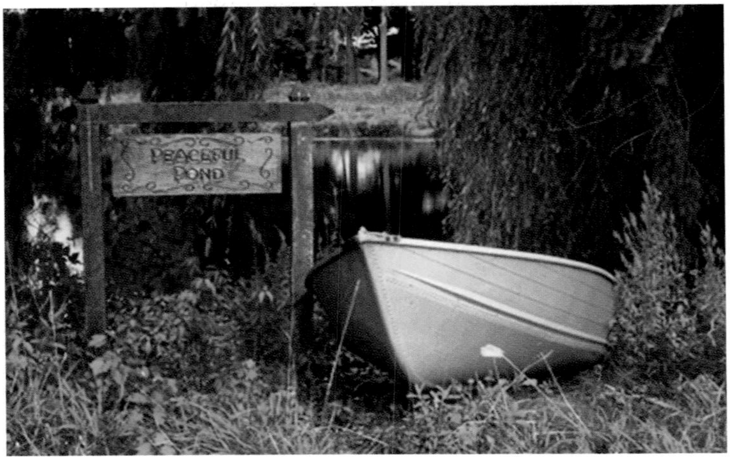
PEACEFUL
POND

But using a digital camera isn't the only way to create digital images. In fact, there are several other ways to obtain digital pictures, including scanners, online images, and more. The following list gives you a good idea of the many sources of digital images:

✦ **Using a scanner.** Suppose you're planning to attend a family reunion and you want to create a scrapbook of old family photographs for the other attendees. Instead of paying to have the images reprinted at a photo shop, you can use a scanner, like the one shown in Figure 3-1, to copy the images and save them as files on your computer. Then you can print the images using your own printer.

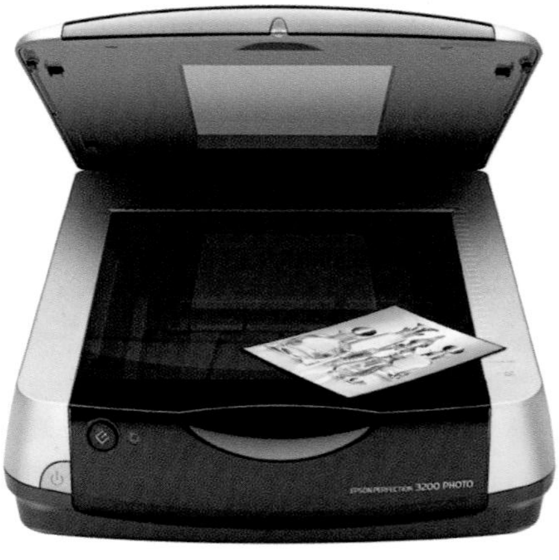

Figure 3-1 You can use a scanner to transfer traditional prints to your computer.

- **Using a CD.** Many photo developers will place your images on CD when you develop film. You can open these files from the CD and work with them on your computer.

All new computers come with a recordable CD or DVD drive which you can use to record (or burn) your own CDs or DVDs. Because photo files can be quite large, storing them on CDs is a great way to keep your photos organized.

- **Using the Web.** In addition to placing your images on CD, many photo developers will place your photos on a Web site from which you can view, download, share, and print them. Alternatively, some Web sites offer clip-art illustrations or photographs that you can download and use, as shown in Figure 3-2.

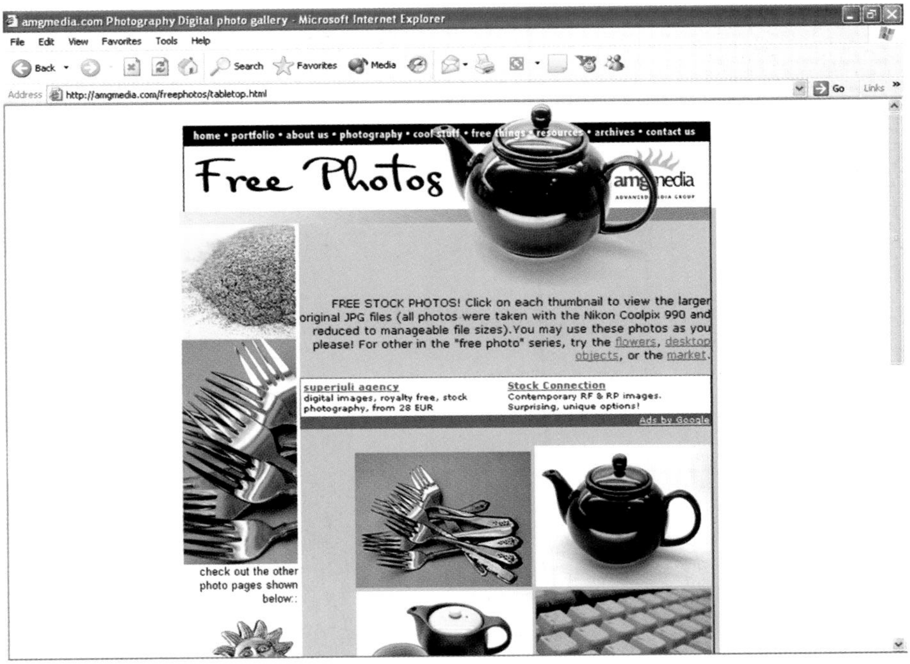
amgmedia.com Photography Digital photo gallery - Microsoft Internet Explorer
File Edit View Favorites Tools Help
Back Search Favorites Media
Address http://amgmedia.com/freephotos/tabletop.html
Go Links
home • portfolio • about us • photography • cool stuff • free things • resources • archives • contact us
Free Photos
amgmedia
FREE STOCK PHOTOS! Click on each thumbnail to view the larger original JPG files (all photos were taken with the Nikon Coolpix 990 and reduced to manageable file sizes).You may use these photos as you please! For other in the "free photo" series, try the flowers, desktop objects, or the market.
superjuli agency
digital images, royalty free, stock photography, from 28 EUR
Stock Connection
Contemporary RF & RP images. Surprising, unique options!
Ads by Google
check out the other photo pages shown below::

Figure 3-2 You can find many sources of digital images online.

Some images are copyrighted. Just because you find a picture you like on the Web does not mean you have permission to use that image as you see fit. Many clip-art and photo sites spell out what you can and cannot do with their images.

Taking Advantage of Digital Images

Because digital cameras are easy to use and provide immediate results and endless editing capabilities, professional photographers were among the first to welcome digital photography. But even though they were among the first, they aren't the only ones who've found uses for digital cameras. Now you'll explore some examples of using digital photography for your business or family photographs and documents.

In addition to highlighting some uses for digital images, this section will also discuss some of the techniques for enhancing or repairing pictures using special photo-editing software.

Photo Possibilities

Digital photos are easy to transfer to your computer, and you can use them in countless different ways. Here are just a few ideas to get your creative wheels turning for your own photographic works.

- **Slideshows and albums.** You can combine your pictures into a slideshow or use a picture album on your computer to organize your photos. You can also burn these slideshows and albums to a CD or DVD and even view them on your home entertainment center using a special type of DVD player.

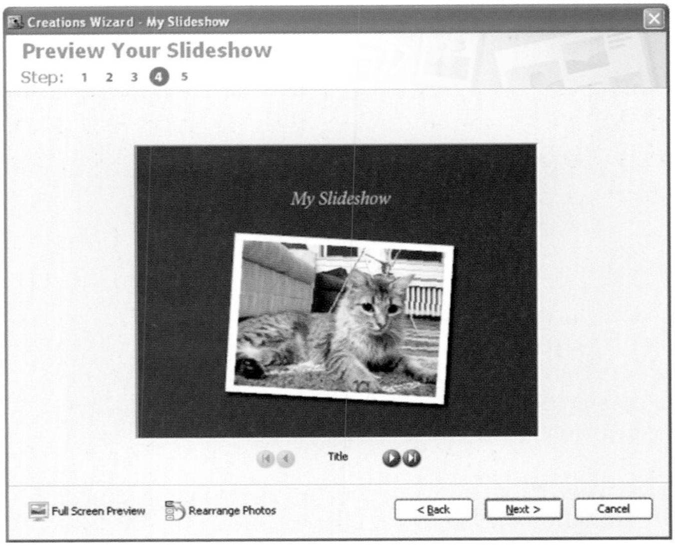
Creations Wizard - My Slideshow
Preview Your Slideshow
Step: 1 2 3 4 5
My Slideshow
Title
Full Screen Preview
Rearrange Photos
< Back
Next >
Cancel

- **Web pages.** Liven up your personal or business Web page with photographs. For example, you can showcase your best-selling products on your business site or include pictures of your pet on your personal page. If online auctions are your passion, you'll want to include one or more good pictures of the item you want to sell. Your imagination and the possibilities offered by the Web are limitless!

Microsoft FrontPage - C:\Documents and Settings\KMiller\My Documents\My Webs\index.htm
File Edit View Insert Format Tools Table Frames Window Help
Normal
Times New Roman
4 (14 pt)
Views
index.htm
Page
Folders
Reports
Navigation
Hyperlinks
Tasks
Dan's Custom Ceramics
These one-of-a kind pieces are now showing at my real as well as online studio. Choose from hundreds of custom made items, or commission your own. I will take orders for mugs, lamps, bowls, plates, you name it. Flower pots are also a popular item. Please email me with any questions you have about my truly unique collection.
Dan Barrow Ceramics
Normal
HTML
Preview
43 seconds over 28.8

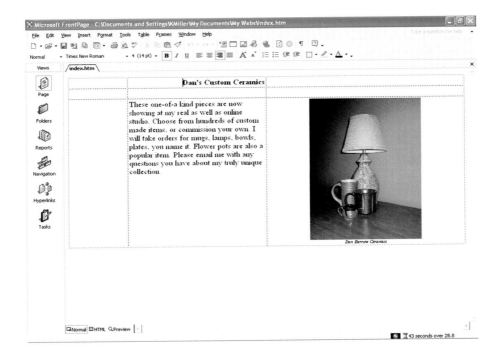

- **Online auctions.** If you ever list items for sale on an online auction site, a digital camera can be a great investment. In a matter of minutes, you can take a picture of the item you are selling and post it to your page. Showcasing your item with a digital image attracts potential buyers who generally want to see the condition of an item before placing their bids.

- **Family scrapbooks.** Scrapbooking is one of the latest crazes. Just visit any craft store and you'll see aisles and aisles of supplies. With a scanner or camera (or both), you can organize your photographic memories so they tell a story. Using digital images, you can create a highlight book of your grandchildren's school years or surprise your children with a family history that includes scanned photographs of their storied past.

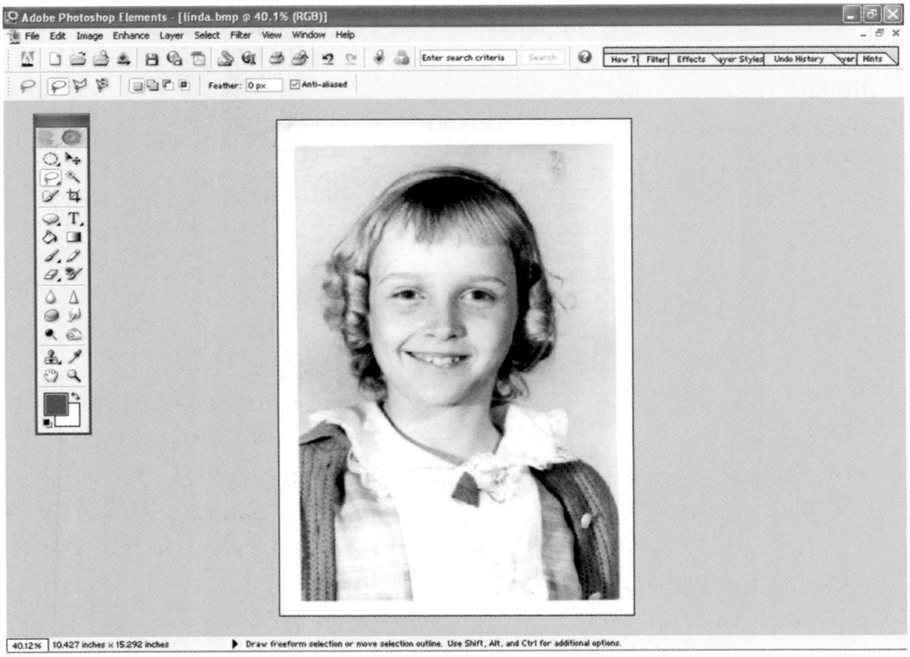
Adobe Photoshop Elements - [linda.bmp @ 40.1% (RGB)]
File Edit Image Enhance Layer Select Filter View Window Help
Enter search criteria
Search
Filters
Effects
Undo History
Hints
Feather: 0 px
Anti-aliased
40.12%
10.427 inches x 15.292 inches
Draw freeform selection or move selection outline. Use Shift, Alt, and Ctrl for additional options.

- **Craft projects.** In addition to printed projects such as invitations, you can also use your pictures for craft projects. For example, you can apply your images to memory quilts, T-shirts, mugs, and so on.

Many craft projects require that you print your images on special transfer paper. You can find this paper—as well as craft-related computer programs—at a variety of locations, including hobby or craft stores, computer outlets, office supply stores, or even general purpose retail stores.

✦ **Cards, invitations, and banners.** With digital images, you can design your own holiday letter and include pictures of the family. Having a party? Create a fun invitation using digital photos or make a banner for an office party with photos of everyone in the company. You can create many types of documents for entertainment and other purposes!

Creations Wizard -
Preview Your Greeting Card
Step: 1 2 3 4 5
Season's Greetings!
Title
Full Screen Preview
Rearrange Photos
< Back
Next >
Cancel

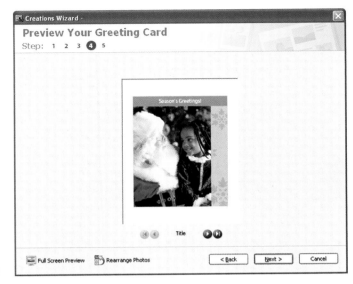

✦ **Business reports.** Pictures are a great way to improve the content and readability of many business reports, including newsletters, annual reports, and more. Do you want your clients to get to know you? Include your picture. Do you need to share a complex plan or diagram with customers? Scan it and then include it in the document. Regardless of your business, you can dress up reports by including photographs.

Marketing
We have assembled the top professionals in the field, ready to serve your advertising needs. Each staff member draws upon many years of experience in his or her field of expertise and is specially suited to address the demands of your market.
We can reach your audience on many levels, including print media, online publishing, and television and radio broadcasting
Our marketing staff can help you meet all your advertising needs, and create media campaigns that get results!
Please call our offices to set up a consultation to explore how marketing can meet and exceed the quality your organization requires.
1234 Street Address
City, ST 01234
Phone (555) 555-5555
Fax: (555) 555-5555

- ✦ **Business cards.** Personalize your business card by adding your picture or company logo. By including your picture, you make sure the recipient will remember your smiling face.

- ✦ **Product sales sheets and brochures.** If you are in sales, the old adage "a picture is worth a thousand words" couldn't be truer. You can show your potential clients one or several pictures! For example, realtors use digital images to prepare virtual tours of the homes they're selling—providing a picture of hardwood floors and built-in bookcases makes for an easier sale than simply describing these features.

 Scientists and doctors use digital images to photograph microscopic subjects to study them in detail. Digital photography is even used in space. The Hubble Space Telescope, for instance, takes digital images that are then sent back to the space center and distributed to astronomers and the news media.

More About . . . Uses for Digital Photos

For insurance purposes, it's a good idea to keep a list of all your major possessions. That way, in case of a catastrophe, you have a record of the items that may have been lost or damaged. A digital camera is a perfect tool for this project; you can use it to photograph your belongings and insert the images into the document containing your list!

Editing Possibilities

In addition to the many uses for digital images, you also have a great deal of freedom in working with your digital pictures. The programs that enable you to edit digital images are called image-editing programs.

If you own a digital camera, it probably came with its own editing program, which you can use to manipulate your photos. Alternatively, you can purchase programs created by other companies if your needs are more advanced. The following is a quick overview of the types of things you can do with photo-editing programs.

- ✦ If your photos have flaws, such as red-eye, you can correct them. You can also remove blemishes and wrinkles, giving yourself or a friend a virtual facelift!

◆ You can crop out portions of the picture to frame your subject better.

◆ You can change the orientation of the image, flipping or rotating it.

◆ You can apply special effects, such as converting a color image to black and white or warping the image.

◆ You can repair old pictures that are torn or stained.

◆ You can manipulate pictures or add and combine them to create a totally new picture. For instance, suppose your friend cannot attend your son's wedding. You can take an existing photo of your friend and place him or her in a wedding picture, just as if he or she were there!

No Computer Required

Ideally, you have a computer on which to copy, edit, and print your pictures. But if you don't, you can still access many of the features and fun of a digital camera. For example, your digital camera's display acts as a portable photo album, so you can view and show off all the pictures (or even the short movies) you've recently taken. Also, some cameras come with removable media, such as CompactFlash and the SmartMedia cards. You can take pictures, store them on these media cards, and then take them to a local print shop. You can also purchase printers that will read media cards and print the images from the card directly without the need for a computer.

Exploring Your Camera's Features

Unless you're an expert, you might view most of the dials, buttons, and other gizmos on your digital camera as mysterious at best. Getting a handle on how these features and settings work will pave the way to using your digital camera to its fullest potential. A number of common features are displayed in Figure 3-3.

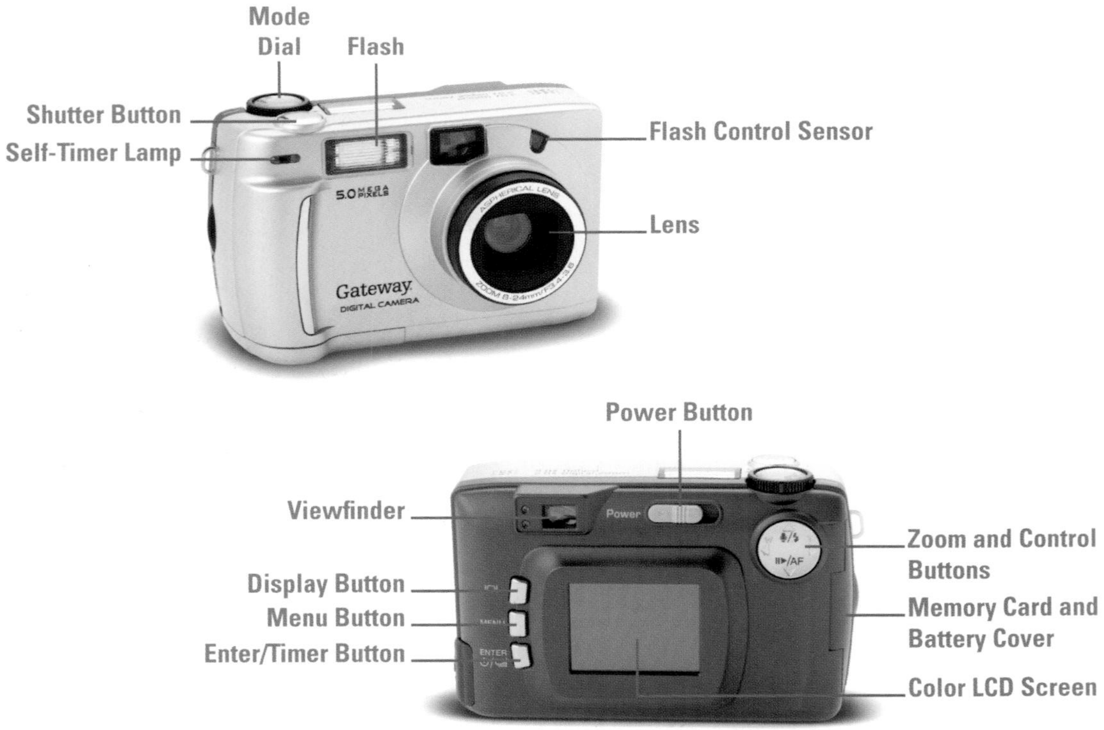
Mode Dial
Flash
Shutter Button
Self-Timer Lamp
Flash Control Sensor
Lens
5.0 MEGA PIXELS
Gateway
DIGITAL CAMERA
Power Button
Viewfinder
Display Button
Menu Button
Enter/Timer Button
Zoom and Control Buttons
Memory Card and Battery Cover
Color LCD Screen
Power

Figure 3-3 Most digital cameras include the features shown here.

Every camera offers different features. Even when two cameras boast the same features, you probably access them in different ways. The best way to determine your camera's features and the best use of them is to read the camera's user manual.

The features that are typically found in digital cameras include the following:

- **Lens and lens cover.** The lens and lens cover are easy to locate on the camera's front side. To take pictures, you remove the lens cover or slide it to the side to expose the lens.
- **Power button.** To turn on your camera, you need to press the power button, which is typically located either on the side or the top of the camera.
- **Connection port.** To transfer pictures from your camera to your computer, connect the cable that came with your camera to your camera's port. The port is usually found on the side of the camera.
- **Viewfinder.** The viewfinder is a tiny window on the camera's body that you look through to frame your shots. It is generally found on the back of your camera.
- **Shutter button.** You press this button, which is almost always located on the top of the camera, to take a picture.
- **Flash.** You use a flash to illuminate the subject of your photograph if the setting is too dark.
- **Mode dial.** Most digital cameras have several modes—one for taking pictures, another for reviewing or playing back photos, and so on. You use the mode dial, typically found on top of the camera, to switch modes. Figure 3-4 shows a mode dial.

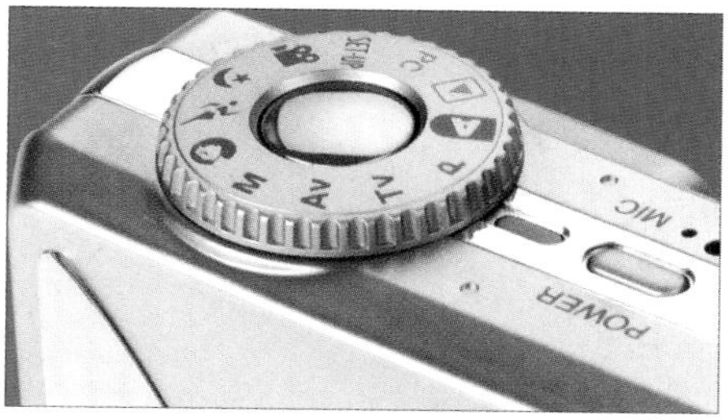
M
Av
TV
P
A
PC
MIC
POWER
Figure 3-4 Use the mode dial to switch from taking pictures, to recording movies, to reviewing them.

Many digital cameras also feature a video mode, which allows the camera to shoot short videos in addition to still photos.

- **LCD screen.** The LCD screen shows you a preview of a picture you've just taken. You also have the option of switching to playback or review mode, enabling you to view the pictures currently stored on your camera on the LCD screen.

◆ **Menu button.** Many cameras feature a menu button (or something similar) that enables you to access the commands on your camera, such as the Delete command.

◆ **Scroll buttons.** Scroll buttons, which usually look like arrows, enable you to navigate among commands or move from picture to picture.

◆ **Media slot.** If your camera can use a media card such as a SmartMedia, xD, SD, or CompactFlash card, it will have a slot where you insert the card.

◆ **Battery compartment.** One source of a camera's power is supplied by batteries, which are stored in a battery compartment like the one shown in Figure 3-5.

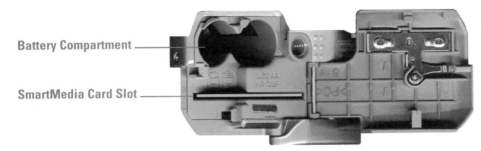

Battery Compartment

SmartMedia Card Slot

Figure 3-5 The door to the battery compartment is usually located on the bottom of the camera.

 In addition to the standard features listed here, your camera may include additional features, such as a strap mount, a tripod mount, or a timer.

Before you can use your camera, you might need to complete a few steps. For specific instructions on completing each of these steps, refer to your camera's user manual.

❶ If necessary, insert batteries into the camera's battery compartment. (In some cases, you'll need to charge them first.)

 Many digital cameras come with a rechargeable battery and a power adapter. When the battery is low, you can simply connect the power adapter to the camera to charge the battery. If you need to purchase replacement batteries, be sure to check your digital camera's manual to ensure you purchase batteries compatible with the camera.

❷ If your camera uses a media card, insert it into the appropriate slot.

❸ You might need to set certain camera options, such as the date and time.

Understanding Basic Photography Principles

One of the very first things you must learn about photography—digital or otherwise—is the terms used by photographers. Learning just a few key photographic terms and concepts will help you decipher your camera's user manual as well as any articles or how-to information you encounter later.

3

This section introduces you to some of the key terms and concepts relating to digital and film-based photography. You don't need to master all these concepts in order to begin taking pictures with your digital camera. However, as you become more skilled, you'll appreciate this foundation.

Composition

Composition refers to the way you frame the subject of your photograph, or compose your image. When composing images, the basic rule is to frame your picture for optimal presentation of its subject. To this end, most beginning photographers frame the subject in the center of the picture. As your photography skills advance, however, you may decide to experiment with other compositions. For example, you may decide to shoot your subject off-center to create a different balance in the picture. Alternatively, you may decide to include more of the background to better show the contrast between your subject and its surroundings. In the photograph shown here, the photographer has incorporated the landscape to convey the magnitude of the scenery in comparison to the prairie in the foreground.

Depth of Field/Focus

When you photograph a subject of any kind, you typically want that person or object to be in focus. Your digital camera uses a lens for focusing, a process that often occurs automatically. With your camera's manual controls, however, you can manipulate your image's depth of field—the area of the photograph that's in focus—by using zoom controls to change the lens's focal length and by adjusting aperture settings. A camera's aperture is the opening through which light enters before striking the film or digital sensors. You can make the diameter of this opening larger or smaller by changing the aperture settings, also called f-stops. A lower f-stop indicates a larger aperture diameter, and vice versa.

Exposure

In photography, be it digital or film-based, you must expose your camera's digital sensors or film to light in order to take a photograph. The term exposure refers to the amount of light allowed to travel through the camera's lens and aperture and strike its digital sensors or film when the shutter is opened.

There are two ways to alter the amount of light that strikes the camera's digital sensors or film. One is to adjust the camera's aperture settings, increasing or reducing the amount of light that can pass through by making the aperture larger or smaller. The other is to increase or decrease the camera's shutter speed—that is, the amount of time the shutter remains open. The longer the shutter is open, the more light can pass through.

Rather than make you adjust the aperture and shutter-speed settings manually, most digital cameras have an automatic-exposure mode that determines the best focus, aperture, and shutter speed for each picture. Some digital cameras, however, enable you to fiddle with the automatic exposure settings.

Lighting and Flash

As you photograph your subject or scene, be sure to consider lighting. If you're outdoors, the sunlight overhead may be intense and cast shadows on your subject that may or may not be visually pleasing. If you're indoors, the lighting may be insufficient for correct exposure.

One way to adjust the lighting for your image is to move the subject to a position where the lighting is more pleasing or robust. Alternatively, you can use artificial lighting—be it lighting designed with photography in mind or lighting designed simply to illuminate a room—to enhance available light. Finally, you can use a built-in camera flash to supplement natural or available light.

Taking Photographs

Using your digital camera to take photographs is extremely simple—especially if the camera is set to automatic mode. After you've grasped the basics, undoubtedly you'll want to move on to more advanced photographic techniques. In this section, you'll learn how to take basic pictures, and you'll get a few tips and tricks to move you to the next step of digital photography.

Using Automatic Mode

Although the preceding section briefly discussed how you can change camera settings to affect focus, exposure, and flash, most digital cameras can adjust these settings automatically. In automatic mode, you only need to point and shoot to take the picture. You'll find that using your camera's automatic mode works for most pictures and frees you to concentrate on the basics of composing and shooting photographs.

To take a photograph in automatic mode, follow these steps:

The steps outlined here are general; they may differ somewhat from camera to camera. Read your digital camera's user manual for specific instructions on taking photographs.

1. Turn the camera on.
2. Set the camera to automatic mode.

The Gateway™ DC-T50 features a dial on top with several icons. The "A" icon represents automatic mode; turn the dial to this mode.

3. Open the lens cover.

If you can't get your camera to display or shoot an image, make sure the lens cover is entirely open. With some cameras, the lens cover must be pushed all the way open until it clicks.

4. Point your camera at the subject you want to shoot, using the viewfinder or LCD screen to center the subject.

5. Press the shutter button halfway down to engage the camera's auto-focus feature.
6. Press the shutter button the rest of the way down to take the picture.

The auto-focus features on most cameras automatically focus on the object or person in the center of the viewfinder. However, you may decide that you want to compose your image differently, perhaps with the subject to one side. Fortunately, many digital cameras offer a workaround. Center the subject in the viewfinder and then push the shutter button down halfway. Doing this locks the focus. Then, offset the viewfinder to one side or the other before taking the shot. Your subject will remain in focus.

7. Check the LCD screen to preview your image. You can either keep the image or discard it.

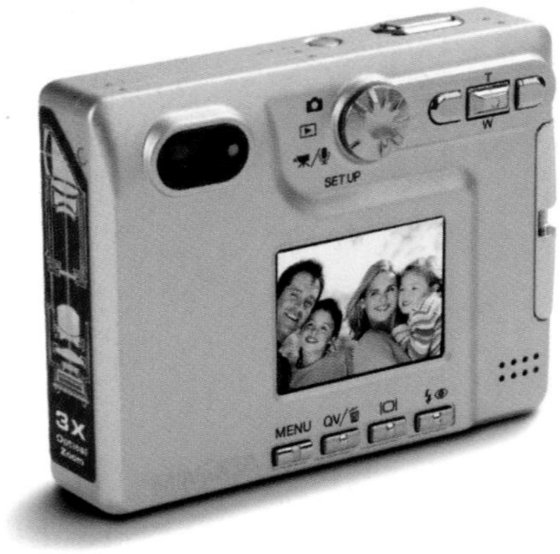
SETUP
MENU
QV/
3X

Using Zoom Controls

When you're comfortable using your camera in automatic mode, you're ready to start experimenting with other features, such as flash settings or zooming. As mentioned previously, your camera uses zoom controls to change its focal length. A shorter focal length yields a wider angle of view (or zooms out), whereas a longer focal length yields a narrower angle of view (or zooms in).

To get the hang of your camera's zoom features, try the following steps:

The steps outlined here are general; they may differ somewhat from camera to camera. Read your digital camera's user manual for specific instructions on using its zoom feature.

1. Point your camera at the subject and preview the photo using the LCD screen.
2. Press the zoom button. You might see the current zoom settings on the LCD screen.
3. Press the zoom adjustment buttons to change the zoom. Continue pressing the buttons until you're satisfied with the size of your photograph's subject in relation to the background.

4 Reframe your shot, placing your subject in the position you want.

5 Press the shutter button halfway down to use the camera's auto-focus feature to refocus the shot at the new zoom level.

6 Press the shutter button the rest of the way down to take the picture.

Improving Your Picture-Taking Skills

There are a number of other tricks that can help improve the results of your photographs. Without delving too deeply into advanced techniques, here are some quick ways to create better-looking photographs:

- ✦ **Use the right lighting.** When you're outside, make sure that your subject isn't looking into the sun and that you are not pointing your camera into the sun. This can cause you to underexpose your subject because the camera will adjust itself to expose for the bright light of the sun. When you're inside, look for soft light, which you can often find by windows. In addition to placing your subject in flattering lighting, you may also want to use a flash.

- ✦ **Select an appropriate background.** If you want the background to be part of the picture, use something simple. This ensures that the background doesn't detract from your subject.

- ✦ **Shoot from a good angle.** In most cases, the best angle is eye-level, but you can also get good shots by shooting from a higher point.

- ✦ **Capture your subject's personality.** As the saying goes, "the eyes are the windows to the soul." Focus on eyes to capture your subject's personality. You'll also find that capturing your subject in a relaxed pose improves your portraits.

- ✦ **Use a tripod when possible.** Keep the camera steady while taking photos. In other words, limit movement as much as possible while the shutter is open. Particularly in nighttime photos, you might consider placing the camera on a platform. Though a tripod is perhaps the best choice, setting your camera on a rock or post can work just as well.

- ✦ **Zoom in for action photos.** Try stepping back and zooming in. In addition to using your camera's macro setting to take a picture just inches from your subject, you can also move back a bit and use the camera's zoom controls. This technique can alleviate problems with distorted backgrounds inherent with close-ups, and may produce a more desirable-looking image.

- ✦ **Take a sample picture and adjust where necessary.** Don't be afraid to take test shots. Try different angles, zoom in, use the flash, etc., and then view results on the camera's display. You can then make any necessary adjustments to the flash or exposure settings.

- ✦ **Be ready for your action shot.** You never know when a dramatic moment will occur. The key to taking action photos is to be ready for that magic moment. Get as close to the action as possible, both physically and by zooming in. Also, some cameras feature a multi-frame mode, which is useful for action photographs because it enables you to take a series of photographs by simply pressing the shutter button and holding it down.

- ✦ **Use a flash when appropriate.** Use the flash during the daytime to eliminate dark shadows cast by the bright sun. Most cameras include a Force Flash setting that allows you to use the flash regardless of the lighting conditions.

- ✦ **Use a lens for extreme close-ups.** When photographing small objects close up, consider the background very carefully. It should generally be clean and uncluttered, not drawing attention from the subject. If possible, lay the small object flat and photograph it from above. For telephoto images or extreme close-ups, you might consider purchasing an additional lens for your camera.

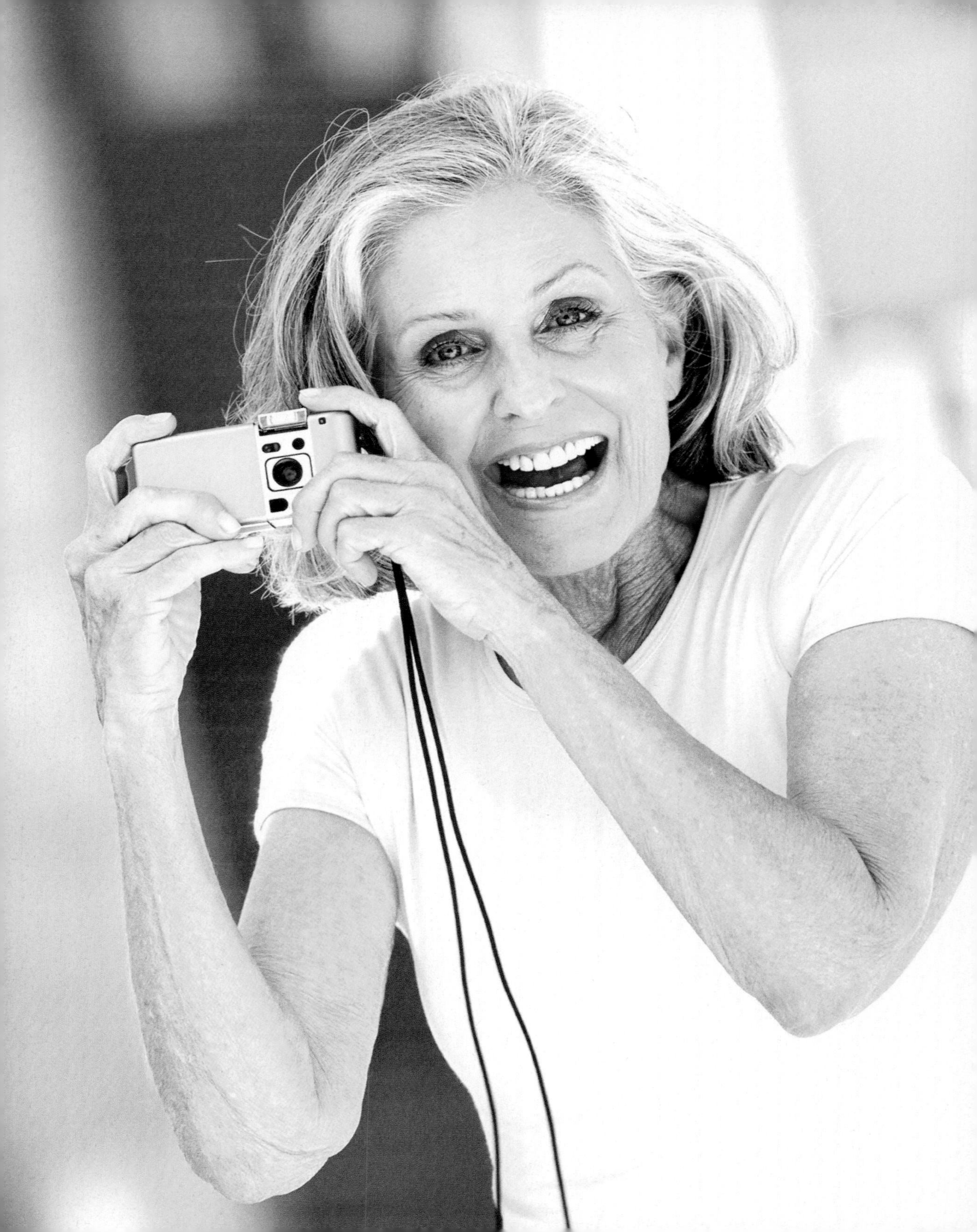

CHAPTER **4**

Manage Your Digital Images

Many people use a photo album to organize and protect their printed photographs. You probably have a stack of your own photo albums. Each album may represent a year in your life, or you might have albums containing photos from a single significant event, such as your anniversary party or your trip to Hawaii.

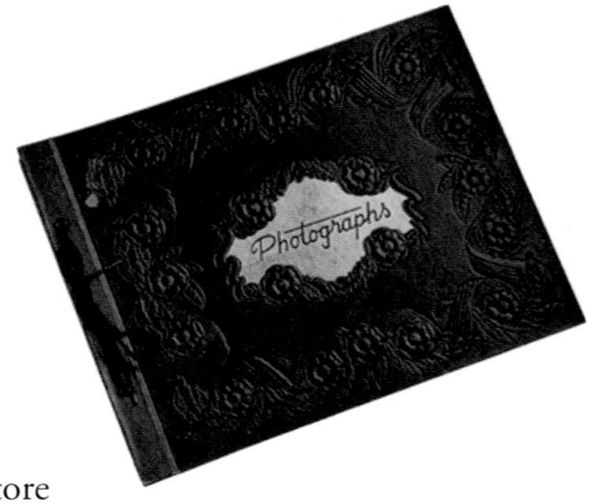
Photographs

Just as you organize your print photos in albums, you likely need some way to organize and protect the digital images stored on your computer. That way, you won't waste time looking all over your hard drive for a particular image.

You can even group related photos in virtual albums that act much like their real-world counterparts by using specialized image management software. You might also decide to store your digital images on other media such as CDs or DVDs, either to free space on your hard drive or to have backup files in the event that something happens to the files on your machine. In this chapter, you'll learn how to do all that and more.

The steps outlined throughout this chapter are general ones. As you read through steps outlined in this chapter, you might find that buttons and menus are named differently on your digital camera. If you are having trouble finding the corresponding button or menu on your camera, consult your camera's user manual.

Using Your Digital Camera to Manage Photographs

Unlike film-based photographs, which must be developed and printed either by you or a photo lab before they can be seen, digital photos are available for viewing instantly. Added to this convenience is the fact that if an image isn't up to par, you can delete it from your camera's memory right away—no messy chemicals or hefty processing fees required. When your camera or removable media device finally runs out of memory, you can transfer the digital images you choose to save to your computer, which you can then use to store, manipulate, print, and e-mail your photos.

More About . . . Tracking Available Memory

Unlike a roll of film, which allows you to take only a set number of photographs (typically 12, 24, or 36), the number of photos you can store in your camera's memory or removable media device depends on how much memory you started with, as well as the image quality of the photographs you take. Fortunately, many cameras calculate how many more photos will fit in memory and display this information on the LCD screen. In addition, most cameras display an error message when they've run out of memory.

In this section, you'll learn how to preview and discard images, as well as how to transfer images to your computer.

Take as many pictures as you want with your digital camera! Because you can discard the ones that don't turn out well before they're ever printed, you don't have to worry about wasting film.

4

Previewing Photographs

With most digital cameras, you use one mode to take photos and another—typically called Playback or Preview—to preview them on your camera's LCD screen. In this mode, you can scroll through all the pictures you've taken. To preview your images, follow these steps:

1. Switch your camera to **Playback** mode.

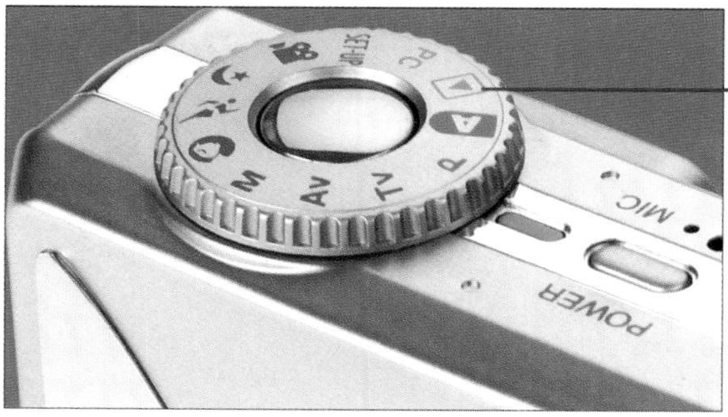
Playback Mode
M
Av
Tv
P
PC
MIC
POWER

The name of this mode varies by camera. Read your camera's user guide to determine which mode is used for deleting photos.

2. Press the **Back** and **Forward** buttons to scroll through your pictures.

Some cameras enable you to magnify a picture to view it in more detail. Most can also display several photographs at once so you can easily navigate to a specific shot. The zoom controls are often used for these functions when the camera is in Playback mode. Check your camera's user manual for information about using these features.

Deleting Photographs

No doubt you'll take a photo that doesn't turn out as you expected, especially when you're getting used to using your new digital camera. Not to worry! You can delete any pictures you don't want, thereby freeing up space on your camera or removable media device for pictures that make the grade.

To delete images from your camera, follow these steps:

1. Change to **Playback** mode.
2. Scroll through your photos until the one you want to delete is displayed.
3. Press the **Menu** button.

 This button lets you scroll through and select different commands, including the command for deleting pictures. If your camera has a dedicated Delete button (which might look like a trash can), simply press that button to delete the current photo.

4. Using the camera's arrow buttons, scroll to the Erase command (or a command with a similar name, such as Delete).

 If you want to delete all the photos currently stored in your camera's memory, use the camera's menu to locate a command named Erase All Frames, Delete All, or something similar.

5. Press the **Select** button to select the command.
6. To confirm the deletion, use your camera's arrow keys to select **OK** or **Yes**.

Understanding Digital File Formats

Chances are, your digital camera stores its images in JPEG format. After you transfer these files to your computer, you can copy, move, rename, or delete them like other file types. Virtually all image-editing software can open JPEG images, and most are capable of saving your JPEG images to TIFF or other file formats. Simply open the JPEG file in the image-editing program, and then choose Save As from the File menu. You can choose to save the image in a variety of different formats.

Following is a list of common digital image formats and how they are most often used:

✦ **JPEG (Joint Photographic Experts Group).** Used by most digital cameras for storage, JPEGs can have up to 16.8 million colors. Although some information is lost to preserve a small file size, you can lower compression settings to achieve higher quality.

- **TIFF (Tagged Image File Format).** Although graphics in this format are generally larger than JPEG files, they can offer very high-quality images and they are capable of 16.8 million colors. This format is commonly used for image editing and publication.

Some high-end digital cameras can store photos in TIFF format.

- **GIF (Graphics Interchange Format).** Because of their small size and features such as animation, GIF graphics are often used for Web pages. However, because they are limited to 256 different colors, they are not the best choice for photographs.

- **EXIF (Extended File Format).** Digital cameras use this format to store additional information along with the image data, such as the date, time, or whether the flash was used. This data can be useful when you're editing an image. Figure 4-1 shows EXIF data accessed from Adobe Photoshop Elements.

File Info
Section: EXIF
OK
Cancel
Make CAMERA
Model SMP-9A3
X Resolution 72.0
Y Resolution 72.0
Resolution Unit Inches
Software Adobe Photoshop Elements 2.0
Date Time 2003:08:29 11:26:25
Exposure Time 1/200 sec
F-Stop 6.7
Exposure Program Normal program
ISO Speed Ratings 100
ExifVersion 0220
Date Time Original 2003:01:01 20:46:57
Date Time Digitized 2003:01:01 20:46:57
Components Configuration Unknown
Shutter Speed 1/208 sec
Aperture Value 5.5
Exposure Bias Value 0.0
Preserve Additional Information

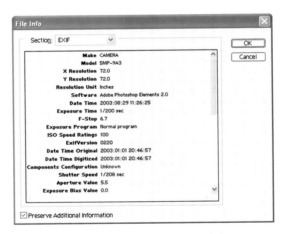

Figure 4-1 You can use EXIF data, which accompanies digital photos taken with most digital cameras, for reference while editing the image.

- **BMP (Microsoft Bitmap Format).** This is the format used for Microsoft Paint. BMP files can be up to 16.8 million colors, but they are larger than JPEG files.

- **PDF (Portable Document Format).** You can open files in PDF format for onscreen display using Adobe's Acrobat Reader, which is offered as a free download from Adobe (http://www.adobe.com/products/acrobat/readermain.html). Because of their small size and versatility, PDF files are often used for Web pages and transfer over the Internet. They can only be saved using one of Adobe's products, such as Photoshop Elements or Photoshop Album.

 Because PDF files can be created from Adobe's image-editing, illustration, or page-layout software, electronic documents of all types are commonly found in PDF format. You can also optimize PDF files for printing.

+ **PSD (Photoshop Format).** This is the native format of Adobe Photoshop and Adobe Photoshop Elements. Unlike generic formats, such as TIFF or JPEG, image-editing data (such as layers and selections) is saved with PSD files. You can open files saved in this format in Photoshop products. Some other image-editing programs are also capable of opening PSD files.

Now that you've learned the basics and available formats for managing your photographs, it's time to actually get those photos onto your computer so you can explore the full potential of digital images.

Transferring Images to Your Computer

After you've taken a series of photos and deleted the ones you don't want, you can transfer the remaining photos to your computer. In addition to enabling you to store, manipulate, print, and e-mail your photos, transferring photos from your camera has the added benefit of allowing you to free up space so you can store additional photos in your camera's memory or removable media device.

Before you can transfer your photos to your computer, however, you must set it up to handle this operation. In this section, you'll learn how to configure your computer and camera for easy transfer and how to use Windows XP to perform the transfer operation. In this section, you will also learn how to set up a scanner and import scanned images.

Setting Up Your Computer

Before you can transfer digital images to your computer, you must install the camera or scanner on your computer, just as you would a printer or any other hardware device. The installation process copies the drivers your computer needs to communicate with your camera.

The first step to installing your camera or scanner is to connect it (or removable media) to the appropriate port on your computer using the connection cable that came bundled with the camera or scanner. (You might need to pull back a cover to reveal the camera's connection port.)

Most cameras or camera media connect to computers via a USB (Universal Serial Bus) or FireWire port. Sometimes these ports are found on the front of the computer, but some computers have USB and/or FireWire ports on the back or the back and front. If your port is on the back, it should be right below the cables for the mouse and the keyboard.

After you've connected your camera or scanner to your computer, you'll use one of two methods to install it—plug-and-play setup or manual setup. The process which you use will depend largely on the type of digital camera or scanner you have and the version of Windows you have on your computer.

Try installing your camera or scanner via plug-and-play first. If that doesn't work, use one of the manual methods.

Importing Images from Your Camera

Microsoft Scanner and Camera Wizard leads you through the process of downloading images from your camera to your computer. Simply follow these steps:

❶ Connect the camera or camera media to the appropriate port on your computer and, if necessary, turn on the camera.

❷ When you are prompted by the Removable Disk dialog box, select **Copy pictures to a folder on my computer using Microsoft Scanner and Camera Wizard**, and then click **OK**.

Removable Disk (E:)
Windows can perform the same action each time you insert a disk or connect a device with this kind of file:
Pictures
What do you want Windows to do?
Copy pictures to a folder on my computer using Microsoft Scanner and Camera Wizard
View a slideshow of the images
using Windows Picture and Fax Viewer
Print the pictures
using Photo Printing Wizard
Open and edit the pictures
using Microsoft Picture It! Photo 7.0
Edit pictures
Always do the selected action.
OK
Cancel

If you are not prompted by the Removable Disk dialog box, click the **start** button and select **My Computer**. If the camera is properly connected to the computer, you will see an icon labeled Removable Disk. Double-click **Removable Disk**, and open any folders therein until you see your image files. Then, you can drag them to another folder, such as My Pictures, to copy them to your hard drive as you would any other file. Or, select the images, and then in the Task pane on the left, under File and Folder Tasks, choose **Copy the selected items**. Then choose the destination folder and click **OK**.

❸ Windows will read the camera or removable media and then display the Wizard's Welcome screen. Click **Next**.

Scanner and Camera Wizard
Choose Pictures to Copy
Pictures with check marks will be copied. To rotate a picture or view its properties, click it, and then click the appropriate button.
Clear All
Select All
8 picture(s) selected of 8
< Back
Next >
Cancel

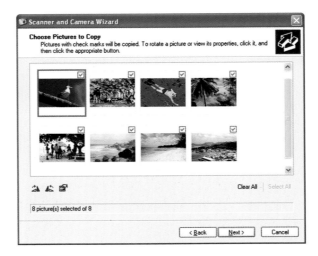

4. The Wizard will display thumbnail versions of each picture stored on the camera or camera media. By default, all the images are selected. To prevent Windows from downloading an image, click it to cancel the selection. Alternatively, you can click **Clear All** to clear all image selections, and then click the images you want. After you have selected the images you want to transfer, click **Next**.
5. By default, Windows places all the selected images in a folder within the My Pictures folder, which is located in the My Documents folder. To specify a name for this folder, type it in the text box labeled **1. Type a name for this group of pictures**, or select a name from the drop-down menu.

Every Windows XP user has a unique My Pictures folder that is the default location for storing images.

6. To specify a different location for the new folder, click **Browse** and navigate to the drive and folder where you want the new folder containing your pictures to be stored.
7. To delete the pictures from your camera after they've been copied to your computer, click **Delete pictures from my device after copying them**.

It's a good idea to delete the photos from your camera after you've transferred them because it frees up space for any new photos you take. However, the first few times you transfer pictures, you might want to leave them on the camera just to make sure the transfer went through without a hitch. After you've verified that the images were successfully transferred, you can use the commands in your camera's menu to delete the images from the camera's memory.

Scanner and Camera Wizard
Copying Pictures
Please wait while the wizard copies your pictures.
Location:
My Pictures\Picture
Picture:
Picture 004
Picture progress: 70% complete
Currently copying picture 4 of 8:
To stop copying, click Cancel.
< Back
Next >
Cancel

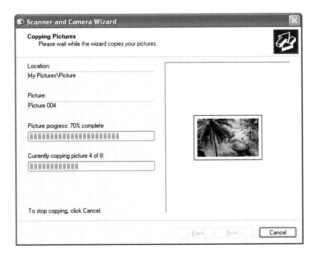

8. Click **Next**. The images will be copied to the folder you've specified.
9. Now you'll be prompted to select what you want to do next. You can publish the pictures to a Web site, order prints online, or do nothing.

10. Click **Nothing. I'm finished working with these pictures**, and then select **Next**.
11. Click **Finish** to close the Wizard. After you have transferred the images to your computer, you can open the folder they're stored in and review, modify, or print them.

Now that you have downloaded your images to your computer, you are ready to enhance and print them. However, you don't have to have a digital camera to transfer images to your computer. You can also use a scanner to capture existing photographs and send them to your computer. The following sections explain how to set up your scanner and transfer traditional prints to your computer as digital image files.

Scanning Existing Photographs

Transferring scanned images to your computer works much the same way as transferring images with a digital camera. A scanner basically takes a high-resolution picture of a photograph and sends the image data to your computer. Once the image file is on your computer, you can copy, delete, or manipulate it just like images transferred from your digital camera.

Your scanner works much like a copy machine. You place the image you want to scan on the scanner's bed, and then you scan it. The scanner copies the image data, converts it to digital information, and displays it on your computer in the scanner's software program.

The specific steps for scanning—such as the commands to select and the range of scanning options—vary across scanner models, but the basic steps are essentially the same. The following list illustrates the general steps for a flatbed scanner. For specific information, check the manual for your particular scanner and scanner software.

1. Click on **start**, **All Programs**, and then point to the scanner program folder and select the program. Alternatively, you can scan from another program.

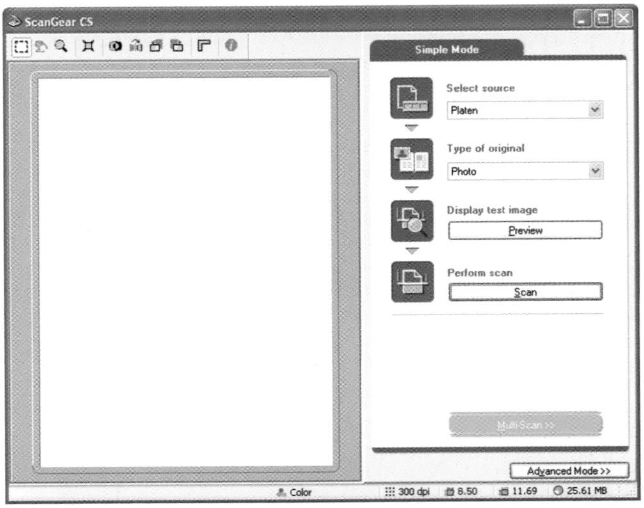
ScanGear CS
Simple Mode
Select source
Platen
Type of original
Photo
Display test image
Preview
Perform scan
Scan
Multi-Scan >>
Advanced Mode >>
Color
300 dpi
8.50
11.69
25.61 MB

In Adobe Photoshop Elements, for example, you can click the **File** menu and choose **Import** and then your scanner device to access Photoshop Album's scanning utility. If you use this method, the scanned photo opens directly in Photoshop Elements.

2. When the scanning program window opens, place the image you want to scan facedown in the top corner of the scanner's view area. (Check your scanner manual to find out exactly where to place the image. Like copiers, scanners usually indicate the start area with an arrow and include paper dimensions.) Close the scanner lid.
3. Set any available scanning options. For instance, you might be able to select the purpose for which the scanned document will be used (such as editing text, faxing, filing, or copying) and the type of image (black and white, color, and so on). You can also select mode (color, grayscale, or black and white), resolution, size, and other options. These options vary depending on the scanner. In Office XP's scanning program, you can select the color, (black and white, black and white from color page, color, or grayscale) as well as options for the paper (whether it is double-sided, for instance).
4. Some programs display a preview of the scan automatically. Others, such as Adobe Photoshop Album's scanning utility (shown in Figure 4-2), require you to click on a preview button to preview the scan.

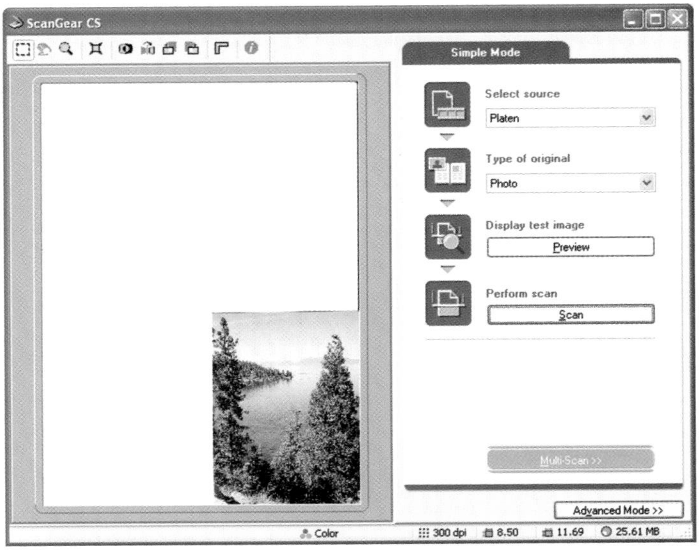
ScanGear CS
Simple Mode
Select source
Platen
Type of original
Photo
Display test image
Preview
Perform scan
Scan
Multi-Scan >>
Advanced Mode >>
Color
300 dpi
8.50
11.69
25.61 MB

Figure 4-2 Photoshop Album's ScanGear CS window displays a preview of the image before you scan to a file.

5. Click on the menu command or button to start the scan. Most programs include a menu command such as File, Acquire, as well as a toolbar shortcut. Check with your program for the particular command to start the scan. In Photoshop Album, you click **Scan**.

Archiving Your Digital Images

Just as you might keep negatives of your pictures as an archive in case something happens to your prints, you can also archive your original digital image files. One major reason to do so is that image files are large and consume significant space. When you archive your digital image files, you free up space on your hard drive, making room for other files. Another major reason to archive files is for protection: You can archive your favorite image files as backups in case the original files become damaged.

One way to archive your digital image files is to keep them on your hard drive in a compressed format; that way, they consume considerably less space. Alternatively, if your computer has a drive that lets you record CDs, you can copy your image files to a CD and archive them that way. The next two sections discuss these options.

Archiving Images on Your Hard Drive

No matter how large your hard drive is, it will fill up if you add large numbers of image files to it. One solution is to add another drive to gain more disk space. Another solution is to store your images in a compressed (or zipped) folder. That way, the images remain on your hard drive, but in a different, more compact format.

 In addition to the compression utility included with Windows XP, you can download programs from the Internet to compress files. These include shareware programs, for which you pay a small fee, and freeware programs, which are free.

To use Windows XP to store images in a compressed folder, follow these steps:

1 Locate and open the folder that contains any images you want to compress.

2. Click the image(s) or folder(s) you want to compress. (To select multiple images or folders, hold down the **CTRL** key while you click each item you want to compress. To select a contiguous list of files or folders to compress, hold down the **SHIFT** key while you click the first and last file or folder in the range.)

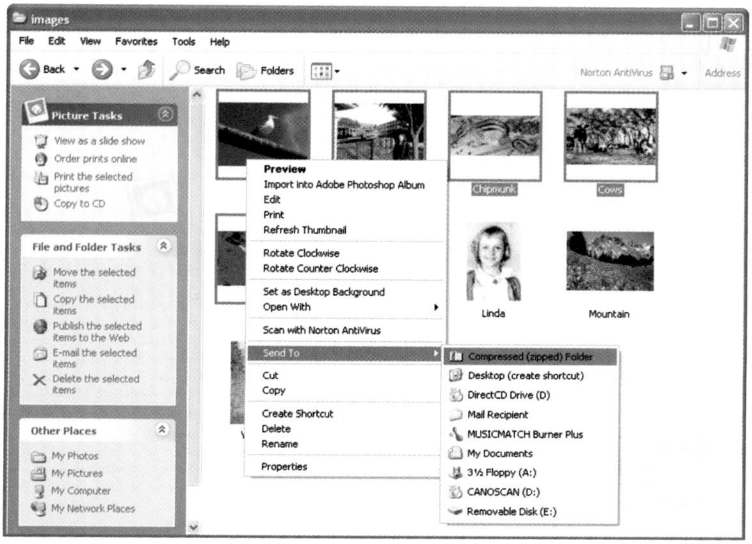

images
File Edit View Favorites Tools Help
Back Search Folders
Norton AntiVirus Address
Picture Tasks
View as a slide show
Order prints online
Print the selected pictures
Copy to CD
File and Folder Tasks
Move the selected items
Copy the selected items
Publish the selected items to the Web
E-mail the selected items
Delete the selected items
Other Places
My Photos
My Pictures
My Computer
My Network Places
Preview
Import into Adobe Photoshop Album
Edit
Print
Refresh Thumbnail
Rotate Clockwise
Rotate Counter Clockwise
Set as Desktop Background
Open With
Scan with Norton AntiVirus
Send To
Cut
Copy
Create Shortcut
Delete
Rename
Properties
Compressed (zipped) Folder
Desktop (create shortcut)
DirectCD Drive (D)
Mail Recipient
MUSICMATCH Burner Plus
My Documents
3½ Floppy (A:)
CANOSCAN (D:)
Removable Disk (E:)
Chipmunk
Cows
Linda
Mountain

3. Right-click any of the selected files, choose **Send to** from the shortcut menu that appears, and click **Compressed (zipped) Folder**. Windows XP's built-in compression utility will compress and store the images in a compressed folder within the current folder. A progress window will indicate the progress of the compression operation.
4. The compressed folder's default name usually consists of the name of one of the compressed images. To give the compressed folder a more descriptive name, right-click it and choose **Rename** from the shortcut menu that appears. The folder's name will be selected.
5. Type a new name for the folder and press **ENTER**.

When you send images to a compressed folder, they are copied, not moved. That means the original image files remain on the disk. To free up disk space, delete the original versions of the images you compressed. (To select multiple images, hold down the **CTRL** key while you click on each file you want to delete. Or, hold down the **SHIFT** key to select a range of contiguous files.)

Although you can't open images when they're compressed, you can decompress or extract them when you want to work with them. To do so, follow these steps:

1. Locate and open the folder that contains the compressed folder with the images you want to extract.

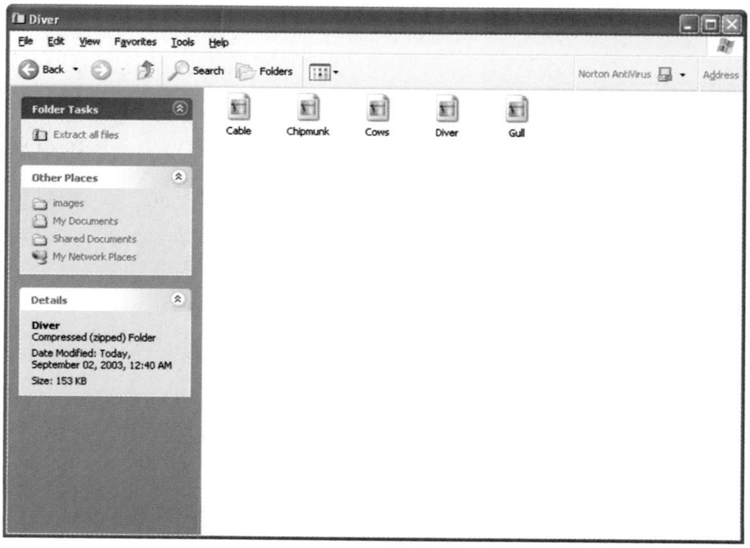
Diver
File Edit View Favorites Tools Help
Back
Search
Folders
Norton AntiVirus
Address
Folder Tasks
Extract all files
Other Places
images
My Documents
Shared Documents
My Network Places
Details
Diver
Compressed (zipped) Folder
Date Modified: Today, September 02, 2003, 12:40 AM
Size: 153 KB
Cable
Chipmunk
Cows
Diver
Gull

2. Double-click the compressed folder. Its contents will be displayed in a window, but the files aren't yet extracted.
3. Select the file(s) you want to extract.
4. Right-click any one of the selected files and click **Copy** in the shortcut menu that appears.
5. Open the folder or drive to which you want to copy the files.
6. Right-click in a blank area of the folder window and click **Paste** in the shortcut menu that appears. The files will be extracted and copied to the open folder.

Don't close the window with the compressed files before pasting them. If you close a compressed folder, copied contents are erased from the clipboard.

If you want to extract all the files in the folder, click **Extract All Files** in the compressed folder window's task pane. This will start the Compressed (Zipped) Folders Extraction Wizard. Read the Welcome screen and click **Next**. When prompted, select the folder in which you want to place the extracted images, and then click **Finish**. The images will be extracted and copied to the folder you selected.

Saving Images on a CD

CD-ROM drives have been standard equipment on most computers for nearly a decade, making it easy to install programs, view data, and so on. However, CD-ROM drives have one major limitation. Although they can read data from discs, they can't write data to discs—you can't use a CD-ROM drive to save data on a CD.

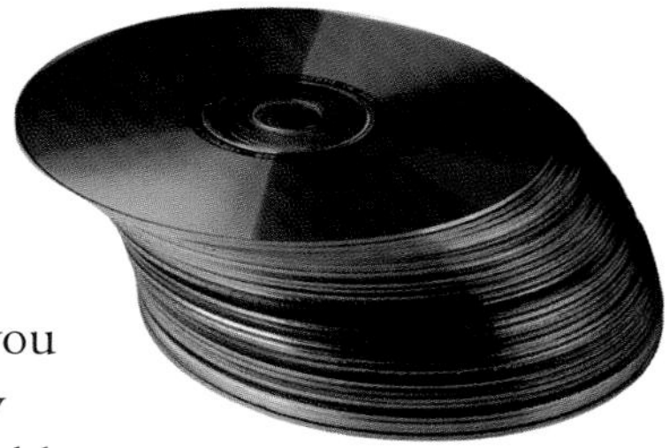

In recent years, technology has given rise to a new generation of recordable CD drives that not only read data from discs, but also record data to discs. In other words, if you insert a blank CD into a recordable CD drive, you can copy information from your computer to the disc. With a recordable CD drive, you can back up data files (including image files) to CDs, allowing you to free up even more hard-drive space than you can free when you compress image files.

4

The advantage of using CDs instead of other storage media, such as floppy disks, to store your digital images is that CDs can store anywhere from 650 to 700 MB of data—the equivalent of nearly 500 floppy disks! This provides ample storage for your digital images.

There are two different types of recordable CD drives:

- **CD-R drives.** A CD-R drive (R for read) can read data from CD-ROM discs and write to CD-R discs. A CD-R disc is a CD on which you can save or write data one time only. Once it has been written to, a CD-R becomes a CD-ROM.

- **CD-RW drives.** A CD-RW drive (RW for read-write) has the same capabilities as a CD-R drive, but you can use it to record data to the same CD multiple times. You can even erase a CD and reuse it. To take advantage of these additional capabilities, you must use a special type of CD called a CD-RW.

You can also record image files to DVDs (Digital Video Discs) if you have a recordable DVD drive installed on your computer. Some DVDs can hold up to 17 GB of data, the equivalent of over two dozen CDs.

You can use Windows XP to copy your images to a CD just as you would use it to copy to any other type of drive. In addition to enabling you to archive images you no longer need, copying images to a CD is a good way to create backups of your important image files—the ones you really don't want damaged or lost. If you want, you can archive copies of these files on CD, leaving the original versions intact on your computer. Here's how:

Some recordable CD drives come bundled with their own software for writing data to a CD (a process also known as burning a CD). Consult the user guide that came with your computer to find out whether your drive requires you to use its accompanying software instead of Windows XP to burn files to CD.

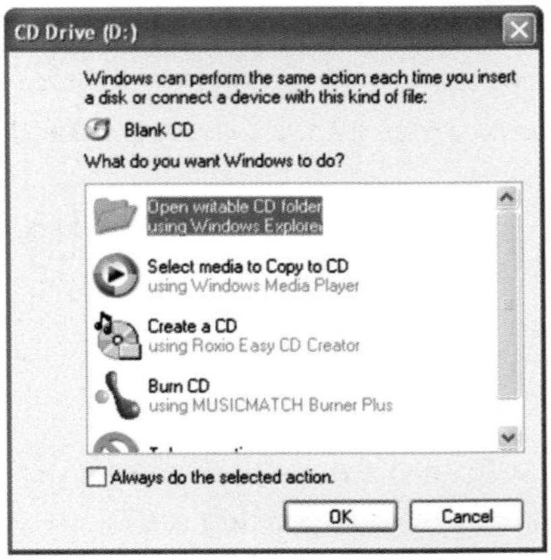
CD Drive (D:)
Windows can perform the same action each time you insert a disk or connect a device with this kind of file:
Blank CD
What do you want Windows to do?
Open writable CD folder using Windows Explorer
Select media to Copy to CD using Windows Media Player
Create a CD using Roxio Easy CD Creator
Burn CD using MUSICMATCH Burner Plus
Always do the selected action.
OK
Cancel

1. Insert a blank CD into the recordable CD drive. The CD Drive dialog box will appear. Click **Cancel**.
2. Click **start** and select **My Computer**. The My Computer window will open.
3. Locate and open the drive and folder that contain the image files you want to copy to CD.
4. Select the file or files you want to copy.

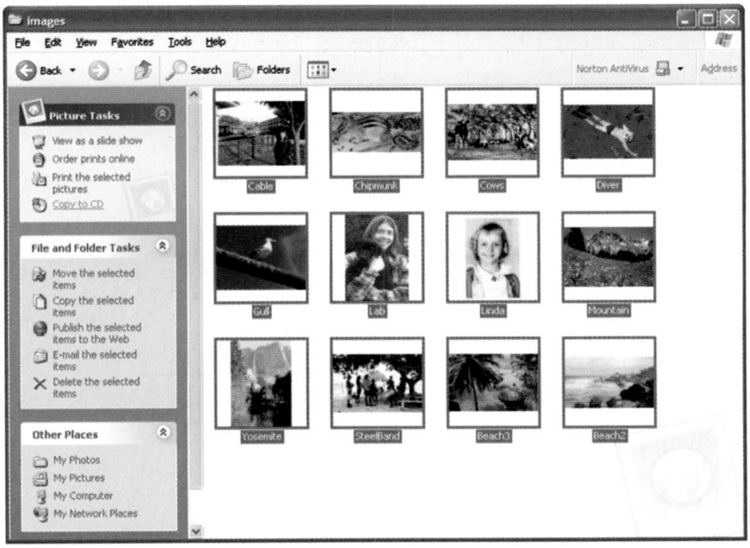
images
File Edit View Favorites Tools Help
Back
Search
Folders
Norton AntiVirus
Address
Picture Tasks
View as a slide show
Order prints online
Print the selected pictures
Copy to CD
File and Folder Tasks
Move the selected items
Copy the selected items
Publish the selected items to the Web
E-mail the selected items
Delete the selected items
Other Places
My Photos
My Pictures
My Computer
My Network Places
Cable
Chipmunk
Cows
Diver
Gull
Lab
Linda
Mountain
Yosemite
SteelBand
Beach3
Beach2

5. The next step depends on the folder in which your image files are stored. If your pictures are stored in the My Pictures folder, click **Copy to CD** in the task pane. If your pictures are stored in another folder, click **Copy this file** (for a single file), **Copy this folder** (for a folder), or **Copy the selected items** (for multiple files). The Copy Items dialog box will open.
6. Click the CD-R or CD-RW drive, and then click **Copy**. The files will be copied to the CD-R or CD-RW drive.

You can purchase blank CDs at computer stores, office supply stores, warehouse stores, and other places. Remember: CD-R drives can write only to CD-R discs, but CD-RW drives can write to both CD-R and CD-RW discs. DVD recorder drives require media designed for the type of DVD burner. For example, DVD-R drives can burn DVD-R discs, but not other types of recordable DVDs. DVD-RAM drives are capable of recording DVD-RAM, DVD-R, DVD-RW, CD-R, and CD-RW discs and can read information from discs of any of these formats.

Because you have copied the files rather than moved them, they are still taking up space on your hard drive. To free up this space, empty the Recycle Bin. Alternatively, you can leave the originals intact and save the files on CD or DVD as a backup in the event that the original files are damaged or deleted.

Using Image-Management Software

In addition to using Windows XP to manage and organize your images, you can also use image-management software specifically designed to help you organize your photo collection. Using one of these programs, such as Adobe Photoshop Album (see Figure 4-3), you can easily find, consolidate, organize, and edit images on your computer and images imported from a scanner or digital camera. You can also create albums, slideshows, and even Web pages with ease.

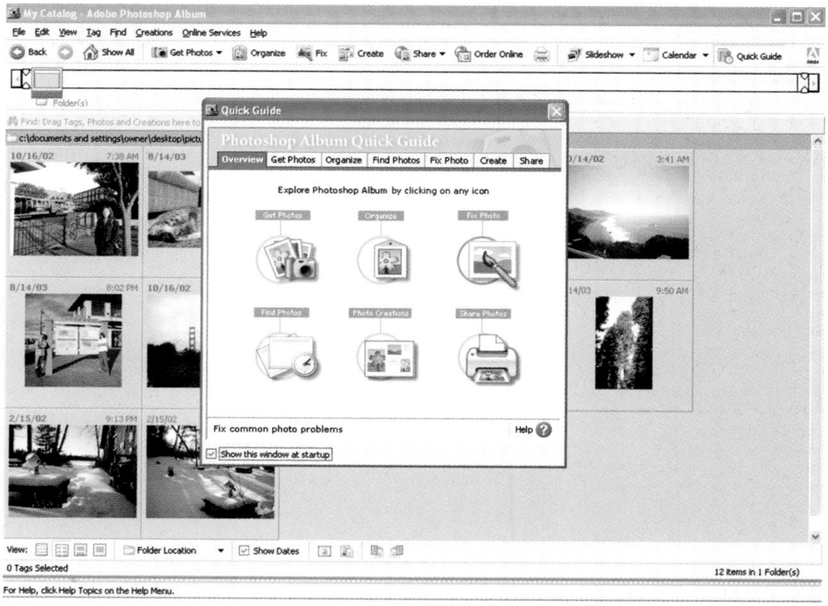
My Catalog - Adobe Photoshop Album
File Edit View Tag Find Creations Online Services Help
Back Show All Get Photos Organize Fix Create Share Order Online Slideshow Calendar Quick Guide
Quick Guide
Photoshop Album Quick Guide
Overview Get Photos Organize Find Photos Fix Photo Create Share
Explore Photoshop Album by clicking on any icon
Fix common photo problems
Help
Show this window at startup
View: Folder Location Show Dates
0 Tags Selected
12 items in 1 Folder(s)
For Help, click Help Topics on the Help Menu.

Figure 4-3 Adobe Photoshop Album is one image-management program.

Before you can take advantage of an image-management program, you need to instruct the software to acquire, or import, the images. Importing images that are already on your computer into Photoshop Album is easy. Just follow these steps:

1. From the File menu, choose **Get Photos**, and then select **By Searching**.
2. The Get Photos By Searching for Folders dialog box will appear. Click on the **Look in** drop-down menu and choose the location you want to search for image files. Choose **All Hard Disks** to search your entire computer. Alternatively, you could look in a specific drive or folder.

Get Photos By Searching for Folders
To find and import photos, select search options and click Search. Then select the desired folders and subfolders from the search results (use shift-click and control-click to select multiple folders) and click Import Folders.
Search Options
Look In: My Documents
Exclude System and Program Folders
Exclude Files Smaller Than: 100 k
Search
Import Folders
Cancel
Preview
Search Results
C:\Documents and Settings\Owner\My Documents\
C:\Documents and Settings\Owner\My Documents\My Pictures\
C:\Documents and Settings\Owner\My Documents\My Pictures\Adobe\Scanned Photos\
14 files found
Clear
Select All
Tip
To browse to a particular photo yourself, go to Get Photos > From Files and Folders.
Take me there (This will exit this dialog and cancel any pending search)
+ 7 More

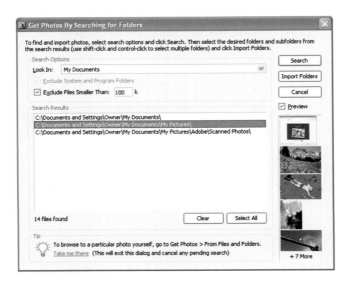

3. Click **Search**. All folders in the location you selected that contain image files will appear in the Search Results list. Click a folder to preview its contents.
4. Click **Import Folders** to open the image files in the main Photoshop Album window for further management or to perform other operations.

To import images directly from a digital camera, card reader, or scanner, click the **File** menu, choose **Get Photos**, and then select **From camera or card reader or from scanner**. Importing images directly from a scanner was covered earlier, in the "Scanning an Image" section.

After you have consolidated your photos, it's time to assign them to categories. By adding some custom information to your photographs, Photoshop Album can make organizing them and finding them later a snap. Computers are best at finding files by looking at the size or file name, but you are more capable of distinguishing pictures you took in Germany versus those you took in Paris. For this reason, Photoshop Album lets you create your own categories and assign each picture in your collection to one of these categories.

A category you assign to a file is called a tag, and this assignment will define some characteristic of the file. You can use pre-defined categories, such as People, Places, or Family, or you can create new categories with any criteria you want to use that will help you find the picture later. After you have established the criteria and tagged your photos accordingly, you'll find it easy to track down any of your photos.

More About . . . Assigning Tags with Photoshop Album

Personally assigning your own tags is the best way to keep track of your photos. To assign a tag to a photo in Photoshop Album, from the main window, right-click the thumbnail in the main window, and then choose **Attach Tag**, followed by the appropriate submenu item, and then the tag.

In addition to the convenience of managing all of your images in one place, there are a variety of other advantages to using image-management software. For example, you can generate slideshows and albums with a single command. Photoshop Album then runs a wizard that asks you how to display your pictures, and with what style of background. The results can be sent to a friend over e-mail, archived on a CD, or posted to a Web site.

4

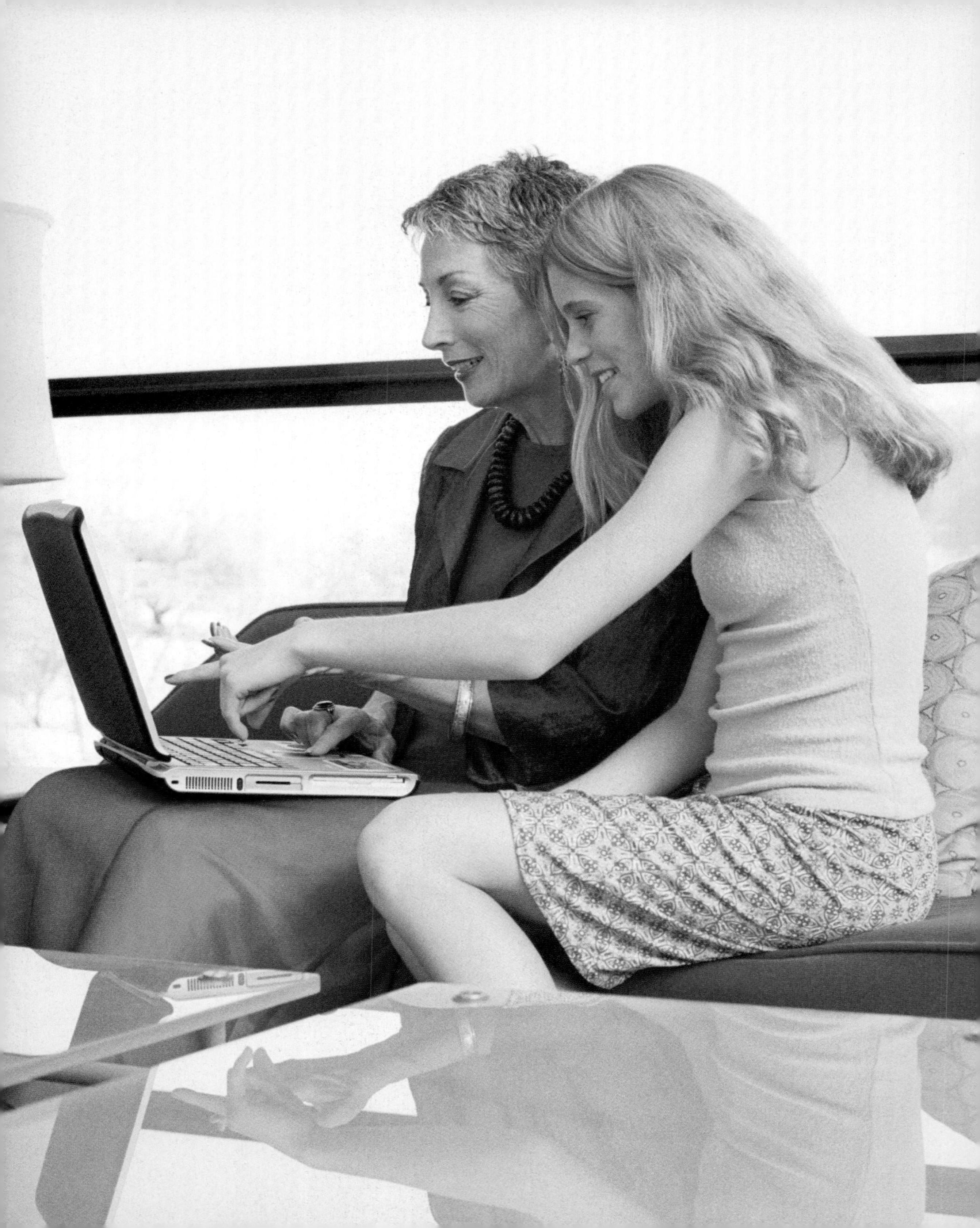

CHAPTER 5

Edit and Manage Your Digital Photos

Remember that photo you took of Rover where his eyes were red and glaring? Or how about the one of all your cousins at the family reunion that turned out too dark? Everyone has that one photograph that simply got away. Sometimes the photograph eludes you because you didn't have your camera with you. Other times you manage to snap the scene, only to discover that it wasn't in the best lighting or setting. Image-editing software can't help you if you missed a shot because you forgot your camera. It can, however, rectify photographic mistakes like red-eye or image brightness. Using image-editing software, you can crop out unnecessary portions of a photo, as well as correct images that are too dark or too bright, fix red-eye, rotate images, and more.

In addition, you can use image-editing software to apply a wide variety of special effects to your images and create special projects such as greeting cards, calendars, and slide shows. In this chapter, you'll gain an overview of what you can accomplish using your photo-editing program, and you'll learn some specific skills that will help you perfect your images.

Understanding Image Editing Basics

Many digital cameras or camera bundles include an image-editing program that will probably work perfectly for your needs. But if your camera doesn't include an editing program, or if you think you'd prefer to use a different program, you can also buy one. Although each image-editing program on the market works a little bit differently, most offer the same basic set of features. For example, nearly every program enables you to open, edit, organize, share, and print your pictures. However, image-editing programs often differ in precisely how you accomplish each of these actions.

In this section, you'll learn some common characteristics of image-editing software and preview some of the tools you can expect to find in such a software package.

 This chapter provides detailed steps for tasks using Photoshop Elements and Picture It!. If you use a different program, check its user guide for specific instructions. Typically, the steps are very similar.

Before you can use your image-editing program, you must first install it. The specific steps for this process differ from program to program. Usually you can simply insert the CD into your CD drive and follow the directions. If you have problems with installation, consult the program's manual for additional instructions. After you install your image-editing program, you start it just as you would any other program.

When you start your image-editing program, it will probably display a Welcome screen with icons and/or links (underlined menu commands) for common tasks. This Welcome screen can help you familiarize yourself with your image-editing program. For example, Photoshop Elements displays a Welcome screen with options for opening a file on your computer, connecting to a camera or scanner, and going through a tutorial (see Figure 5-1).

Adobe Photoshop Elements
File Edit Image Enhance Layer Select Filter View Window Help
Adobe Photoshop Elements 2.0
New File
Browse for File
Connect to Camera or Scanner
Common Issues
Tutorial
Exit Welcome Screen
Show this screen at startup

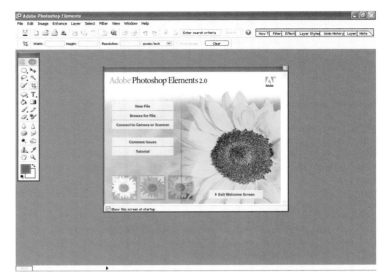

Figure 5-1 Open a file, import an image from your camera or scanner, or go through a tutorial from the Photoshop Elements Welcome screen.

In Photoshop Elements, as in some other image-editing programs, the Welcome screen appears each time you start the program unless you remove the checkmark from the Show This Screen at Startup box in the lower-left corner.

Microsoft Picture It! Photo Premium 9
Common Tasks
Quick Links
Startup Window...
Create a Project...
Touchup
Levels Auto Fix
Brightness and Contrast...
Fix Red Eye...
Adjust Tint...
Sharpen or Blur...
Hue and Saturation...
Batch Edit in Mini Lab...
Format
Effects
Edges
Add Something
Microsoft Picture It! Photo Premium 9
Picture It! PHOTO PREMIUM
Open
Open from Camera
Scan a Picture
Edit Multiple Pictures
Create a Project
Take a Tour
Instructional Videos
Help
Online Photo Tips
Register Online
Discover Even More
Recent Files
[More Files...]
Kittens.tiff
Coast.jpg
Beach.jpg
Seagull.jpg
Show on startup
Close

Figure 5-2 When launched, Picture It! displays a startup window that contains various options for opening files and viewing reference materials.

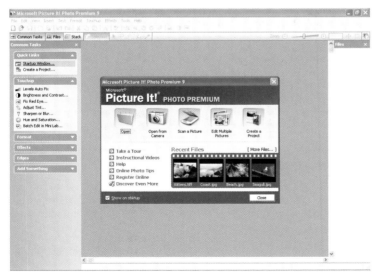

Likewise, Picture It! displays a Welcome screen upon startup, listing your main choices: Open, Open from Camera, Scan a Picture, Edit Multiple Pictures, or Create a Project (see Figure 5-2). From this screen, you can also take a tour of the program and access help and reference materials. Also, recently opened images appear in this window for easy access.

Opening and Saving Your Images

Now that you're familiar with your image editor's program window and tools, it's time to get down to the business of using the program to work with your images. First, however, you must learn how to open images on your computer.

Before you can open an image on your computer, you must download it from your digital camera, scan it using your scanner, or obtain it in some other way—perhaps by downloading it from the Internet or copying it from a photo CD. In many cases, you can use your image-editing program to complete this task. When the image is stored on your computer, you can use your image-editing program to open it.

In this section, you'll learn how to open images stored on your computer and save the changes you make to an image.

Opening an Image for Editing

You have already discovered several different sources for digital images, including digital cameras, scanners, the Web, and your computer. Most image-editing programs enable you to obtain pictures from the following sources:

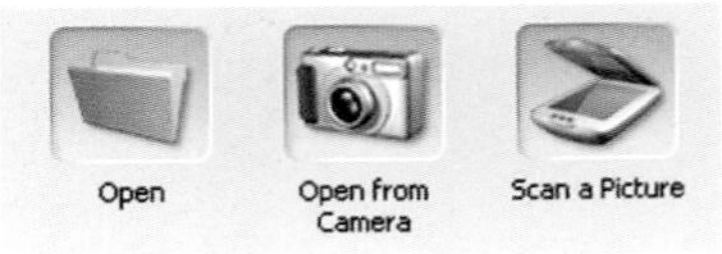
Open
Open from Camera
Scan a Picture

- **Your computer.** In most cases, you transfer images from your digital camera or other device, such as a scanner, directly to your computer. You probably store images found on the Internet on your computer as well. You can use your image-editing program to open image files directly from your computer. When you choose this method, you select the drive and folder where your images are stored, including your CD-ROM drive, and then open the images.
- **Your digital camera.** Many image-editing programs enable you to download and open pictures directly from your camera. For help transferring pictures from your camera to your computer, review Chapter 4.
- **Your scanner.** In most cases, you can start a scan from your image-editing program and scan the image directly into the image-editing program window. The option for doing this might be called Scanner or TWAIN.

TWAIN is the official technical standard for scanning images. Almost all scanners come with a TWAIN driver (software that allows the device to communicate with the computer). This makes such scanners compatible with any other device that supports the TWAIN standard.

- **The Internet.** You can use your image-editing program to access online photo and image sources and download image files to your computer.

Let's take a look at the most common method of opening pictures—from the computer. The following sections cover opening images using Photoshop Elements and Picture It!.

Often you may want to open and work with several pictures at once or in order. Most programs enable you to open a set of pictures and select the image you want to work with first. The image you've selected appears in the image-editing program's work area, and the remaining images are displayed in a library or Files palette. In the following sections, you'll learn how to open and manage multiple images.

Opening an Image in Photoshop Elements

To use Photoshop Elements to open an image stored on your computer, follow these steps:

1. On the Welcome screen, click **Browse for File**. The File Browser dialog box will appear; it will display the contents of the My Pictures folder automatically.

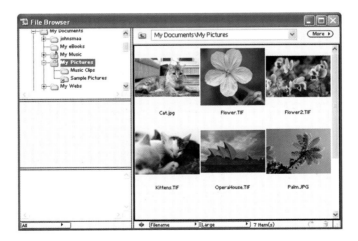

File Browser
My Documents
johnsmaa
My eBooks
My Music
My Pictures
Music Clips
Sample Pictures
My Webs
My Documents\My Pictures
More
Cat.jpg
Flower.TIF
Flower2.TIF
Kittens.TIF
OperaHouse.TIF
Palm.JPG
All
Filename
Large
7 Item(s)

2. Navigate to the file using the folder list in the upper-right corner of the dialog box. Click the + (plus sign) to the left of a folder to expand it; click the – (minus sign) to the left of a folder to collapse it. Click a folder to display its contents in the preview pane on the right side of the dialog box.

By default, most image-editing programs only list image files when you browse for files to open. Photoshop Elements automatically filters out word processing documents, digital music files, and other file types, which makes finding images easier.

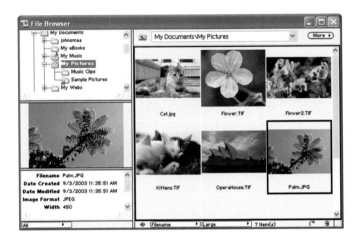

File Browser
My Documents
johnsmaa
My eBooks
My Music
My Pictures
Music Clips
Sample Pictures
My Webs
My Documents\My Pictures
More
Cat.jpg
Flower.TIF
Flower2.TIF
Kittens.TIF
OperaHouse.TIF
Palm.JPG
Filename Palm.JPG
Date Created 9/3/2003 11:35:51 AM
Date Modified 9/3/2003 11:35:51 AM
Image Format JPEG
Width 450
All
Filename
Large
7 Item(s)

❸ Click the image file you want to open. The image and additional file information will appear in the preview area beneath the folder list. To select multiple files, hold down the **CTRL** key and click each file you want to open. If you select multiple images, no preview will be displayed in the left preview pane.

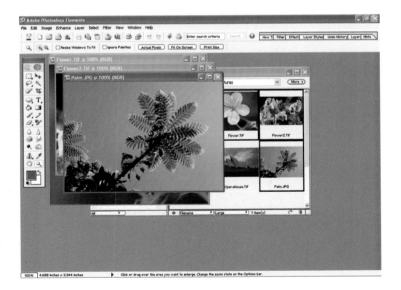

Adobe Photoshop Elements
File Edit Image Enhance Layer Select Filter View Window Help
Flower.TIF @ 100% (RGB)
Flower2.TIF @ 100% (RGB)
Palm.JPG @ 100% (RGB)

❹ Double-click a selected file to open all selected files; or, right-click a file and choose **Open**. If you selected a single image file, it will open in the work area. If you selected multiple files, they will all open in the work area.

Opening an Image in Picture It!

Follow these steps to open an image using Picture It!:

1. On the Welcome screen, click **Open**. The File Browser dialog box will appear.

   Picture It! also lists recently opened files on the Welcome screen; you can reopen these files by clicking on them.

2. Using the list on the left side of the dialog box, locate the folder that contains your image files. Click the + (plus sign) to the left of a folder to expand it; click the – (minus sign) to the left of a folder to collapse it. Click a folder to display its contents in the preview pane on the right side of the dialog box.

3. On the right side of the File Browser dialog box, click the image file you want to open. To select multiple files, hold down the **CTRL** key and click each file you want to open.

File Browser
All Files
MSN Groups
Look in:
Nature
Desktop
My Documents
My albums
My eBooks
My Music
My Pictures
Animals
My Photos
Nature
New Folder
Picture
Slideshows
My PSP8 Files
My Videos
My Computer
3½ Floppy (A:)
Local Disk (C:)
DVD-RAM Drive (D:)
Shared Documents
Mountain
Yosemite
Palm
Waterfall
File name:
"Mountain.TIF" "Yosemite.TIF" "Waterfall.tiff"
Files of type:
All Pictures or Projects (*.png;*.php;*.mix;*.fpx;*.psd;*.d
OK
Cancel

Waterfall.tiff - Microsoft Picture It! Photo Premium 9
File Edit View Insert Text Format Touchup Effects Tools Help
Common Tasks
Files
Stack
Zoom
21%
Common Tasks
Quick Links
Startup Window...
Create a Project...
Touchup
Levels Auto Fix
Brightness and Contrast...
Fix Red Eye...
Adjust Tint...
Sharpen or Blur...
Hue and Saturation...
Batch Edit in Mini Lab...
Format
Effects
Edges
Add Something
Files
Mountain.TIF
Yosemite.TIF
Waterfall.tiff

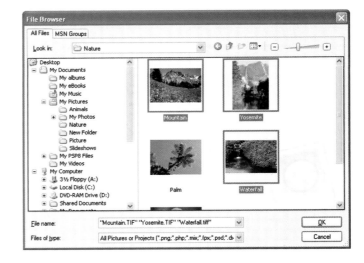

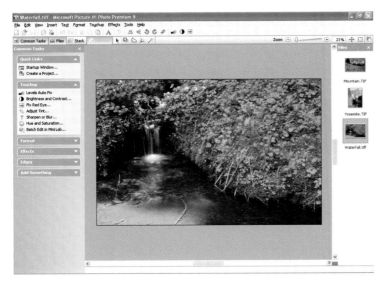

4. Click **OK**. If you selected a single image file, it will open in the work area. If you selected multiple files, click the **Files** button in the upper-left corner of the screen to show the Files palette, which displays all opened files to the right of the main project area.

Saving an Image

In most cases, before you begin to make changes to an open image, you should create a working copy of it. That way, any changes you make to the image will occur on the working copy, while the original remains intact. You can then save the copy as a new file with a different name than the original. If your edits are disappointing, this ensures that you can always return to the original and start over.

When you save an image file, observe the following guidelines:

+ **Select the correct command from the File menu.** Choose **Save As** the first time you save the file, and give it a new name or store it in a new location, thereby preserving the original. After you've saved the file using the Save As command, click **Save** periodically as you continue to edit the image.

 Don't wait until you've put the final touches on your image to save it, and be sure to keep saving as you work. Otherwise, if some disaster befell your computer (for instance, if it lost power), all your work would be lost.

+ **Rename downloaded images.** When you download pictures from a digital camera, the file names are usually not very descriptive. For example, images might be named according to the date they were taken, or the camera might use a numbering scheme to identify the order in which they were taken. To help you remember which image is which, it's a good idea to save each image file using a descriptive file name.

 Even if you don't open pictures for editing and then save them, you should still rename your files if their names are not descriptive. This will help you keep your image files organized. You can rename files in a Windows folder by right-clicking the file, selecting **Rename** from the menu that appears, and typing a new name.

+ **Select a file format.** If your image-editing program saves image files using a default proprietary file format, you might decide to change a file's format to share it with people who use different image-editing programs. The JPEG format is used frequently for images placed on the Web because JPEG images are compressed and therefore require less space. The TIF and PCX formats are used commonly for printed illustrations. For more information about file formats, refer to Chapter 4. To change the file type, click the **Save as Type** drop-down menu, and then select the format you want.

Saving an Image in Photoshop Elements

To save an image that is open in the Photoshop Elements work area, follow these steps:

1. Click **File**, and then click **Save As**. The Save As dialog box will open.

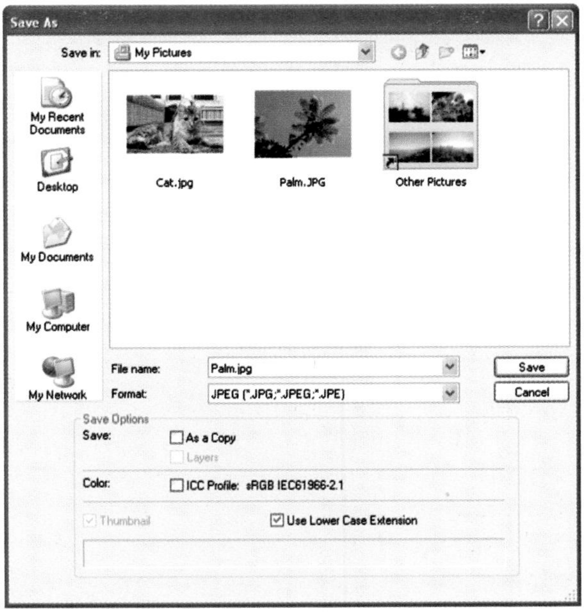
Save As
Save in: My Pictures
My Recent Documents
Desktop
My Documents
My Computer
My Network
Cat.jpg
Palm.JPG
Other Pictures
File name: Palm.jpg
Format: JPEG (*.JPG;*.JPEG;*.JPE)
Save
Cancel
Save Options
Save: As a Copy
Layers
Color: ICC Profile: sRGB IEC61966-2.1
Thumbnail
Use Lower Case Extension

2. Navigate to the drive and folder where you want to store your image.
3. Locate and open the folder in which you want to save your image.

> If you want to create a new folder for your images, click the drive or folder in which you want to place the new folder, and then click **Create New Folder**. The new folder will appear. Type a name for the folder and press **ENTER**. Double-click the new folder to open it.

4. Type a name for the file in the File name text box. Make sure this name describes the contents of the image file.
5. Click **Save**.

Saving an Image in Picture It!

To save an image that is open in the Picture It! work area, follow these steps:

1. Click **File**, and then click **Save as** to open the Save As dialog box.

Save As
All Files
Save in:
Nature
Desktop
My Documents
My albums
My eBooks
My Music
My Pictures
Animals
My Photos
Nature
My PSP8 Files
My Videos
My Computer
3½ Floppy (A:)
Local Disk (C:)
DVD-RAM Drive (D:)
Shared Documents
My Documents
My Network Places
camera
1029-12
1066-07
Palm
Waterfall
File name:
Waterfall.tif
Save as type:
Tagged Image File Format (*.tif;*.tiff)
Options...
Save
Cancel

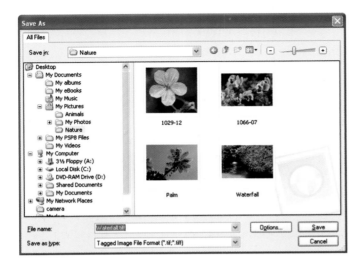

2. Locate and open the folder in which you want to save your image.
3. Type a file name in the File name text box. Make sure this name describes the contents of the image file.
4. Click **Save**.

Enhancing Pictures

Now that you understand the basics of your image-editing program, it's time to get into the meat of the program—using it to enhance your images.

One of the most common reasons to edit an image is to correct problems in it. For example, you might discover that the image is too light or too dark, that it lacks contrast, or that the eyes of your photograph's subject may appear to be red, a common problem with flash photography. You might want to eliminate unwanted elements of the picture and keep only part of it. In this section, you'll learn how to correct these common problems.

Most image-editing programs offer many more tools for fixing problem pictures than the ones covered here. For information about some other types of enhancements you might be able to apply using your image editor, see your image-editing software manual.

Adjusting Color

Many factors affect the color in your image, including brightness, contrast, and tint. If your picture is too dark, you can use your image-editing program to brighten it. Or perhaps the details in your image are not sharp—in that case, you can adjust the image's contrast. Finally, if you want to add a special effect, you can adjust an image's tint. In this section, you'll learn how to adjust basic color settings using Photoshop Elements and Picture It!.

Every picture is different, so there are no set rules for determining what color settings will work best for you. To get the color in your image just right, you'll need to experiment a bit with the various settings. Don't be afraid; you can always undo your edits if you don't like the results.

Enhancing Color in Photoshop Elements

Photoshop Elements can adjust the color, brightness, and contrast of your image automatically, or you can use the program to adjust the color manually. It's always best to try the automatic features first to let the software do the work for you. Then, if you don't like the results, you can adjust the settings manually. To instruct Photoshop Elements to handle color and contrast settings automatically, follow these steps:

1. Make sure the image you want to change is open in the Photoshop Elements work area.
2. From the Enhance menu, choose **Auto Levels, Auto Contrast,** or **Auto Color Correction**. When you choose one of these options, Photoshop Elements takes the necessary steps to enhance the image's color settings.

   Figure 5-3 demonstrates an image before and after these automatic enhancements.
3. To reject these changes, choose **Undo** from the Edit menu (or press **CTRL+Z**).

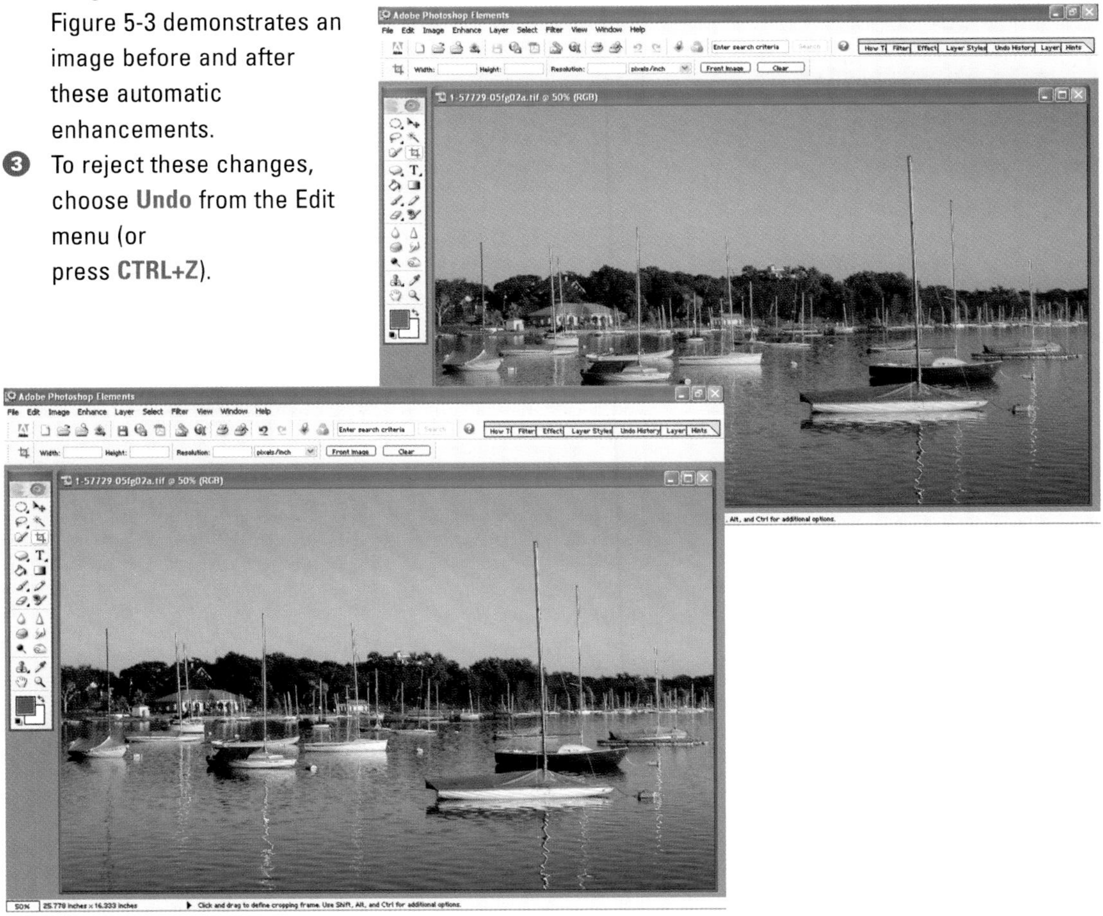
Adobe Photoshop Elements
1-57729-05fg02a.tif @ 50% (RGB)
Adobe Photoshop Elements
1-57729-05fg02a.tif @ 50% (RGB)

Figure 5-3 Using Auto Levels, Auto Contrast, and Auto Color Correction, you can easily improve the appearance of your photographs.

To adjust the color settings manually, you can use Photoshop Element's Quick Fix utility. Using this method, you can apply to your image several effects related to color, brightness, and contrast before you confirm your changes.

If an area is selected, Quick Fix applies changes to the selected area only. You'll learn about selection in the "Cropping an Image" section later in this chapter.

To use Photoshop Elements' Quick Fix feature to adjust color settings, follow these steps:

1. Make sure the image you want to change is open in the work area.
2. From the Enhance menu, choose **Quick Fix**. The Quick Fix dialog box will appear.
3. In the Select Adjustment Category section, choose **Brightness** or **Color Correction**.

   In addition to color and brightness, you can adjust focus and rotation settings from the Quick Fix dialog box. You will learn more about these features later in this chapter, in the "Rotating an Image" and "Adding Other Special Effects" sections.

4. In the Select Adjustment section, choose the desired effect. For example, choose **Brightness/Contrast** to compensate for exposure problems.
5. In the third column, your options will depend on the adjustment you selected. Click the **Apply** button. Alternatively, you can click and drag a slider to preview the adjustment in the preview pane at the top of the Quick Fix dialog box. Figure 5-4 demonstrates how you can improve brightness by using Quick Fix.

Quick Fix
OK
Cancel
Help
Before
After
Tip:
Brightness/Contrast: Adjusts the overall brightness or contrast of a photo. Use to make small adjustments only. To make larger adjustments, use Auto Contrast or Auto Levels.
Undo
Redo
Reset Image
1. Select Adjustment Category
Brightness
Color Correction
Focus
Rotate
2. Select Adjustment
Auto Contrast
Auto Levels
Brightness/Contrast
Fill Flash
Adjust Backlighting
3. Apply Brightness/Contrast
Brightness:
Contrast:
0

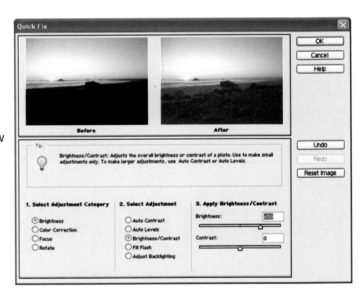

Figure 5-4 Adjust the color and brightness using Photoshop Elements' Quick Fix feature.

6. Click the **Undo** button to undo the previous change. Click the **Reset** button to revert to the original image. Click **OK** to accept the changes and return to the main window.

Adjusting Color in Picture It!

Like Photoshop Elements, Picture It! affords you several options when it comes to adjusting the color in your image—and using them is just as easy. For example, to adjust image brightness and contrast automatically, follow these simple steps:

1. Make sure the image you want to change is open in the Picture It! work area.
2. In the Common Tasks pane on the left side of the screen, open the **Touchup pane** (if it's not already open).
3. Choose **Brightness and Contrast**. The Brightness and Contrast task pane will open.
4. Click **Levels auto fix** and **Contrast auto fix**. Picture It! will update the image, correcting brightness and contrast problems automatically. Figure 5-5 demonstrates these results.

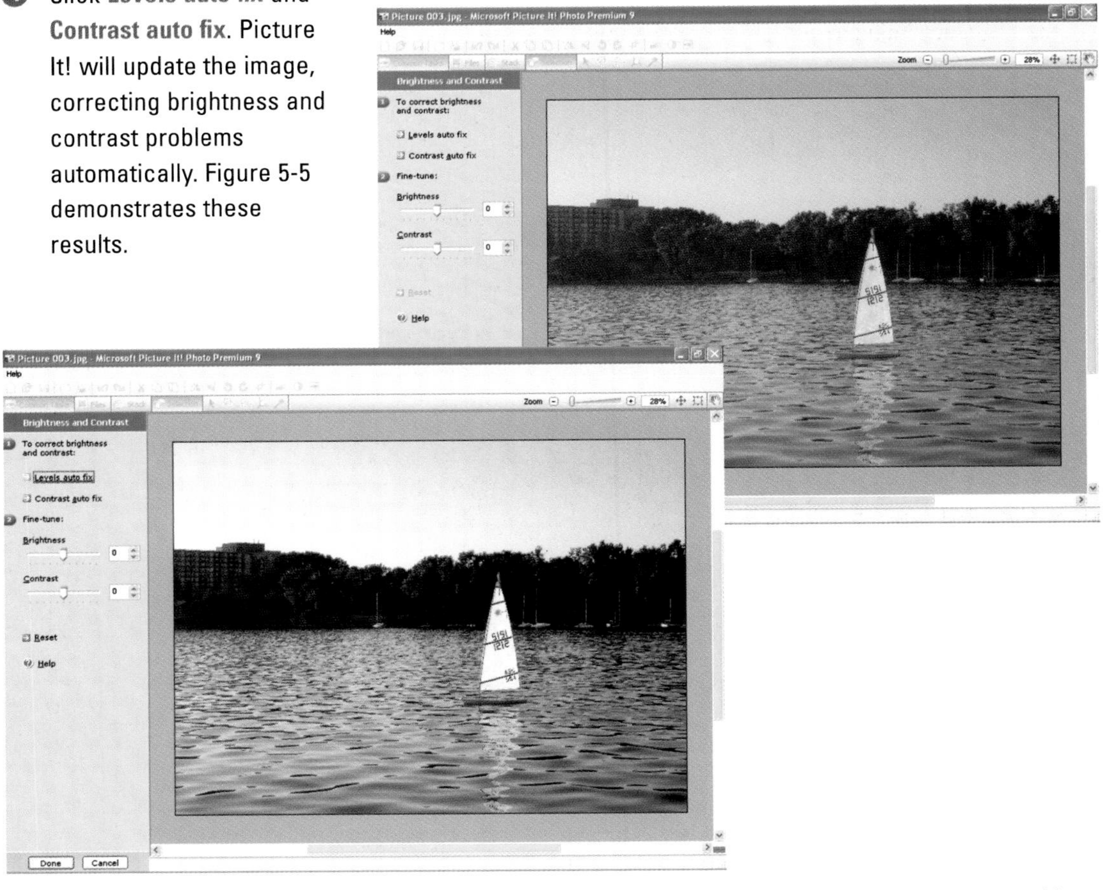
Picture 003.jpg - Microsoft Picture It! Photo Premium 9
Help
Zoom
28%
Brightness and Contrast
To correct brightness and contrast:
Levels auto fix
Contrast auto fix
Fine-tune:
Brightness
Contrast
Reset
Help
Done
Cancel

Figure 5-5 Use the Levels and Contrast Auto Fix features to resolve common color and contrast problems.

5. If you like the results, click **Done**. To reject the results, click **Cancel**.

If you prefer to adjust color settings manually, drag the Brightness and Contrast slider bars until the image is the way you want it. Picture It! defines brightness as "the amount of light that appears to emanate from a color" and contrast as "the degree of difference between the lightest and darkest parts of an image."

In addition to adjusting the brightness and contrast in your image, you can adjust the tint automatically or manually.

1. Make sure the image you want to change is open in the work area.
2. In the Touchup pane, choose **Adjust Tint**. The Adjust Tint task pane will open, displaying settings for Color and Amount.
3. To instruct Picture It! to adjust the tint in your image automatically, click **Tint auto fix**. Figure 5-6 displays an image whose tint was adjusted automatically.

Picture 006.jpg - Microsoft Picture It! Photo Premium 9
Help
Adjust Tint
To correct tint:
Tint auto fix
Or
Click an area in the picture that should be white.
Fine-tune:
Color
Amount
Redo
Help
Zoom
22%
Picture 006.jpg - Microsoft Picture It! Photo Premium 9
Help
Adjust Tint
To correct tint:
Tint auto fix
Or
Click an area in the picture that should be white.
Fine-tune:
Color
88
Amount
2
Reset
Help
Done
Cancel
Zoom
22%

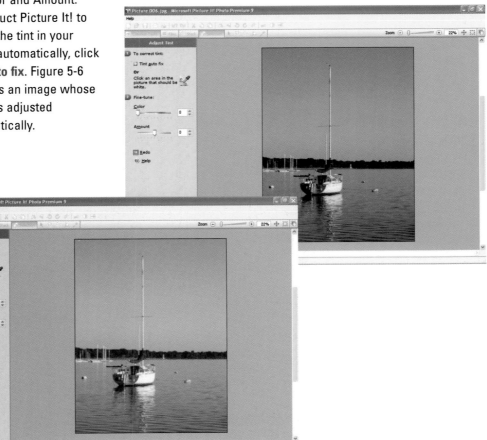

Figure 5-6 Automatically adjust the tint of an image in the Adjust Tint pane.

4. To adjust tint settings manually, drag the Color slider bar to select the color you want to change. Then drag the Amount slider bar to add more or less of the color tint.
5. If you like the results, click **Done**. To reject the results, click **Cancel**.

Fixing Red-Eye

Have you ever captured a perfect moment on camera, only to discover that your camera's flash turned your subject's eyes an unattractive shade of red? Fortunately, some cameras are designed to prevent red-eye in flash pictures. If your camera does not have this option, however, or if you forgot to turn it on, then you can use your image-editing program to return your photographed subject's eyes to a normal color.

Fixing Red-Eye in Photoshop Elements

To fix red-eye in Photoshop Elements, follow these steps:

1. Make sure the image you want to fix is open in the Photoshop Elements work area.
2. For more precision, click the **Zoom tool** and zoom in so the red in the eye is viewable.

   To choose the viewable area (in this case, the eye), select the Zoom tool and click and drag a box around the subject's eye.

3. Click the **Red Eye Brush tool** in the Tools palette.
4. In the options bar at the top of your screen, make sure that First Click is selected.
5. Point the brush on a red area you want to remove, and then click it (see Figure 5-7). Photoshop Elements will remove the red coloring within the circular drawing area. To use a different brush size, click the drop-down palette in the options bar in the upper-left corner of your screen.

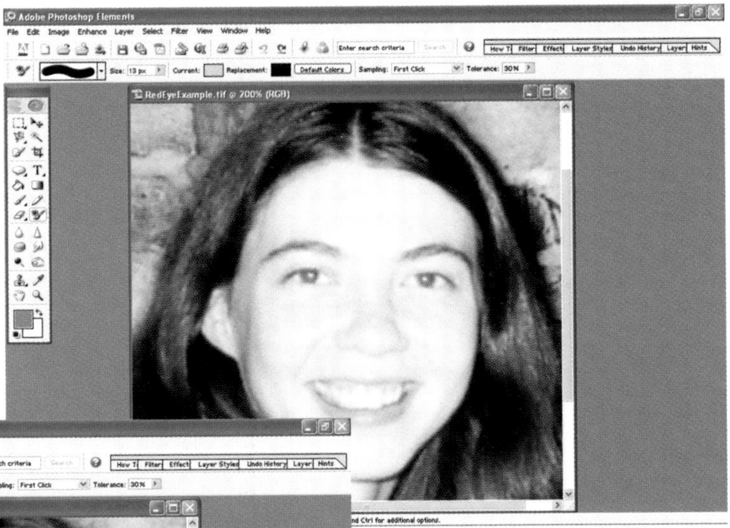
Adobe Photoshop Elements
RedEyeExample.tif @ 200% (RGB)
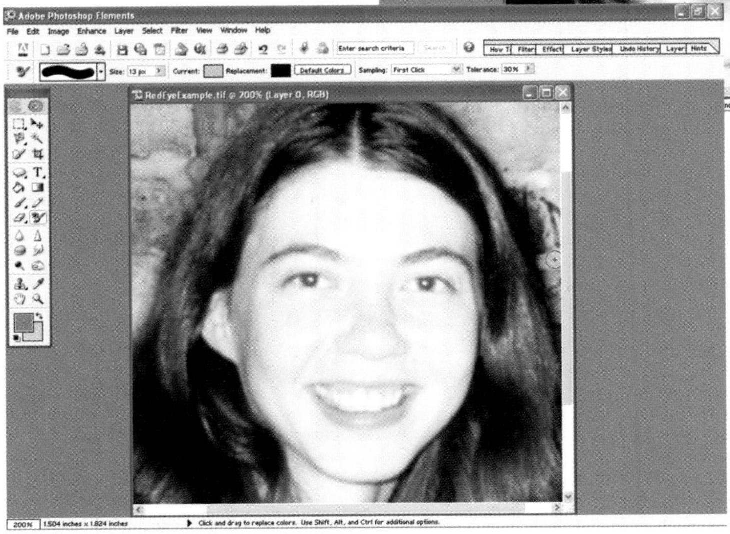
Adobe Photoshop Elements
RedEyeExample.tif @ 200% (Layer 0, RGB)

Figure 5-7 Use Photoshop Elements' Red Eye Brush tool to remove red-eye from a picture.

Fixing Red-Eye in Picture It!

To fix red-eye in Picture It!, follow these steps:

1. Make sure the image you want to fix is open in the work area.
2. Click **Touchup** in the Common Tasks pane (if it isn't already open), and then click **Fix Red Eye**.
3. Drag the zoom slider in the Fix Red Eye toolbar to zoom in on the part of the image you want to fix.
4. Using the scroll bars in the picture work area, scroll so that you can see the red-eye.
5. Place the round pointer over the first eye and click on it.
6. Repeat Step 5 for the second eye.
7. Click **Red-eye auto fix** (see Figure 5-8).
8. Click **Done** to return to the main editing screen.

RedEyeExample.tif - Microsoft Picture It! Photo Premium 9
Help
Zoom
200%
Fix Red Eye
Zoom in on the eyes.
Click the red part of the eyes.
To fix the red eyes, click:
Red-eye auto fix
Reset
Help
RedEyeExample.tif - Microsoft Picture It! Photo Premium 9
Help
Zoom
200%
Fix Red Eye
Zoom in on the eyes.
Click the red part of the eyes.
To fix the red eyes, click:
Red-eye auto fix
Reset
Help
Done
Cancel

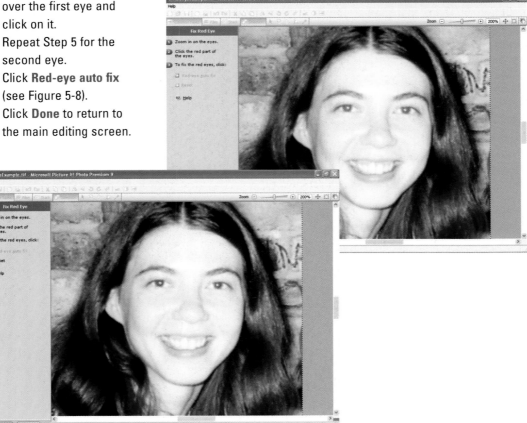

Figure 5-8 In Picture It!, use the Fix Red Eye pane to eliminate red-eye from a photograph.

Cropping an Image

If you have an out-of-place object in the background of an image, or if the subject isn't properly centered, you can cut out the unnecessary parts to better focus on your subject. Cutting out part of a picture is called cropping. As will be discussed in this section, you can use your image-editing program to crop your picture. You can even use special cutout features to create unusually shaped images, such as stars or suns.

Cropping an Image in Photoshop Elements

To crop in image in Photoshop Elements, follow these steps:

1. Make sure the image you want to crop is open in the Photoshop Elements work area.
2. Click the **Crop tool** in the Tools palette.

   Right-click the **Crop tool** to choose between a rectangular or elliptical marquee.

3. Click and drag around the part of the photograph you want to keep, as shown in the top image in Figure 5-9.
4. Click and drag the handles at the edge of the cropped area to make adjustments.
5. From the Image menu, choose **Crop**. The region surrounding the crop box will disappear, and the overall image will be resized, as shown in the bottom image in Figure 5-9.

Adobe Photoshop Elements
File Edit Image Enhance Layer Select Filter View Window Help
Picture 023.jpg @ 30.7% (RGB)
Adobe Photoshop Elements
File Edit Image Enhance Layer Select Filter View Window Help
Picture 023.jpg @ 54.5% (RGB)

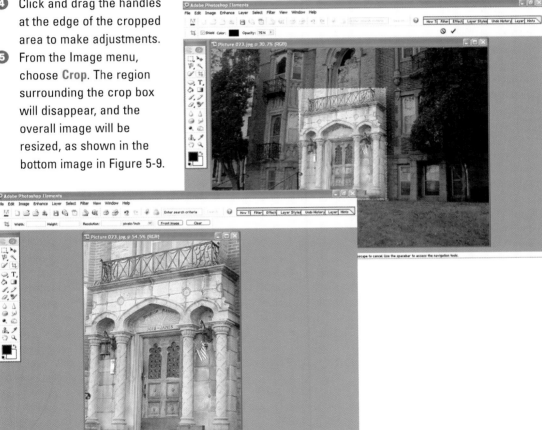

Figure 5-9 In Photoshop Elements, you can use the Crop tool to crop an image.

The cropped image will appear smaller than the original image at first. To resize the canvas to fill the screen, choose **Fit on Screen** from the View menu.

Cropping an Image in Picture It!

To crop an image in Picture It!, follow these steps:

1. Make sure the image you want to crop is open in the Picture It! work area.
2. Click the **Format** pane in the Common Tasks pane.
3. Choose **Crop Canvas**. The Crop screen will appear.
4. Drag the resizing handles so the part of the image you want to keep is boxed. You can also drag the rotate handle to change the orientation of the cropped shape.
5. When you're ready, click **Done** to crop the picture (see Figure 5-10).

Picture 023.jpg - Microsoft Picture It! Photo Premium 9
Help
Zoom
29%
Crop
Select a proportion:
Custom
Click a starting point, and then drag the outline.
Set a size:
827
1113
pixels
Width
Height
You can also:
Show guidelines for the rule of thirds.
Reset
Help
Picture 023.jpg - Microsoft Picture It! Photo Premium 9
File Edit View Insert Text Format Touchup Effects Tools Help
Common Tasks
Files
Stack
Zoom
52%
Common Tasks
Quick Links
Startup Window...
Create a Project...
Touchup
Levels Auto Fix
Brightness and Contrast...
Fix Red Eye...
Adjust Tint...
Sharpen or Blur...
Hue and Saturation...
Batch Edit in Mini Lab...
Format
Rotate...
Crop Canvas...
Straighten Picture...
Resize Image...
Flip...
Effects
Edges
Add Something

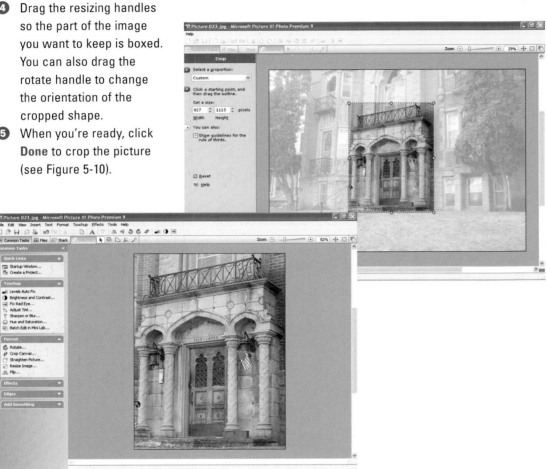

Figure 5-10 In Picture It!, use the Crop Canvas option to crop a portion of an image.

Picture It! also enables you to crop your images using any of a series of predefined proportions. In the Crop window, select the proportion you want to use from the Select a Proportion drop-down list. (Your choices include wallet, square, and widescreen, among others.)

Rotating an Image

Sometimes digital images need to be rotated so they are displayed correctly on your monitor (for example, if you accidentally place an image upside down on the bed of your scanner). Simply use your image-editing program to rotate the image so it's displayed properly. Additionally, if a photo is slightly crooked when you scan it, you can rotate the image in your image-editing program until it is set with the proper orientation.

Rotating an Image in Photoshop Elements

To rotate an image in Photoshop Elements, follow these steps:

1. Make sure the image you want to rotate is open in the Photoshop Elements work area.
2. From the Image menu, choose **Rotate**, and then select a rotation angle (90 degrees left, 90 degrees right, or 180 degrees).

   Figure 5-11 shows an image rotated 90 degrees right.
3. From the Image menu, choose **Rotate**, and then **Custom** to rotate the image by a specified amount. The Rotate Canvas dialog box will appear.

Adobe Photoshop Elements
File Edit Image Enhance Layer Select Filter View Window Help
Clock Tower.jpg @ 25% (RGB)

Adobe Photoshop Elements
File Edit Image Enhance Layer Select Filter View Window Help
Clock Tower.jpg @ 25% (RGB)

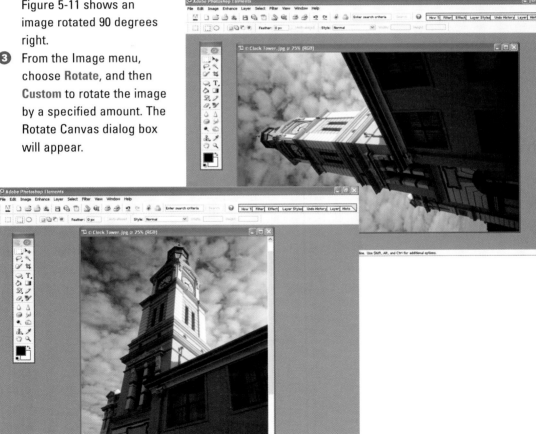

Figure 5-11 Rotate images to adjust the orientation of a photograph.

4. Enter the angle (in degrees) in the text box, and then choose whether you want to rotate the image left or right.
5. Click **OK**. You will return to the main work area, and the image will be rotated by the degree you specified.
6. After you rotate the image manually, crop it to the desired area as discussed in the previous section.

Rotating an Image in Picture It!

To rotate an image in Picture It!, follow these steps:

1. Make sure the image you want to rotate is open in the Picture It! work area.
2. Click the **Format** pane in the Common Tasks pane.
3. Choose **Rotate**.
4. Click the rotation you want—**Left**, **Half turn**, **Right**, or **Custom** (see Figure 5-12).
5. If you rotated the image manually, the edges will be slanted. To restore the orientation of the photograph, crop it to the desired area as discussed in the previous section.

Picture 006.jpg - Microsoft Picture It! Photo Premium 9
Help
Zoom
28%
Rotate
Click a direction:
Left
Half turn
Right
Custom
0
Help

Picture 006.jpg - Microsoft Picture It! Photo Premium 9
Help
Zoom
22%
Rotate
Click a direction:
Left
Half turn
Right
Custom
270
Reset
Help
Done
Cancel

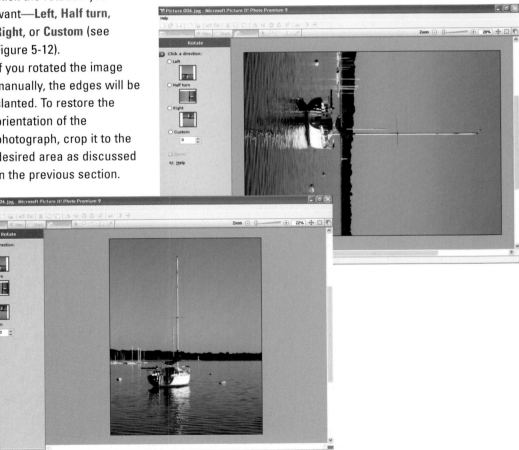

Figure 5-12 Use the Rotate window to change the orientation of a photograph in Picture It!.

More About . . . Adding Special Effects

In addition to correcting problems, you can use your image-editing program to add some fun and artistic effects to your picture. For example, you can convert a color photo to black-and-white or add a sepia tone (a brownish tint) to artificially age the image. You can create a cutout by removing a selected portion of a photo and then pasting it into another image. If you're feeling really funky, you can warp the picture to make it like a reflection in a funhouse mirror, turn it into a mosaic, add shadows, apply 3D effects, and much more.

The best way to learn how to use these features is to experiment! Try different features to see how the results look. If you don't like the effect, simply undo your changes.

The following lists just a few of the different special effects available with Photoshop Elements or Picture It!:

- **Apply filters.** You can use filters to apply a number of general effects to your image. You can blur the image, apply textures, and add artistic effects.
- **Draw effects.** Draw on your image to apply colors and effects using brushes, erasers, and predefined shapes.
- **Combine photos.** Photoshop Elements includes a Photomerge option, from which you can create panoramic sweeps.
- **Annotate your images.** Add text, clip art, or other graphic objects to your image.
- **Apply effects and filters.** You can apply several common effects to your photographs using filters and effects.
- **Use frames and edge effects.** Add polish to an image by applying frame and edge effects. Frame effects add a digital picture frame around your image, whereas edge effects change the photo's edge. You can highlight or soften the edges or apply some other effect.

5

Creating Greeting Cards

Hunting for the perfect greeting card isn't always easy, and these days it's not even necessary. You can make your own professional-looking holiday cards, thank-you notes, and other greetings from home. With the help of image-editing software, you can include your own customized messages and images.

To create a greeting card using Picture It!, follow these steps:

1. In Picture It!, open the picture you want to include on the greeting card.
2. In the Common Tasks pane, on the left side of your screen, under Quick Links, choose **Create a Project**.

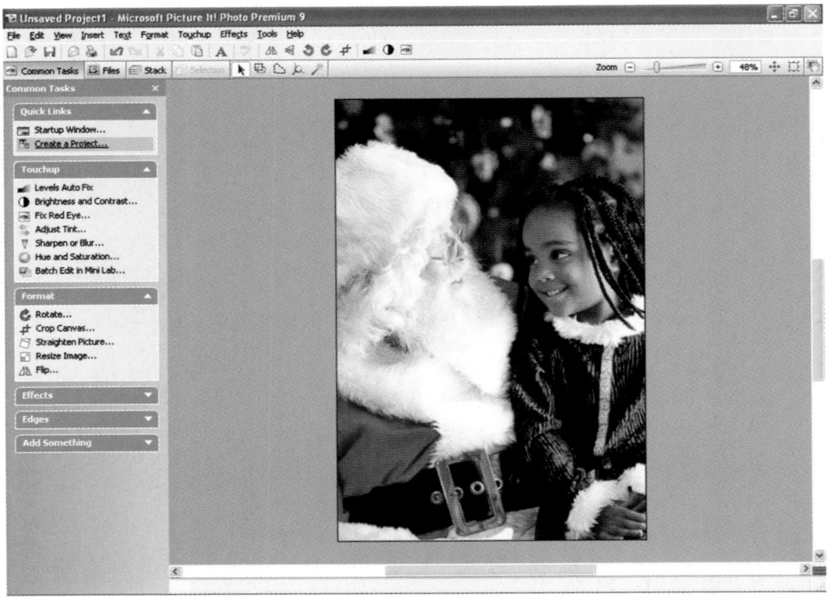

Unsaved Project1 - Microsoft Picture It! Photo Premium 9
File Edit View Insert Text Format Touchup Effects Tools Help
Common Tasks Files Stack
Zoom
48%
Common Tasks
Quick Links
Startup Window...
Create a Project...
Touchup
Levels Auto Fix
Brightness and Contrast...
Fix Red Eye...
Adjust Tint...
Sharpen or Blur...
Hue and Saturation...
Batch Edit in Mini Lab...
Format
Rotate...
Crop Canvas...
Straighten Picture...
Resize Image...
Flip...
Effects
Edges
Add Something

3. Click **Cards** and then click the theme you want to use. For this example, we'll use the **Holiday** theme.
4. In the Themes pane on the left side of the screen, choose **Photo Frames**.
5. Click the design you want to use for your card, and then click **Open**.

Although Picture It! displays several designs, some may not be installed on your computer. If you select a design that isn't installed, Picture It! will prompt you to insert one of the program installation discs. Insert the disc and click **Retry**.

6. Drag the image from the Files palette on the right side of your screen into the middle of the picture frame. The picture snaps to the middle of the frame as shown in Figure 5-13. Click **Next**.

Unsaved Project2 - Half side-fold card - Microsoft Picture It! Photo Premium 9
Help
Files
Zoom
50%
Photo Project
If your picture is in the Files palette, drag it onto the collage.
Or
If the pictures are not in the Files palette, you can:
Open a picture
Scan in a picture
Download from digital camera
Help
Files
Unsaved Pro...
Next >
Cancel

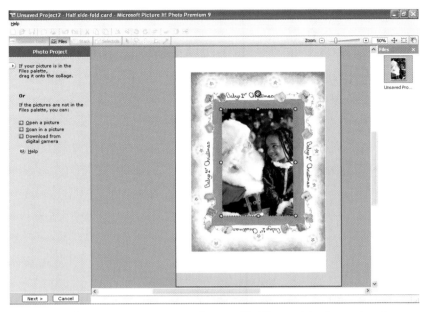

Figure 5-13 Creating a custom greeting card in Picture It! takes only minutes.

7. Now, you can click the corner handles and drag to resize the image. Or, click the image and drag to move it. When the image is sized and positioned, click **Done**. The card appears in the main work area.
8. You can view the inside spread of the card or the back by choosing from the three icons in the window to the lower left of the work area. To add text, click the **Text** tool in the toolbar at the top of the screen. Choose the font and size from the drop-down menus to the left of the Text tool. Then, type the desired text and drag it into position.
9. From the File menu, choose **Save** to save the card project. After printing the card, fold if necessary.

If you need to create several copies of the same card, as you might do with a holiday card or invitation, simply choose to print multiple copies when the Print dialog box appears.

Creating Calendars

Creating a calendar that features your own photography can be a fun way to put your digital images to use. Personalized calendars are good for at least a year of memories and can make great gifts. You can print your calendar at home or send it to a professional for production. In this section, you'll learn how to design and produce your own custom calendar.

Creating Your Own Calendar

To create a custom calendar using Picture It!, follow these steps:

1. In Picture It!, open the pictures you want to include on the calendar.
2. In the Common Tasks pane, on the left side of your screen, under Quick Links, choose **Create a Project**.
3. Click **Calendars**, and then click the type of calendar. For this example, we'll choose **Twelve Month**.
4. Click the design you want to use for your calendar, and then click **Open**.

   If you select a design that isn't installed, Picture It! will prompt you to insert one of the program installation discs. Insert the disc and click **Retry**.

5. In the Calendar Project pane, choose the year and which day you want to begin each week. Then click **Next**.

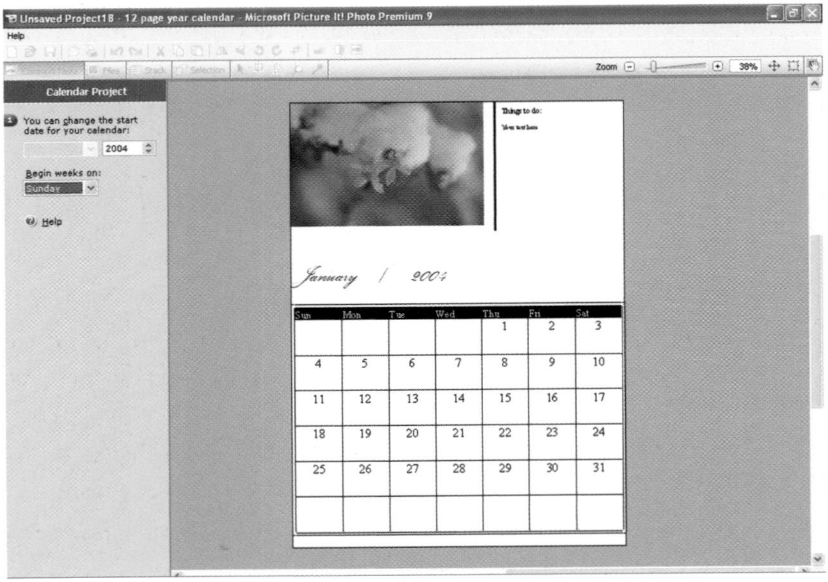
Unsaved Project18 - 12 page year calendar - Microsoft Picture It! Photo Premium 9
Calendar Project
You can change the start date for your calendar:
2004
Begin weeks on:
Sunday
Help
Zoom
Things to do:
Sun
Mon
Tue
Wed
Thu
Fri
Sat

6. Drag the image from the Files palette on the right side of your screen into the photo area of the calendar (over the existing image). The picture snaps to the image frame as shown in Figure 5-14.

Unsaved Project18 - 12 page year calendar - Microsoft Picture It! Photo Premium 9
Help
Files
Stack
Zoom
38%
Calendar Project
If your picture is in the Files palette, drag it onto the calendar.
Or
If your picture is not in the Files palette, you can:
Open a picture
Scan a picture
Download from digital camera
You have selected a project with multiple pages. This wizard helps you replace the picture on the first page.
When you are finished with the wizard, use the View menu to change pages, and then replace the pictures on those pages.
Help
Next >
Cancel
Things to do:
January / 2004
Sun
Mon
Tue
Wed
Thu
Fri
Sat
Stack
Files
Winter.jpg
Yosemite.jpg
Picture 010.j...

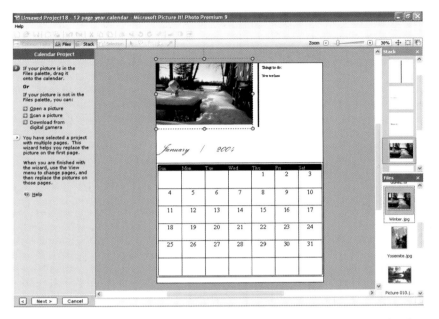

Figure 5-14 Drag an image from the Files palette to create a custom calendar with PictureIt!.

7. Click **Next**. Now, you can click the corner handles and drag to resize the image. Or, click the image and drag to move it. When the image is sized and positioned, click **Done**. The calendar appears in the main work area.

As noted in the Calendar Project pane, the wizard only guides you through placing an image on the first page of the multiple-page calendar project. To place pictures on the remaining pages, continue with these steps.

8. From the View menu, choose **Next Page** (or, in the calendar list to the lower left of the work area, click **February**). The February page of the calendar appears in the main area.
9. Click the existing image and press the **DELETE** key to remove it.
10. Drag an image from the Files palette on the right side of the screen. Then, use the handles to resize the image, and click and drag the image to move it into place. Repeat steps 8 through 10 until you have placed images on each page.
11. From the File menu, choose **Save** to save the calendar project. When the project is printed, all pages of the calendar will be sent to the printer.

After you've finished designing the calendar, you can send it to your own printer and assemble it yourself or use a professional calendar service, which you'll learn about in the next section.

Using Professional Calendar Services

If you don't want to go to the trouble, or you don't have the utilities necessary to put together your calendar, have someone do it for you. From Picture It!, you can send an electronic copy of your calendar design to a professional, who will print the calendar and send you the final product. To use a calendar service after designing a calendar with Picture It!, follow these steps:

1. Follow the steps for creating a calendar listed in the previous section.
2. With the calendar project open, from the File menu, choose **Print Professionally Online**, and then choose **Prints and Enlargements**.
3. In the Prints and Enlargements pane, choose **All pictures** on the Files palette, and then click **Next**. A screen appears giving you several print options (see Figure 5-15).

Unsaved Project18 - 12 page year calendar - Microsoft Picture It! Photo Premium 9
Prints and Enlargements
To print your picture(s), follow the instructions on the right.
When you have finished, click Done.
Done
Browse Gifts & Prints
Prints
Film & Photo Development
Frames
Cards
Photo Gifts
Clothing
Posters
Photo-editing Software
Cameras & Gear
Do More with Picture It!
Customer Service
Read Before Ordering
Prints
Print FUJICOLOR
Only the best will do for prints and enlargements of your digital photos. Our Fujicolor processing captures your special memories on the high-quality Fujicolor paper you trust for traditional film processing.
Simply select a single photo or multiple photos, and then choose the sizes and quantities you want.
Friends and family can also order Fuji prints of your digital photos that are shared online.
Size
4" x 6"
5" x 7"
8" x 10"
Pricing
$0.49
$1.29
$3.29
Order Prints

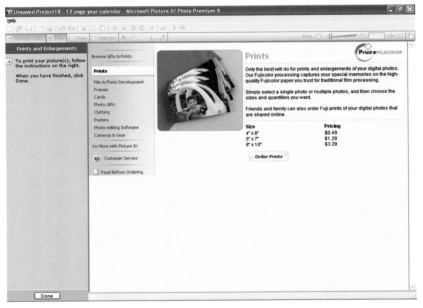

Figure 5-15 Click Order Prints to send your calendar to a professional service.

4. Click the **Order Prints** button, and follow the on-screen directions.

You can also order albums, prints, and other creations using the same method.

Creating Digital Albums

Although using your computer's folder system or recordable CDs to store your digital images is practical, a more creative way to organize your images is by creating digital albums, which are much like the regular photo albums you use to store your photo prints. When you use digital photo albums, you select which pictures you want to include and arrange them in an order you choose. You'll learn how to create digital photo albums in this section. Both Picture It! and Photoshop Album include features for creating photo albums. In the following sections, you'll learn how to use these programs to accomplish this task.

Creating a Digital Album in Photoshop Album

To create an album using Photoshop Album, follow these steps:

1. In Photoshop Album, open the pictures you want to include in the album.
2. Hold down the **CTRL** key and click to select the photos you want to include in the album. Press **CTRL+A** to select all photos in the work area.

My Catalog - Adobe Photoshop Album
Workspace
Start Creations Wizard...
Drag photos for your album here, then select the Start Creations Wizard button. If you plan to include a title page, the first photo will be used.

3. From the Creations menu, choose **Album**. The Workspace window will appear.

You can add photos to the Workspace by dragging them from the catalog.

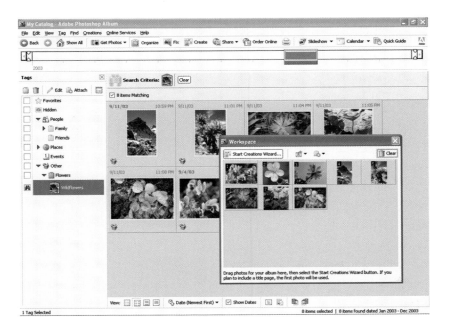

4. Click **Start Creations Wizard**.
5. Choose the album style from the list on the left and click **Next**.
6. Type the desired title for your album in the Title text box. Also, choose the number of photos per page and whether to include page numbers and captions. Here you can also specify a header and footer. When you've made your settings, click **Next**.
7. A preview of your album will appear. Use the arrow buttons to view the pages of your album. Click **Next**.

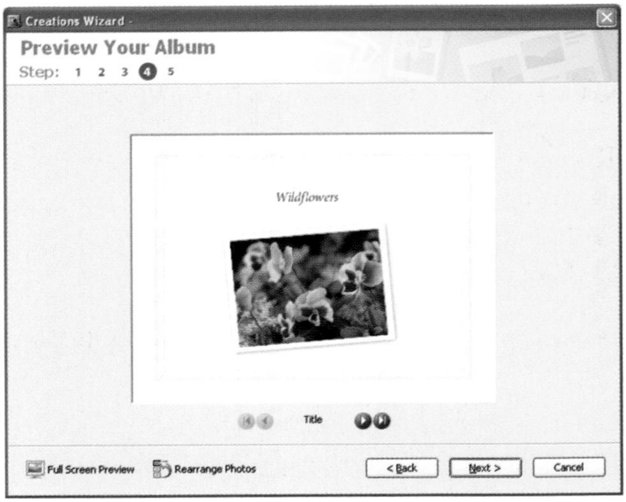
Creations Wizard
Preview Your Album
Step: 1 2 3 4 5
Wildflowers
Title
Full Screen Preview
Rearrange Photos
< Back
Next >
Cancel

8. Choose how you want to publish your album. The options here are identical to those for publishing greeting cards and calendars. For example, Figure 5-16 shows an album saved as a PDF and opened in Acrobat Reader. These PDF files are relatively small in file size and work well for transfer over the Internet.

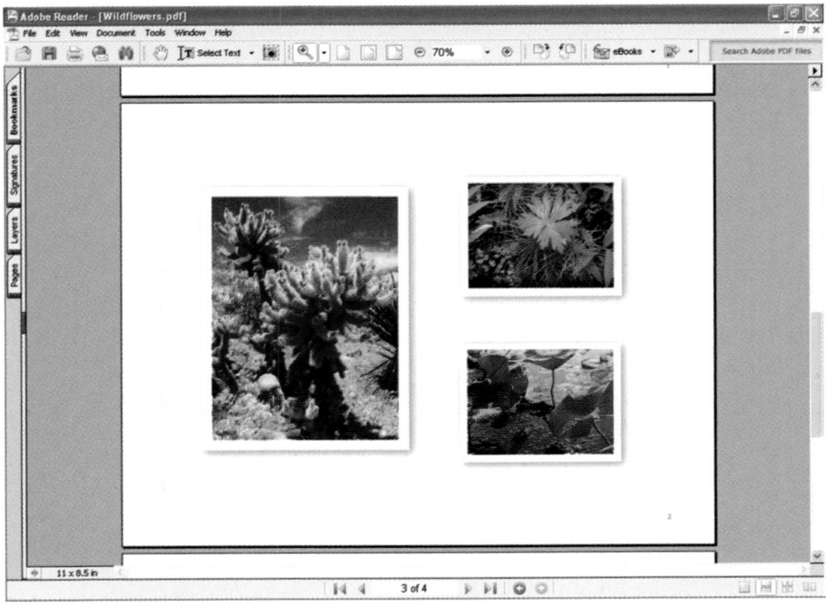
Adobe Reader - [Wildflowers.pdf]
File Edit View Document Tools Window Help
Select Text
70%
eBooks
Bookmarks
Signatures
Layers
Pages
11 x 8.5 in
3 of 4

Figure 5-16 Albums saved as PDF files can be opened in Adobe Acrobat Reader.

PDF files saved in an Adobe family product are compatible with additional features in Acrobat Reader. For example, you can export photos, order prints online, and more. Click **Picture Tasks** in Acrobat Reader to access these features.

Creating a Digital Album in Picture It!

To create an album using Picture It!, follow these steps:

1. In Picture It!, open the pictures you want to include in the album.
2. In the Quick Links section of the Common Tasks pane, click **Create a Project**.
3. Click **Albums**.

Microsoft Picture It! Photo Premium 9
File Help
Back
Cancel
Themes:
Baby
Birthday
Family
General
Holidays
Kids
Seasonal
Sports
Travel
Wedding
9 object(s)
View: Best Thumbnail Size
Photo album page
Photo album page
Photo album page
Photo album page
Photo album page
Photo album page
Photo album page
Preview
Open

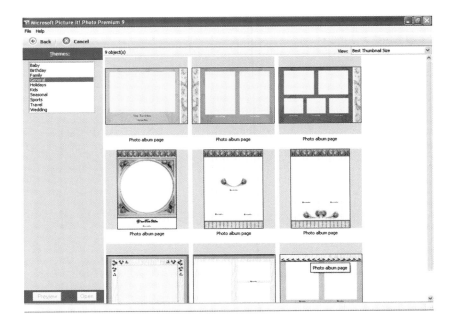

4. Click **Album Sets** to view a list of design options for your album pages, including background images and placeholders for pictures. From the list on the left, you can choose from several designs or themes, including Baby, Birthday, Family, General, Kids, Travel, Wedding, Holiday, Seasonal, and Sports.
5. Click a design that relates to the photographs you want to include, and then click **Open**.

Although Picture It! displays several designs, some may not be installed on your computer. If you select a design that isn't installed, Picture It! will prompt you to insert one of the program installation discs. Insert the disc and click **Retry**.

6. Drag a picture from the Files palette on the right side of your screen to a placeholder on the album page.

If you discover that you forgot to open a picture you want to include in your album, click **Open a Picture** and add it.

7. Drag a sizing handle to move or resize your image as needed. You also can flip images horizontally or vertically.
8. Repeat steps 6 and 7 for all placeholders on the page. When you're finished, click **Next**.
9. Click **Next**, and then click **Done**. The album will appear in Picture It!'s main editor window, as shown in Figure 5-17.

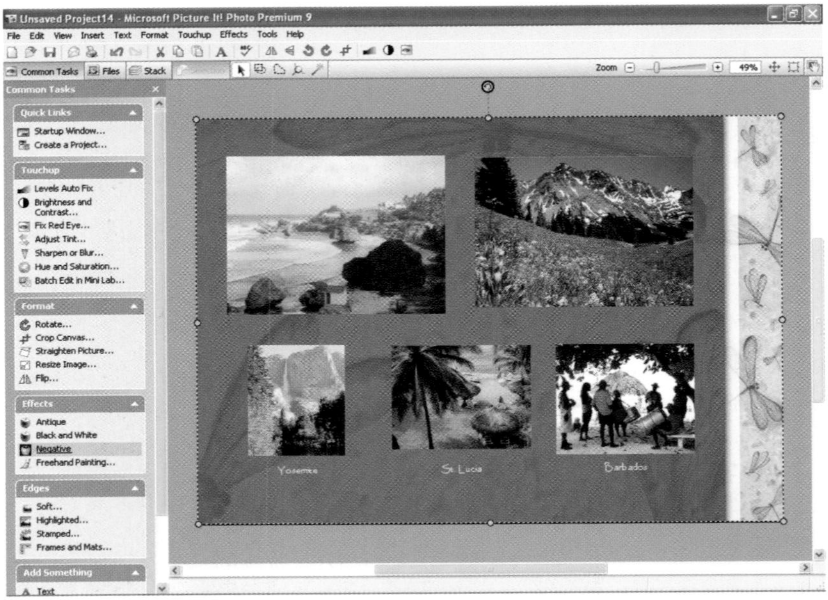
Unsaved Project14 - Microsoft Picture It! Photo Premium 9
File Edit View Insert Text Format Touchup Effects Tools Help
Common Tasks
Files
Stack
Zoom
49%
Common Tasks
Quick Links
Startup Window...
Create a Project...
Touchup
Levels Auto Fix
Brightness and Contrast...
Fix Red Eye...
Adjust Tint...
Sharpen or Blur...
Hue and Saturation...
Batch Edit in Mini Lab...
Format
Rotate...
Crop Canvas...
Straighten Picture...
Resize Image...
Flip...
Effects
Antique
Black and White
Negative
Freehand Painting...
Edges
Soft...
Highlighted...
Stamped...
Frames and Mats...
Add Something
Text
Yosemite
St. Lucia
Barbados

Figure 5-17 Create your own digital photo albums in Picture It!.

10. If the album page includes any text placeholders, delete the text and replace it with your own.
11. Click **File** and then click **Save As**. Navigate to the folder where you want the album stored and give it a descriptive name.

After you've saved your album, you can add pages to it by repeating the steps just listed. When your album is complete, you can print it.

More About . . . Picture It! Designs

An album is only one of the projects you can complete using Picture It! Others include business cards, crafts, envelopes, papers, and collages. To experiment with these options, choose **Create a Project** from the File menu or click **Create a Project** in the Common Tasks pane. For more information, consult Picture It! Help.

Creating Digital Slide Shows

Another way to showcase your pictures is to create a digital slide show. In a slide show, the images are displayed full-screen on your computer, one after another. You can create a slide show of your images using Windows XP or your image-editing program.

A slide show is a great way to broadcast your photos over the Web or share them via e-mail.

Creating a Slide Show in Windows XP

To create a slide show using Windows XP, follow these steps:

1. Place all the photos you want to include in one folder within the My Pictures folder.

   To ensure you can access the slide show option in Windows XP, place photo files in the My Pictures folder or one of its subfolders.

2. Open the folder that contains the pictures.
3. In the task pane on the left side of the window, click **View as a slide show**. Windows XP will display all the images in full-screen mode in a continuously running slide show.
4. Move the mouse pointer to the upper-right corner of the screen. A row of control buttons will appear, as shown in Figure 5-18. Play the slide show, move through the photos, or close the slide show by clicking the appropriate button.

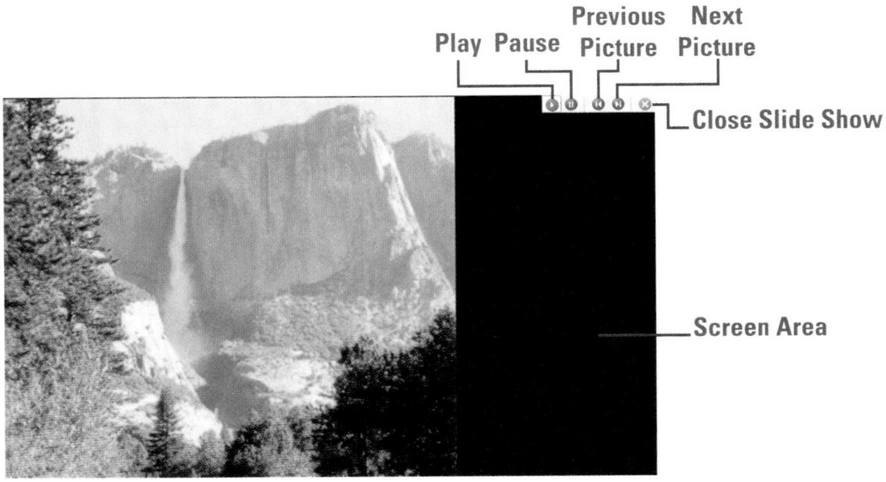
Play
Pause
Previous Picture
Next Picture
Close Slide Show
Screen Area

Figure 5-18 Create your own digital slide shows in Windows XP.

5

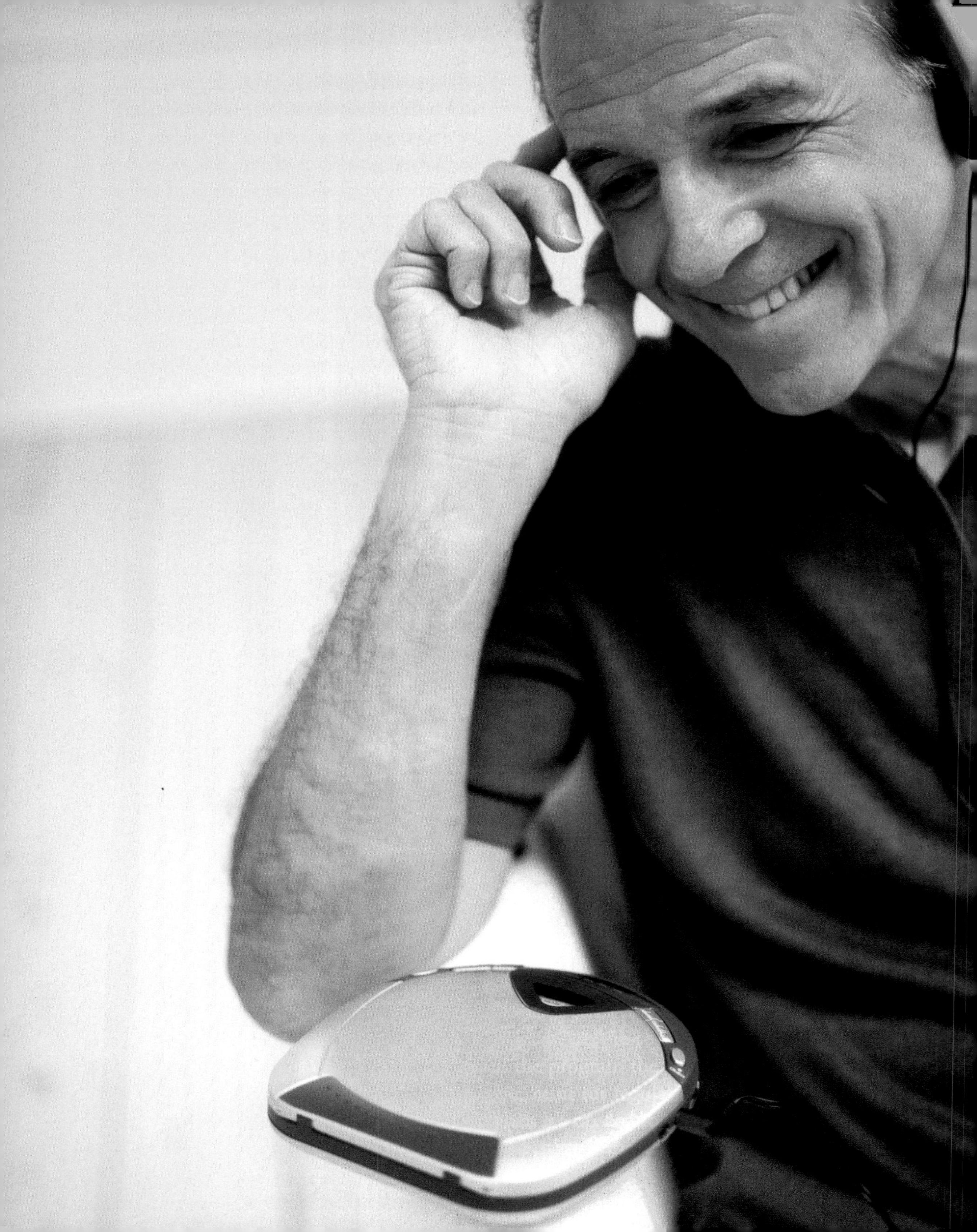

Discover Digital Music

Welcome to the era of digital music! You're about to revolutionize your music experience and discover how easy it is to take advantage of all the latest music technology. New tools have transformed the scratchy, static-filled music from times past into crystal-clear digital music for your computer, your home or car stereo, or to anywhere you can bring a wallet-sized portable MP3 player. With searchable online resources boasting collections of hundreds of thousands of titles, all of your favorite music only a few mouse clicks away. If you have a computer, much of this potential is already at your fingertips. This chapter will show you what you need to know to harness the marvels of today's digital music technology.

Reaping the Benefits of Digital Audio

The benefits and rewards of using digital are bountiful. Many of the obstacles that previously plagued listeners have been solved entirely by digital music, and new advantages are cropping up that were hardly imaginable only a few years ago. Digital listening quality far exceeds anything we've expected, and with the variety of new digital players available, you can listen anywhere, anytime, in a variety of different digital mediums, including digital radio.

Quality

If you've ever listened to the same song on vinyl, then on CD, the difference in quality is often staggering. Digital recordings mirror the original sound far better than analog recordings because most analog recordings are plagued by a low signal-to-noise ratio due to high background noise. That is, the signal, or the part of the recording you want to hear, is weak compared to the background noise. Digital recordings have a very high signal-to-noise ratio, meaning the signal is strong, with background noise virtually nonexistent.

The advantages of digital recording are only further revealed when copies of the recording are made. Unlike an analog recording, a copied digital recording maintains consistent sound quality no matter how far removed it is from the original. That's because instead of storing sound information in grooves on a record or on a magnetic tape, a digital recording is stored in an electronic file that can be copied bit for bit, just as a word-processing document can be copied from your hard drive to a floppy disk with no loss of letters, words, or sentences. Whether a digital recording is the master copy, or is a copy a thousand times removed, quality can remain the same. As a result, the CD you buy in a store has the exact same quality as the original digital studio recording.

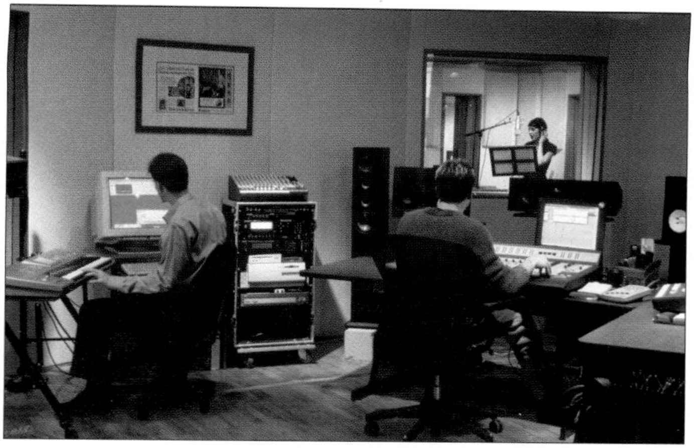

Versatility

Since digital recordings are basically a series of bits in a data file, they can be stored on your computer. Like other files on your computer, they can be copied, edited, deleted, and organized into folders. Of course, this is just the beginning. The types of media you can use to store your music files include CDs, DVDs, high capacity floppy disks, and any new storage hardware that shows up at your local computer store. Figure 6-1 shows music files stored on a computer.

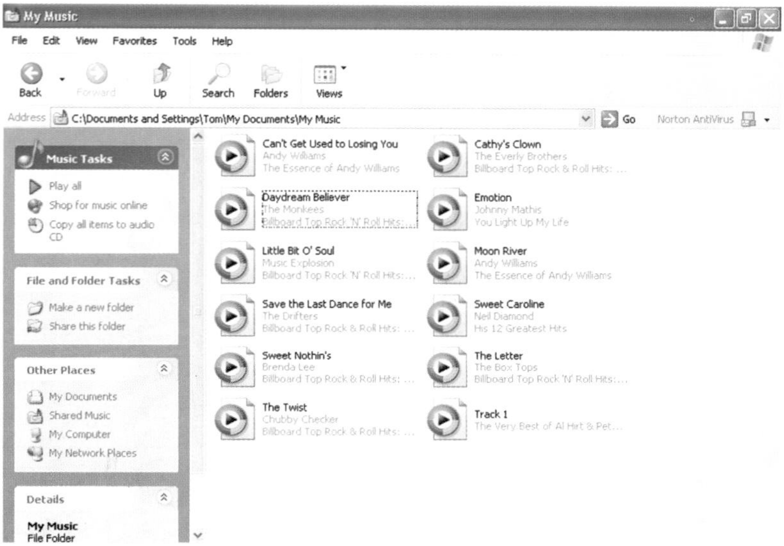
My Music
File Edit View Favorites Tools Help
Back Forward Up Search Folders Views
Address C:\Documents and Settings\Tom\My Documents\My Music
Go
Norton AntiVirus
Music Tasks
Play all
Shop for music online
Copy all items to audio CD
File and Folder Tasks
Make a new folder
Share this folder
Other Places
My Documents
Shared Music
My Computer
My Network Places
Details
My Music
File Folder
Can't Get Used to Losing You
Andy Williams
The Essence of Andy Williams
Cathy's Clown
The Everly Brothers
Billboard Top Rock & Roll Hits: ...
Daydream Believer
The Monkees
Billboard Top Rock 'N' Roll Hits: ...
Emotion
Johnny Mathis
You Light Up My Life
Little Bit O' Soul
Music Explosion
Billboard Top Rock 'N' Roll Hits: ...
Moon River
Andy Williams
The Essence of Andy Williams
Save the Last Dance for Me
The Drifters
Billboard Top Rock & Roll Hits: ...
Sweet Caroline
Neil Diamond
His 12 Greatest Hits
Sweet Nothin's
Brenda Lee
Billboard Top Rock & Roll Hits: ...
The Letter
The Box Tops
Billboard Top Rock 'N' Roll Hits: ...
The Twist
Chubby Checker
Billboard Top Rock & Roll Hits: ...
Track 1
The Very Best of Al Hirt & Pet...

Figure 6-1 Store digital music just like any other file on your computer.

Once you've got some music on your computer, all you need is a digital music player program to play it back through your computer speakers. After the player is installed, you can listen to music files stored on your hard drive or on other media. Figure 6-2 shows the interface for Microsoft Windows Media Player.

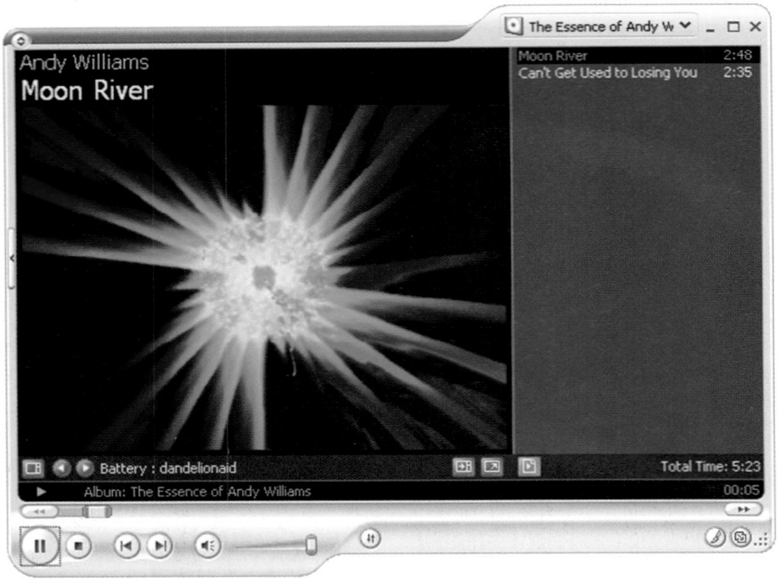

The Essence of Andy W
Andy Williams
Moon River
Moon River 2:48
Can't Get Used to Losing You 2:35
Battery : dandelionaid
Total Time: 5:23
Album: The Essence of Andy Williams
00:05

Figure 6-2 The Windows Media Player is one digital music player option.

These players are easy to use, and in most cases can perform the following functions:

- Play commercial audio CDs from your CD drive
- Play digital music files
- Pause, stop, rewind, and fast-forward playback via push-button controls
- Create and store lists of songs—called playlists—to play in order or randomly
- Download from the Internet the title, album, and artist information for the currently playing song

Of course, just like other files, digital recordings can be downloaded over the Internet or sent from your computer to other electronic devices (which we'll talk more about in the next section). In addition, your entire CD library can be transferred to your hard drive. This process, also known as ripping, immediately transforms your music into the most versatile format available. Overall, the ability to manage music as a file format on your computer allows you the flexibility to benefit from many of today's marvels in computer technology.

Portability

As long as computer technology improves, so will the convenience of digital music. Gone are the days of hefting a giant stereo on your shoulder. You can listen to digital music anywhere, any time, with little or no change in quality or service—a phenomenon commonly referred to as universal access. Thanks to this universal access, you can enjoy your favorite digital music whether you're sitting in front of your computer, baking cookies in your kitchen, driving your car, fishing in the Atlantic, or meandering through your local park. Advances in digital music technology have yielded portable players that enable you to store literally thousands of songs in a compressed digital format, possibly your entire CD collection.

3-IN-1 DIGITAL
MUSIC PLAYER
PLAY/STOP
Gateway

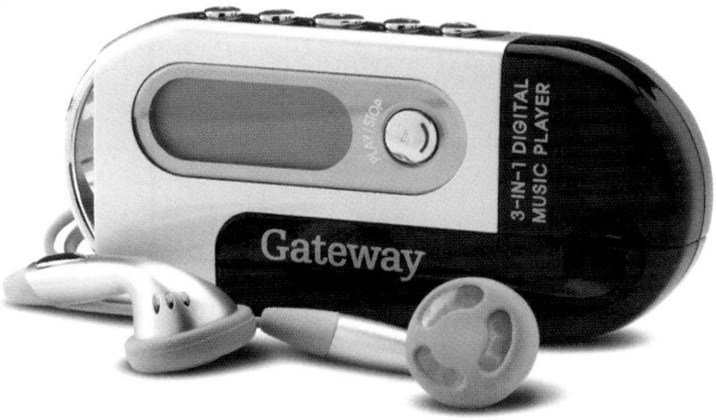

Today's portable digital music players provide more options than just added capacity. For example, many enable you to play music files in a variety of formats. Others include FM radio tuners, for those times when you want to listen to live radio. Incredibly, some of these devices are ev smaller than a portable CD player and fit easily inside a small pocket or fastened to an arm band. Jogging to your music no longer requires a bulky cassette player around your hip. Another benefit of portable digital music players is that the music doesn't skip if the unit is jarred, since there are no moving parts associated with playing the music.

Your daily commute also benefits from digital music. Only a few years ago, digital music players in cars were almost non-existent; these days, however, every major car-stereo manufacturer either has or is planning to release a digital audio-capable unit.

PWR
OFF
SRC
SIRIUS
READY
KENWOOD
RDM
REP
SCAN
THE VAULT -
SRCH/■MENU
SCAN
RDM
REP
M.RDM
DISP
1
2
3
4
5
6

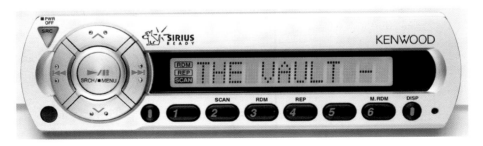

Many models incorporate MP3 CD playback, enabling you to travel with one MP3 CD containing a hundred or more of your favorite songs instead of lugging around dozens of CDs on a road trip.

No longer bound by the need to physically connect to a computer, digital music is even making the leap from your desktop to your mobile phone and PDA. Wireless communication is advancing as fast as digital music, and the combination of the two is exciting. Very soon, you'll be able to store all your digital music files at home and play them from anywhere in the world, even without another computer.

Find and Share New Music

Of course, the Internet has revolutionized many aspects of our culture, and music is no exception. In addition to ripping CDs to your computer, you can also obtain digital audio files by downloading them from the Internet. In fact, the Web features hundreds of sites, each with its own selection of music, offering digital audio file downloads.

Several subscription services, like RHAPSODY pictured in Figure 6-3, offer access to hundreds of thousands of professionally recorded titles in every genre imaginable. For a

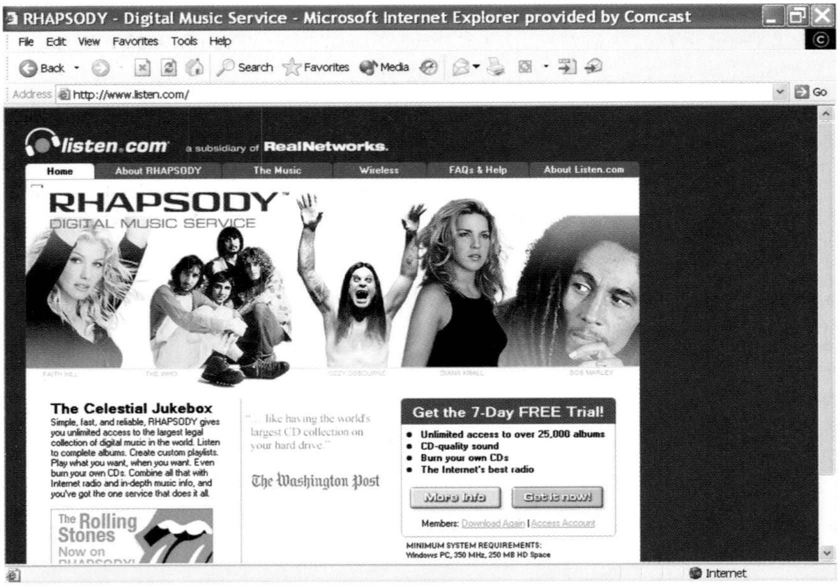
RHAPSODY - Digital Music Service - Microsoft Internet Explorer provided by Comcast
File Edit View Favorites Tools Help
Back Search Favorites Media
Address http://www.listen.com/
Go
listen.com a subsidiary of RealNetworks.
Home
About RHAPSODY
The Music
Wireless
FAQs & Help
About Listen.com
RHAPSODY
DIGITAL MUSIC SERVICE
The Celestial Jukebox
Simple, fast, and reliable, RHAPSODY gives you unlimited access to the largest legal collection of digital music in the world. Listen to complete albums. Create custom playlists. Play what you want, when you want. Even burn your own CDs. Combine all that with Internet radio and in-depth music info, and you've got the one service that does it all.
"... like having the world's largest CD collection on your hard drive."
The Washington Post
Get the 7-Day FREE Trial!
Unlimited access to over 25,000 albums
CD-quality sound
Burn your own CDs
The Internet's best radio
More Info
Get it now!
Members: Download Again | Access Account
MINIMUM SYSTEM REQUIREMENTS:
Windows PC, 350 MHz, 250 MB HD Space
The Rolling Stones
Now on
Internet

Figure 6-3 RHAPSODY is a leading subscription music service where you can find and share music.

small fee, you can easily find, download, organize, and play all your favorite titles. Also, legally burn music to recordable CDs or copy to a portable device.

 Subscription music sites aren't all created equally. You'll learn more about several, and how they differ, in Chapter 7.

Some Web sites, including various digital audio archives, offer music free of charge. Such sites do not always have a vast selection of songs from big-name artists, but they do offer a great way for upcoming artists to reach a large, untapped following of fans.

Still other sites enable you to share music files with other Internet users. Though selections at these sites are often expansive, so is the range of quality; it's sort of like rummaging through a garage sale. Also, not surprisingly, the practice of sharing files with others opens some sticky legal issues. The copyright laws involved are very intricate, and currently, the United States judicial system is reviewing the entire practice. As digital music technology advances, however, we can be fairly certain the technology to prevent copyright infringement will also advance.

Categorize Your Collection

Many of us have experienced finding CDs under couch cushions, behind cabinets, and under car seats. Today, your entire music collection can be neatly organized on your computer, by title, artist, album, or any method you feel like at the time. Search your entire computer in seconds to find any song in your collection, pumped expeditiously through your home stereo. Playlists can store your favorite compilations, primed to break forth with an hour of Calypso in a moment's notice. Your playlists can also be copied to portable players, or even to your car stereo.

Digital Radio

If immediate gratification is important to you, you'll especially appreciate digital radio technology. With streaming audio (also called Webcasting), you can listen to the first part of an audio file while the rest of the file is still downloading. It's also ideal for broadcasting live concerts, news reports, and sporting events. Listeners can hear events

6

unfolding in real time, even though the audio file isn't yet complete. As shown in Figure 6-4, you can easily access many radio stations using your computer's media player.

There are several types of streaming-audio players. You'll learn more about how to use your computer to listen to Internet radio in Chapter 7.

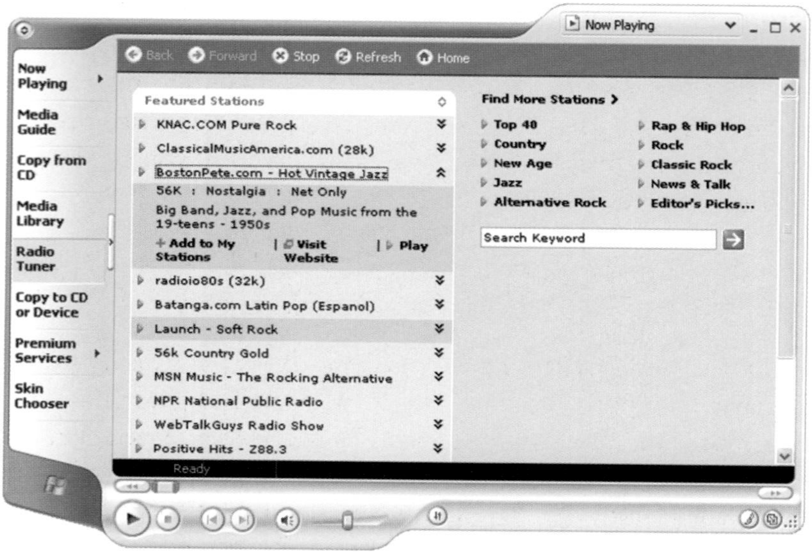

Now Playing
Back
Forward
Stop
Refresh
Home
Now Playing
Media Guide
Copy from CD
Media Library
Radio Tuner
Copy to CD or Device
Premium Services
Skin Chooser
Featured Stations
KNAC.COM Pure Rock
ClassicalMusicAmerica.com (28k)
BostonPete.com - Hot Vintage Jazz
56K : Nostalgia : Net Only
Big Band, Jazz, and Pop Music from the 19-teens - 1950s
Add to My Stations
Visit Website
Play
radioio80s (32k)
Batanga.com Latin Pop (Espanol)
Launch - Soft Rock
56k Country Gold
MSN Music - The Rocking Alternative
NPR National Public Radio
WebTalkGuys Radio Show
Positive Hits - Z88.3
Find More Stations
Top 40
Country
New Age
Jazz
Alternative Rock
Rap & Hip Hop
Rock
Classic Rock
News & Talk
Editor's Picks...
Search Keyword
Ready

Figure 6-4 You can use Windows Media Player to find live Internet radio broadcasts.

Digital music, whether played over your home stereo, in your car, or on your computer, doesn't have to be from your own collection. These days, satellite radio providers use satellites and digital transmission to provide continuous music anywhere in the world. Imagine, no more silent drives through the Sonoran desert: you and a friend can listen to the same song at the same time from the same broadcast even if you're on opposite sides of the country. There are also products on the horizon that will allow you to pause, rewind, and save live radio for later, much like Digital Video Recorders like TiVo do for television broadcasts today. For example, imagine you only caught the tail end of a traffic report—with these new products, you'll be able to rewind the live radio to hear the parts of the report you missed.

Get the Very Most Out of Your Favorite Music

In a nutshell, digital music has the power to maximize your music listening experience, and become a major part of your life. Imagine a ride home from work. You turn on your XM radio and relax to your favorite international station. You hear a new tune you love. As you roll up the driveway, you note the title and artist from the radio display. You step inside, log on to your subscription music service, and download the title, and a number of others from the same artist, to your portable MP3 player. By the time you've donned your biking attire, the songs are ready. Now, you clip on the player and take a ride to your new find. This is just one of many scenarios that demonstrate how the digital age has brought the enjoyment of music closer than ever before.

But you don't need to have a bunch of digital gadgets to benefit from digital music. In fact, if you own a computer, much of this potential is only as far away as your mouse and keyboard. In these chapters, you'll find how to take advantage of the amazing capabilities that already exist on your computer, and then how to take digital music further than ever before. For music lovers everywhere, it's a very exciting time, and you can be a part of it. The next few chapters will show you how.

Understanding Digital Formats

Just as you needed a record player to play 33s, 45s, and LPs, a tape deck to play cassette tapes, and a CD player to play your compact discs, you need a digital music player to play audio files on your computer. The difference? Unlike record players, tape decks, and CD players, all of which are hardware components, a digital music player is a piece of software installed on a computer. In fact, odds are one of them came pre-installed on your computer. Playing digital music on your computer is as easy as using your mouse to click the buttons that appear in the player program's window.

Thanks to the popularity of digital music, recent years have seen an explosion of digital music players on the market. Although you can use all these players to listen to audio files, important differences do exist between players.

Before you get into the nuts and bolts of choosing a digital music player, it's a good idea to gain some understanding of the various digital audio file formats commonly used today. That's because certain digital music players support only certain types of files. There are other differences between file types as well. Some compressed digital audio formats are small in file size and ideal for storing on a computer in mass. Others are large in file size, but may be required for CD burning and other tasks. Conversions from one file format to another may be necessary depending on the player you are using, and what you plan to use the file for. For example, to create an audio CD, you may need to first convert a file into a format compatible with a player that supports CD burning, and then convert the file into an uncompressed format suitable for the burning itself. By knowing the advantages and disadvantages of each file format, you'll have a better idea of which player to choose, as well as a basic understanding of the file format best suited for a specific task.

A "file format" is the way information in a file is encoded; different programs are designed to handle files of different formats. Take word processing programs as an example. NotePad can handle files that use the TXT (text) format and Microsoft® Word can manage files that use the DOC (document) format. Some word processing programs can handle different types of word processing files; for example, you can use WordPad to open and edit a DOC file. Other word processing programs, however, cannot. It's important to also mention that Word is far more more powerful than NotePad and also compatible with more file formats. Of course, the main disadvantage with Word is that it must be purchased, whereas NotePad comes free with Windows. Digital music players are often alike in this respect. Players available as a free download may contain only the basic features, with a purchased upgrade required to perform advanced tasks. Figure 6-5 shows some common file formats and their associated programs.

My Documents
File Edit View Favorites Tools Help
Back Search Folders
Address My Documents
Go Links
File and Folder Tasks
Make a new folder
Publish this folder to the Web
Share this folder
Other Places
Desktop
My Computer
My Network Places
Details
My Documents
System Folder
My Pictures
3/29/2002 6:25 PM
My Music
4/6/2003 9:00 PM
My Webs
4/6/2003 9:03 PM
Document 1
10/11/2002 1:11 PM
Microsoft Word Document
TextDoc
2/26/2003 5:35 PM
Text Document
Sunset
4/6/2003 9:08 PM
800 x 600
Baby_Doll
4/1/2003 9:16 PM
Spreadsheet
1/30/2003 11:33 AM
Microsoft Excel Worksheet
Microsoft Word Document
Image File
Microsoft Excel Spreadsheet
Text Document
Windows Media Player file

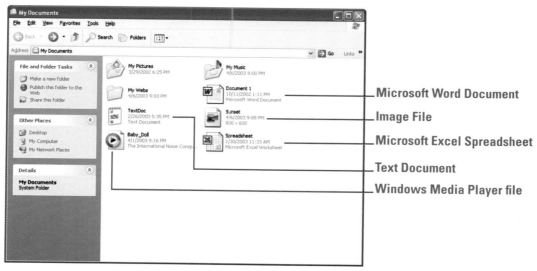

Figure 6-5 File icons represent an associated program used to view or play that file.

Windows Media Player is included in the purchase price of the Windows operating systems, and is a bit more robust than some free players available for download over the Internet. Even so, additional plug-ins may need to be purchased to perform specific tasks, such as encoding an audio file to MP3, whereas some free players have this capability.

Likewise, different digital music players work with different types of files, supporting some file formats but not others. These file formats vary in sound quality and file size, each with its own strengths and weaknesses. For example, WAV, a commonly used uncompressed file format, boasts good quality, but a large file size. If your music files use this file format, they'll quickly consume any available space on your hard drive. Fortunately, other formats offer smaller file sizes.

The two most popular compressed file formats for recording your own digital music files are MP3 (Moving Pictures Expert Group Audio Layer 3) and WMA (Windows Media Audio). Most digital music players work with both formats. MP3 and WMA, however, aren't the only formats in town. As shown in Table 6-1, there are many different digital music file formats.

Table 6-1 Common Digital Audio Formats

EXTENSION	FORMAT
MP3	Widely adopted format using data compression to produce high-quality audio in relatively small files. MP3 files are often used to make hard-disk copies of music from CDs.
WAV	A widely used file format (pronounced "wave"). This is the standard format for Windows system sounds, and is also used on many Web pages.
WMA	MP3 alternative with similar audio quality at a smaller file size.
RA	Developed by Real Networks, this RealAudio format was originally designed for real-time streaming audio feeds.
LQT	MP3 competitor from Liquid Audio, with increased security features.
AAC	New file format from Dolby Labs producing high-quality sound at low sampling rates.
CDA	High-quality file format used on commercial audio CDs.
MID or MIDI	Used to reproduce instrumental music in very compact files, often for background music on Web pages and in online games.
Mcomputer	The supposed successor to MP3, capable of producing higher-quality files; the official name is MPEGplus.
RM	The Real Network format designed for streaming movie (or "media") files; can also be used to stream digital audio files.
VQF	An older digital audio format, inferior to the MP3 format, and no longer officially supported.

6

More About . . . Data Compression

Music files are often made smaller through a process called data encoding. When a music file is compressed to MP3, WMA, or another compressed digital audio format, a digital audio encoder is used to determine what sounds in the file are audible to the human ear, and removes any sounds outside that range. This means that although the quality of the file is technically degraded, you may not be able to tell by listening to it. If you do find that an encoded music file doesn't meet the high standards of your discriminating ear, you'll have to decide for yourself between the highest possible sound quality and benefits of smaller file size.

No matter what type of file, you can determine its format by looking at the three-letter file extension appended to the end of the file's name. For example, files whose names end in ".mp3" are MP3 files. Likewise, files whose names end in ".wma" are WMA files.

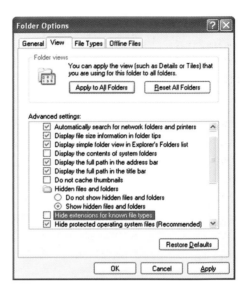

If you're using Windows XP in the default view, you won't see file extensions. However, the computer needs them to know what program to use to access the file. To view the file extensions in the My Music folder, open the folder. Select **Tools**, and then choose **Folder Options**. In the Folder Options dialog box, select the **View** tab, and uncheck the **Hide extensions for known file types** box.

Folder Options
General
View
File Types
Offline Files
Folder views
You can apply the view (such as Details or Tiles) that you are using for this folder to all folders.
Apply to All Folders
Reset All Folders
Advanced settings:
Automatically search for network folders and printers
Display file size information in folder tips
Display simple folder view in Explorer's Folders list
Display the contents of system folders
Display the full path in the address bar
Display the full path in the title bar
Do not cache thumbnails
Hidden files and folders
Do not show hidden files and folders
Show hidden files and folders
Hide extensions for known file types
Hide protected operating system files (Recommended)
Restore Defaults
OK
Cancel
Apply

Windows XP hides the file extensions from users by default because the icons already show the associated program and to protect users from removing this association. If you feel more comfortable not viewing the file extensions, re-select Hide extensions for known file types.

Click **Apply** and then click the **Close** button to close the dialog box. When you open My Music, you'll notice that your file names now display the file extensions.

My Documents
File Edit View Favorites Tools Help
Back
Search
Folders
Address
My Documents
Go
Links
File and Folder Tasks
Make a new folder
Publish this folder to the Web
Share this folder
Other Places
Desktop
My Computer
My Network Places
Details
My Documents
System Folder
My Pictures
3/29/2002 6:25 PM
My Music
4/6/2003 9:00 PM
My Webs
4/6/2003 9:03 PM
Document 1.doc
10/11/2002 1:11 PM
Microsoft Word Document
TextDoc.txt
2/26/2003 5:35 PM
Text Document
Sunset.TIF
4/6/2003 9:08 PM
800 x 600
Baby_Doll.mp3
Spreadsheet.xls
1/30/2003 11:33 AM
Microsoft Excel Worksheet
.mp3 extension

Let's take a look at the most popular digital audio file formats:

MP3

The MP3 digital audio file format compresses music while still maintaining near-CD quality sound. In fact, MP3's data compression reduces digital sound files by about a 12:1 ratio. This combination of features—small file size (and thus quickly downloadable) but high-quality sound—has made MP3 the most popular digital music file format. Indeed, it's no exaggeration to say MP3 has taken the music industry by storm.

In addition to compressing the data in an audio file, MP3 enables you to control the file's sampling rate to reduce file size. The higher a file's sampling rate (also called bitrate), the higher its sound quality—and the larger the file size. When you decrease a file's sampling rate, you decrease its sound quality—but you also reduce the time required to download the file and disk space required to store it. Most MP3s available for download have a sample rate of 128kbps or higher. Streaming MP3s are often sampled at 128kbps for transmission over a broadband connection, but are also sometimes offered at a lower sample rate, usually 64kbps, for dialup connections.

 Because of its obvious benefits, MP3 is the file format you'll encounter most. There is, however, a newer format: MPEGplus. Commonly referred to as the Mcomputer format, MPEGplus encodes CD-quality sound in smaller-sized files than other comparable formats. In the future, MPEGplus may replace the MP3 format.

WAV

If your computer runs Windows, you're already familiar with the WAV file type—even if you don't realize it. That's because the sound you hear each time Windows starts is a built-in WAV file. WAV files store uncompressed sound wave data, making them larger than their MP3 or WMA counterparts. Because WAV files are uncompressed, their audio quality is very good but, as you probably guessed, their file size is quite large. For this reason, you'll rarely find digital music files in the WAV format on the Internet.

 When you burn audio files to a CD, these files will usually be converted to the WAV format. The WAV files are then converted to CDA format so the CD you record can be played in other CD players (besides your computer).

WMA

The WMA format, designed by Microsoft, offers sound quality similar to MP3, but with even smaller file sizes. As with MP3 files, you can control the sampling rate used when recording WMA files. (Remember, the higher the sampling rate, the higher the sound quality, and the larger the file size.) Unlike MP3, however, the WMA format uses copy protection, a feature that works by creating an official license for each song you copy. Copy protected audio files play back only on the system that recorded them. When you copy a file to your computer, your computer—and only your computer—is authorized to play the song. By using Windows Media Player to copy that song from your computer to a CD or portable device, however, you can copy the song's license, enabling you to listen to the song using multiple devices.

 Most digital music players automatically enable WMA copy protection by default. In most cases, you can turn off copy protection for new files you record by accessing the player's recording options. See "Copying Music from a CD" later in this chapter to learn how to access recording options in Windows Media Player.

RealAudio

Real Networks's RealAudio format is the format of choice for streaming audio over the Internet. You can use streaming audio to listen to audio files before and while the entire file is downloading. Broadcasters often use the RealAudio format to transmit audio for live concerts, sports, and other events as they happen.

LQT

LQT isn't widely used for consumer recording, but you will find some commercial music downloads in this format. That's because LQT's built-in security features make copying files more difficult than with other formats. For example, you can't convert LQT files to MP3 or WAV formats, which means you can't burn LQT files to CD. For this reason, many large record companies favor Liquid Audio's LQT format for putting their music online.

AAC

Dolby Labs developed the AAC (Advanced Audio Coding) digital audio format, which creates music files at low sampling rates that sound better than higher rate files encoded with MP3 and other formats. It's not in widespread use yet, but is one of several next-generation formats that could eventually replace MP3 as the digital audio format of choice.

CDA

The CDA (compact disc audio) format is the standard file format used on commercial audio CDs. Unlike most other file formats, such as MP3 and WMA, CDA is uncompressed, resulting in high-quality sound, but also very large files. For this reason, it's not a popular option for storing digital music files on your computer's hard disk. If, however, you want to play your home recorded CDs in your home or car stereo, they will need to be in this format.

MIDI

Although MIDI is a music file format, it doesn't record actual music. Instead, it records information about music. For example, a MIDI file might contain information describing a melody played by a violin—the note values and pitches—without recording the actual performance. It's kind of like how a player piano works. The MIDI player plays back the notes as "recorded" in the original performance.

When a MIDI file is played, its information is fed to a synthesizer built into your computer or other digital music player. This synthesizer, which includes sound samples for any number of instruments, "plays" the notes contained in the MIDI file. Using the violin example, the synthesizer would use its "violin" sound samples to broadcast the information in the MIDI file.

 A MIDI file can sound different from one computer to the next, depending on the quality of the internal synthesizer located either on the sound card or installed as a software device.

Because it doesn't record actual sound waves, MIDI files are very small. Therefore, the MIDI format is an extremely efficient way to store instrumental music. For this reason, it's commonly used by professional musicians. This format is also widely used by Web developers for background music on Web sites. Because it doesn't record any actual instruments or voices, however, it's not (and cannot be) used to digitally copy music from CDs and other sources.

6

Choosing a Digital Music Player

There are many digital music players to choose from, each with its own look and feel. Software vendors usually offer a version of their players free for download over the Internet, so all you need to do is find the right one. Though players vary in appearance, most share a similar basic feature set, meaning no matter which one you choose, you'll enjoy a core set of tools. For example, most digital music players enable you to do the following:

- Play commercial audio CDs.
- Play digital music files in several popular formats, including MP3, WMA, WAV and so on.
- Pause, stop, rewind, and fast forward playback via push button controls, similar to those found on your home CD player. Most digital music players also include Next and Previous Track (song) buttons, along with a volume control and mute button.

All Music
Buy CD
Bikeride
Fakin' Amnesia
Battery : chemicalnova
Artist: Bikeride
Liquid Player 6.1 - Liquid Player
File Tracks View Help
liquid audio
Home
Now Playing
Import CD
Organize Music
Export
Download
Once A Week
Ear_Ring
Album: The Cinch
No art is available.
liquid audio

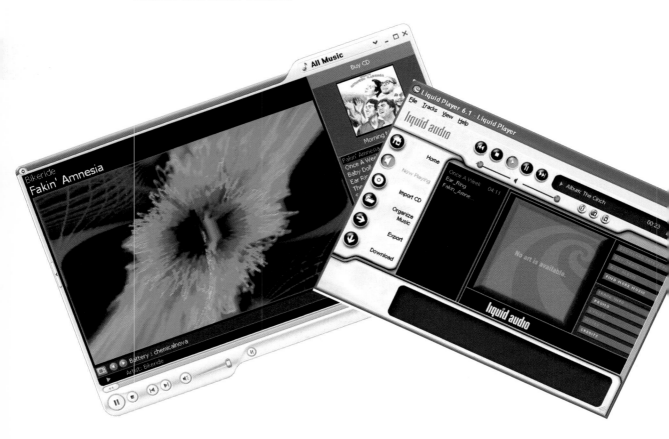

- Store lists of songs, called playlists. A playlist can contain the individual tracks of a CD or individual files on your hard drive. In addition, you can create your own playlists to better organize the music you like to listen to most or to set up a group of songs for burning onto a CD.
- Play songs randomly or in the playlist's predefined order.
- Use the Internet to download song, album, and artist information about the track currently playing. Some players even use the Internet to provide access to detailed artist biographies, or to enable you to purchase the CD online.
- Display CD artwork or colorful visual displays to accompany the music.
- Resize the player on your desktop to consume more or less space.
- Change the look and feel of the player's controls and interface by applying a new "skin."

In addition, many digital music players also include full-blown encoding and CD creation capabilities. These players are often referred to as all-in-one programs. In the next sections, you'll learn about several of the more popular digital music players.

musicmatch
File Edit View Options Help Upgrade
Track
Ear Ring
Artist
Rainer Maria
128 kbps
0:37 / 3:43
1 "Ear Ring" by Rainer Maria
2 "Fakin' Amnesia" by Bikeride
3 "Once A Week" by The Cinch
Open Save Clear
View by Artist
Album
Rock
Bikeride
MUSICMATCH
Owen (Polyvinyl)
Rainer Maria
The International Noise Conspiracy
RealOne Player
(Paused) Ear Ring - Rainer Maria
File Edit View Play
mp3 128Kbps
1:03 / 3:43
Now Playing
Ear Ring - Rainer M...
1 item
Edit
Now Playing
My Library
Audio
My Library
Name
Search Library:
All Audio
Clips
Length
Size
Artist
Album
Genre
Artist/Album
4:11
3,929KB
New Playlist
Burn CD
Copy To
Web
WINAMP
02:04
1. BIKERIDE - FAKIN' AMNESIA
128 kbps 44 kHz
mono
EQ PL
SHUFFLE

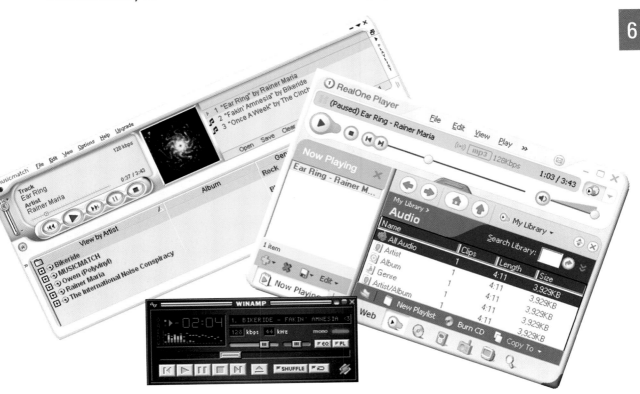

More About . . . Encoding

Also referred to as ripping or copying, encoding is the process of copying a digital audio file to your hard drive from a music CD or from the Internet. While ripping, the .CDA track from the CD is saved to the hard drive as an uncompressed WAV file. Then, another encoding process is used to convert the file into a compressed format such as MP3. Many programs that rip CD tracks to your computer save a WAV file to your computer and compress the file in a single step, so the entire conversion process isn't always apparent.

Windows Media Player

As mentioned earlier, Windows Media Player is a versatile audio/video player Microsoft includes with Windows 98 and later. If your computer runs either of these programs, you already have a copy of Windows Media Player at your disposal.

You can use Windows Media Player to play back audio files in the MP3, WMA, WAV, MIDI, and other formats, organize playlists, and view information about the song you're playing. In addition, Windows Media Player can be used to rip files from audio CDs and, using the WMA format, make custom CDs. Figure 6-6 shows the Windows Media Player Interface. This is probably the most convenient digital player choice, since it is most likely already on your computer. It offers an attractive feature set and user interface.

Playlist
Menu bar
Show menu bar button
Visualization area
Playback controls
Mute button
Volume control
Turn shuffle on/off button
Change player color button
Switch to skin mode button
Windows Media Player
All Music
The International Noise Conspiracy
Baby Doll
Now Playing
Media Guide
Copy from CD
Media Library
Radio Tuner
Copy to CD or Device
Premium Services
Skin Chooser

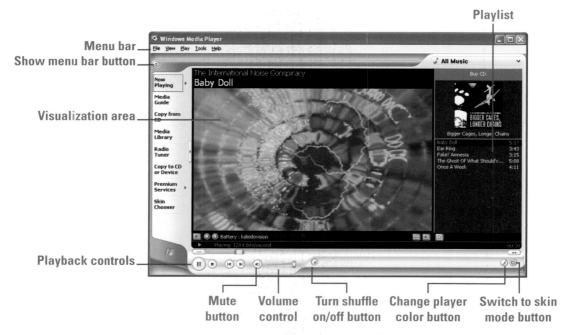

Figure 6-6 Windows Media Player is included with all new Microsoft Windows operating systems.

Although Windows Media Player plays MP3 files, it doesn't record in MP3 format. You can, however, add MP3 recording capabilities to Windows Media Player by adding an optional software utility called the MP3 Creation Pack. Three different companies—CyberLink, InterVideo, and Ravisent—sell versions of this add-on pack.

MusicMatch Jukebox

MusicMatch Jukebox is a favorite among listeners thanks to its many features. For example, using the freeware version of MusicMatch Jukebox, you can play many of the most popular digital music formats, including MP3 and WMA and organize your music files into playlists. If you tire of your own music files, you can use MusicMatch Jukebox to listen to any number of Internet radio stations. Using this program, you can also create custom CDs and encode new digital audio files in MP3 format. Unlike Windows Media Player, MusicMatch Jukebox has built-in MP3 encoding, meaning there's nothing extra to add. In addition, you can use MusicMatch Jukebox to transfer music files to any portable players you might have.

The MusicMatch interface consists of three separate windows—the Player, the Playlist, and My Music Library. However, you can change My Music Library to display the Music Guide on the MusicMatch Web site. All three windows are displayed together, as shown in Figure 6-7. You can also dock or undock these windows and move them to fit your needs. All you do is click the Dock button in the corner of the window you want to dock or undock.

The My Music Library is an area of MusicMatch used to organize your music files. It provides the artist name, album, genre, and length of the song.

Visualization area
Playlist
Menu bar
Volume control
Playback controls
My Library
musicmatch File Edit View Options Help Upgrade
Track
Ear Ring
Artist
Rainer Maria
128 kbps
0:37 / 3:43
1 "Ear Ring" by Rainer Maria
2 "Fakin' Amnesia" by Bikeride
3 "Once A Week" by The Cinch
Open Save Clear Burn Shuffle Repeat Send
View by Artist
Album
Genre
Time
Bikeride
MUSICMATCH
Owen (Polyvinyl)
Rainer Maria
The International Noise Conspiracy
Rock
Blues
Blues
3:15
0:18
5:08
3:43
5:17

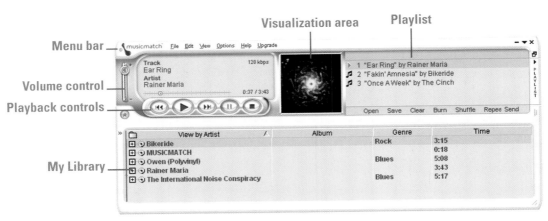

Figure 6-7 MP3 encoding and a variety of other features make MusicMatch Jukebox a popular digital music player.

Other Types of Players

Some digital music players do more than just play digital audio files. For example, several of the players discussed in the preceding sections, including Windows Media Player and MusicMatch Jukebox, are referred to as all-in-one players because you can record your own digital music files as well as play them back. Others, such as Winamp, can't rip digital audio files from music CDs or make custom audio CDs. They simply enable you to play back your music files. As a dedicated digital music player, however, Winamp is one of the most popular because it's been around for a long time—and you download it free from the Internet. Also, this player program loads fast and doesn't display ads in a browser partition like some other players.

Another type of digital music player is a DJ mixer, designed especially for DJ use—complete with advanced audio mixing functions such as cross-fading and pitch change. DJs use these programs to combine songs into long playlists, insert transitions between songs, and automatically adjust the playback volume. With some programs, DJs can even play songs backward and insert simulated vinyl-scratching effects.

Most of these programs are commercial software, which means you can't get them for free. Many, however, do have a shareware option, enabling you to try before you buy.

Copying Music from a CD

Of course, you can't play any digital music files on your hard drive if there aren't any there. Fortunately, Windows Media Player enables you to copy the music files on audio CDs to your hard drive. By default, Windows Media Player uses the WMA format, but you can also choose the format and quality you want to use for your ripped files. If you've installed the MP3 Creation Pack, you'll also have the added option of encoding to an MP3 file. First, open Windows Media Player by clicking the start menu, pointing to **All Programs** and selecting **Windows Media Player**. To set the encoding format and quality level, do the following:

➊ Click the **Tools** menu and click **Options**.

 Windows Media Player will save the file(s) in WMA (Windows Media Audio) format. In the Options dialog box, under the Copy Music tab, click the link "Learn more about MP3 formats" on the right to find utilities you can use to encode these files to MP3 format.

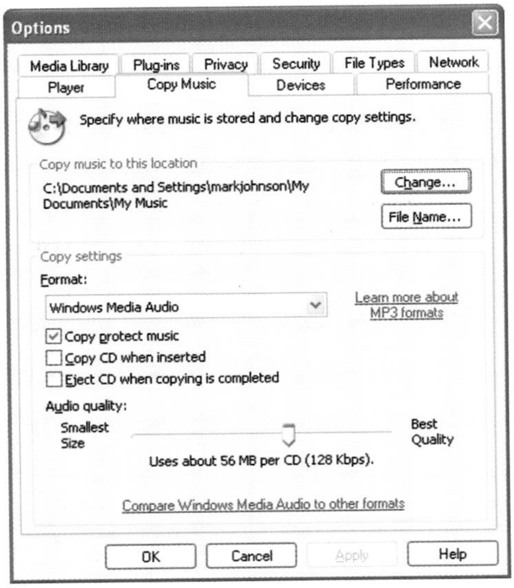
Options
Media Library
Plug-ins
Privacy
Security
File Types
Network
Player
Copy Music
Devices
Performance
Specify where music is stored and change copy settings.
Copy music to this location
C:\Documents and Settings\markjohnson\My Documents\My Music
Change...
File Name...
Copy settings
Format:
Windows Media Audio
Learn more about MP3 formats
Copy protect music
Copy CD when inserted
Eject CD when copying is completed
Audio quality:
Smallest Size
Best Quality
Uses about 56 MB per CD (128 Kbps).
Compare Windows Media Audio to other formats
OK
Cancel
Apply
Help

2. In the Options dialog box, click the **Copy Music** tab.
3. Unless you want to copy-protect the files you're ripping, uncheck the **Copy protect music** option. (This option is available only for Windows Media files.)
4. Adjust the **Audio quality** slider to set the sampling rate for your ripped files. Move the slider to the left for smaller files and lower sound quality, or to the right for larger files and higher sound quality.
5. Click **OK**.

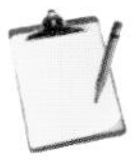

If you want to include information about the songs you're copying, such as the name of the album and the artist, make sure you're connected to the Internet before you encode the files from your CD. Otherwise, Windows Media Player won't be able to download this information.

You can start encoding the files on your audio CD by copying them to your hard drive. Here's how:

1. Insert the CD you want to copy into your computer's CD-ROM drive.
2. Click the **Copy from CD** button on the left side of the Windows Media Player window. The contents of the CD are displayed. If you can't see the names of the CD, click the **Find Album Info** button.

Find Album Info button

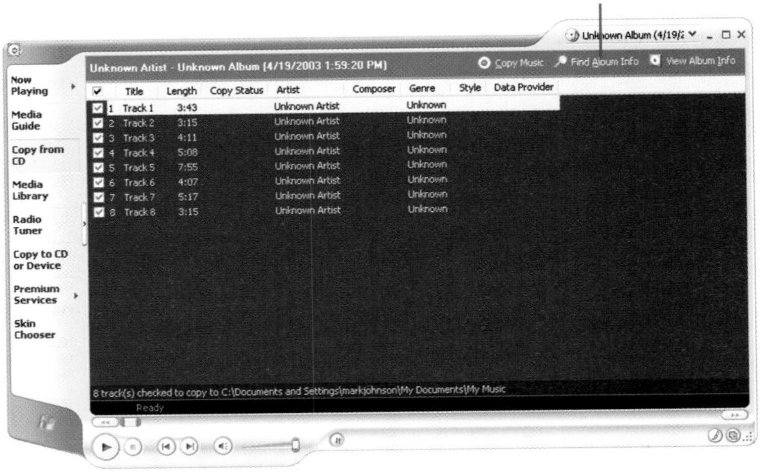
Unknown Artist - Unknown Album (4/19/2003 1:59:20 PM)
Copy Music
Find Album Info
View Album Info
Now Playing
Media Guide
Copy from CD
Media Library
Radio Tuner
Copy to CD or Device
Premium Services
Skin Chooser
Title
Length
Copy Status
Artist
Composer
Genre
Style
Data Provider
8 track(s) checked to copy to C:\Documents and Settings\markjohnson\My Documents\My Music
Ready

3. Make sure the tracks you want to copy are checked, and uncheck those tracks you don't want to copy.
4. Click the **Copy Music** button in the upper-right of the Windows Media Player window. Windows Media Player copies the selected tracks to your hard drive. The status is displayed in the Copy Status area as a progress bar that goes from pending, to copying, to copied.

   If copyright protection is enabled the first time you click Copy Music, a message appears notifying you that you won't be able to copy protected or licensed tracks copied from CDs to another computer. Click **OK**, or clear the **Do not protect content** check box, and then click **OK**.

5. After the file is copied, the Copy Status area reads Copied to Library, at which point you can access your Media Library and play the file from your hard drive rather than from the CD.

   Unless you specify another folder, Windows Media Player copies the music files into your My Music folder. First, however, Windows Media Player creates a subfolder for the artist and, within the artist folder, another subfolder for this CD. If you would like to change to another folder in which to save your music, use the Copy Music tab of the Options dialog box (see step 2 in the previous exercise).

Groovin' to Your Tunes

To use Windows Media Player to play a digital music file, do the following:

1. Click the **Now Playing** button on the left side of the Windows Media Player window.

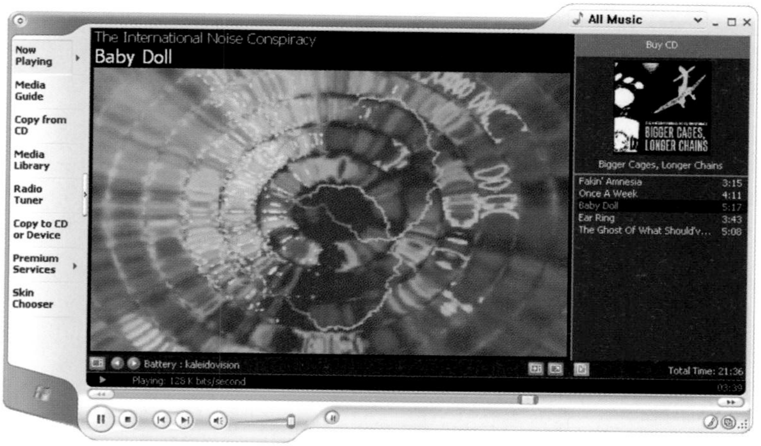
All Music
The International Noise Conspiracy
Baby Doll
Buy CD
Now Playing
Media Guide
Copy from CD
Media Library
Radio Tuner
Copy to CD or Device
Premium Services
Skin Chooser
BIGGER CAGES, LONGER CHAINS
Bigger Cages, Longer Chains
Fakin' Amnesia 3:15
Once A Week 4:11
Baby Doll 5:17
Ear Ring 3:43
The Ghost Of What Should'v... 5:08
Battery : kaleidovision
Playing: 128 K bits/second
Total Time: 21:36

❷ If you can't see the File menu, move your pointer over the top of the player to see the menu bar. To play a file stored on your computer's hard drive, click **File** and choose **Open**.

To load a music file from the Web instead of one stored on your computer, click **File** and choose **Open URL**.

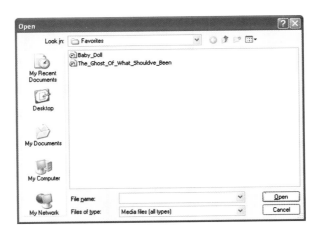

Open
Look in:
Favorites
Baby_Doll
The_Ghost_Of_What_Shouldve_Been
My Recent Documents
Desktop
My Documents
My Computer
My Network
File name:
Files of type:
Media files (all types)
Open
Cancel

❸ In the Open dialog box, navigate to the folder where the file you want to play is located. On most computers, digital music files are stored in the My Music folder. To open this folder, click the **My Documents** folder on the left side of the window, and then double-click the **My Music** folder.

If you have subfolders containing the music you want to listen to, open the appropriate folder.

❹ Select the music file you want to listen to.

Open
Look in:
Favorites
Baby_Doll
The_Ghost_Of_What_Shouldve_Been
My Recent Documents
Desktop
My Documents
My Computer
My Network
File name:
Baby_Doll
Files of type:
Media files (all types)
Open
Cancel

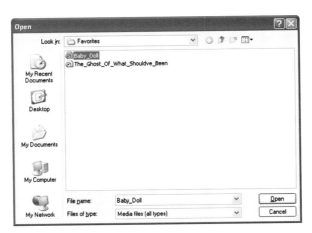

5. Click the **Open** button.
6. Windows Media Player plays the selected file automatically. Use the playback controls to pause or stop play, or adjust the volume.

Playing a CD

Playing an audio CD on your computer is as easy as using a traditional CD player. Put the CD in the CD drive, and the music begins to play in the digital music player designated to play audio CDs. The list of tracks appears in the playlist where you can flip through tracks, fast forward, or rewind using the playback controls. Since Windows Media Player is installed with the Windows operating system, it opens by default. You can configure most other players to play audio CDs by setting that option in the player's preferences.

Your computer can recognize and play traditional audio CDs as well as CDs containing MP3s, WMAs, and other digital music formats. You'll learn more about creating audio and MP3 CDs in chapter 8.

Stopping and Starting Playback

As mentioned earlier, once the music starts playing you can use the playback controls, shown in Figure 6-8, to pause, stop, and restart the song. Click **Pause** to temporarily pause the playback; restart the playback by clicking **Play**. Click **Stop** to completely halt the playback. In addition, most digital music players also have **Forward** and **Back** buttons. Click them to skip forward to the next track, or backward to the last song played.

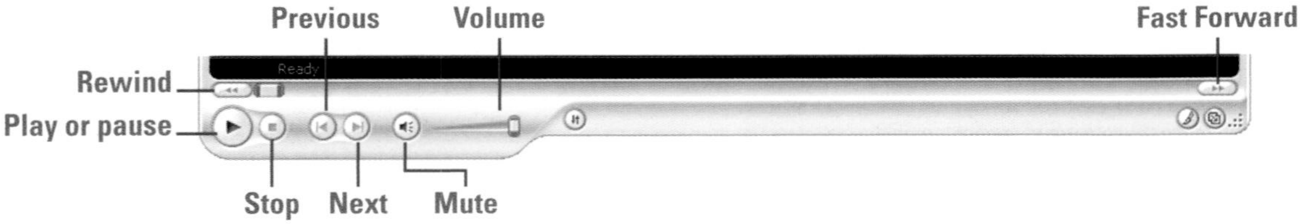
Previous
Volume
Fast Forward
Rewind
Play or pause
Ready
Stop
Next
Mute

Figure 6-8 Manage playback with the playback controls.

Adjusting the Volume

Most digital music players prominently display a volume control near the main controls. You use this control, generally a slider, to change the playback volume. Use your mouse pointer to drag the slider to the right and left (or up and down) to increase or decrease the volume.

Sounds and Audio Devices Properties
Volume
Sounds
Audio
Voice
Hardware
Creative SB Extigy
Device volume
Low
High
Mute
Place volume icon in the taskbar
Advanced...
Speaker settings
Use the settings below to change individual speaker volume and other settings.
Speaker Volume...
Advanced...
OK
Cancel
Apply

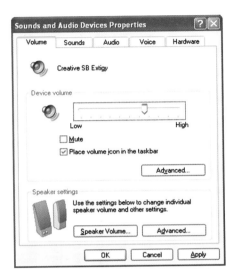

Of course, you can also change your computer's volume with Windows volume controls. In Windows XP, open Control Panel and select **Sounds and Audio Devices**. Then adjust the volume with the slider in the Device volume section.

You can also double-click the **Volume** icon in the Windows notification area, on the far-right end of your taskbar, if available.

Volume Controls
start
10:18 AM

In addition, you can just adjust the volume using the volume controls on the actual speakers.

It's best to set the volume on your music player at its highest level, and use the Windows volume control as your primary volume control.

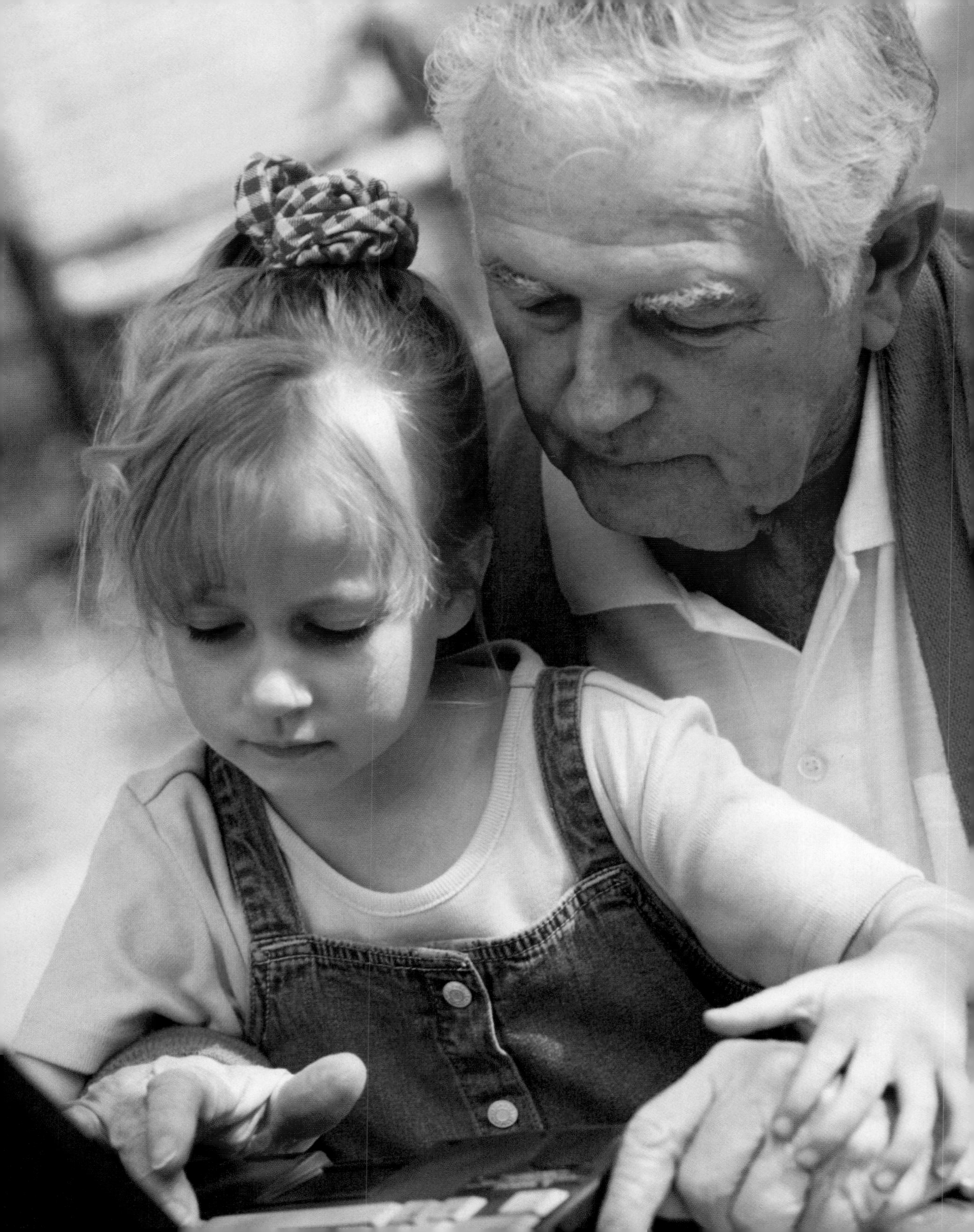

CHAPTER 7

Explore Music Online

The ability to transfer digital music over the Internet has implications hardly imaginable only decades ago. An Internet connection now transforms your computer into a receiver that brings radio stations from across the globe, a searchable database through the world's catalog of music, and an on-demand record store that allows you to purchase that music. Whether you plan to play digital music from your computer, on your home stereo, during your drive to work, or anywhere, you'll first need to acquire that music, and there's no better place than the Internet to do it. There are literally hundreds of Web sites that offer digital audio file downloads, each with its own unique selection of music. That means that no matter how obscure the song you seek or how unknown its performer, chances are you'll find it on the Internet.

In this chapter, you'll learn how to listen to live streaming digital radio broadcasts, search online resources to find any title, and use music services to start downloading your custom collection. You'll also learn how to keep your system safe from viruses and other problems that can result from file transfers over the Internet.

Exploring Internet Radio

There are two basic ways to play digital music you find on the Internet. One requires you to download a complete digital audio file before you can open it in a digital music player and play it, which we'll talk about later in this chapter. Another method, streaming audio, sometimes called Web casting, is used for playing back live radio broadcasts and other programs over the Web, or for offering previews of songs before you download them. In fact, some services on the Web offer large collections of music available only in streaming-audio format, so access to all your favorite music requires no downloads or hard drive space.

 All streaming-audio broadcasts on the Internet are informally called Internet radio.

Streaming Audio

With streaming audio, you don't save a file on your hard drive to listen to it. Instead, the music comes to you a little bit at a time as the player plays it, similar to the way you listen to an AM or FM station on your car radio. Streaming-audio players work by playing the first part of the recording before they finish downloading the rest of the audio file. As shown in Figure 7-1, this process gathers the first part of the audio stream in a small buffer, or storage area, on your hard disk. When the buffer is full, the audio starts playing—while the player continues to download the rest of the song. As a result, streaming-audio files can begin playing almost immediately, eliminating the long wait associated with typical digital audio file downloads. And with live audio broadcasts, the streaming is continuous until the broadcast ends. Depending on the type of Web cast you're listening to, there may or may not be a file for it stored on your hard disk after the broadcast. If not, the audio stream can only be listened to once, in real time.

Incoming stream
Buffer
Now playing stream

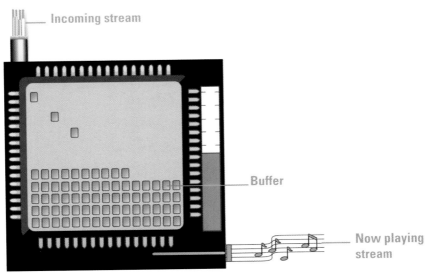

Figure 7-1 Digital radio uses a buffer to store streaming audio data for continuous playback.

Some streaming-audio sites play their audio through your Web browser, using a streaming-audio plug-in. This is a small software program that attaches to your browser and enables it to function like a streaming-audio player. If your browser needs a specific plug-in, you'll be prompted to download it from the Web site; the download and installation—particularly with a broadband connection—is typically fast and automatic.

In the following sections, you'll learn all about Internet radio. You'll find out how to use an Internet radio player to listen to Internet radio, and you'll discover some of the more popular Internet radio sites.

Listening to Internet Radio

Internet radio content covers a broad range, from audio books to news broadcasts, from streamed CDs to live concerts. You'll also find a lot of real-world radio stations streaming on the Internet, making Internet radio a great way to listen to stations you can't pick up on your local AM or FM radio. To listen to Internet radio using your computer, just use your digital music player to dial into a station broadcasting music (or sports or talk shows) that you like. Click **Play** and leave the player running in the background as you work.

> Have you ever heard a song on the radio and wondered what it was called or who sang it? If so, you'll appreciate the fact that many Internet radio stations display the title and performer of the song that is currently playing right on your computer screen.

For example, to listen to Internet radio using Windows Media Player, follow these steps:

1. Click the **Radio Tuner** button in the taskbar on the left side of the player. Windows Media Player connects to the WindowsMedia.com Web site and displays a list of featured stations.
2. To see more stations, click a genre in the Find More Stations section or use the search box to search for specific types of music or station call letters.

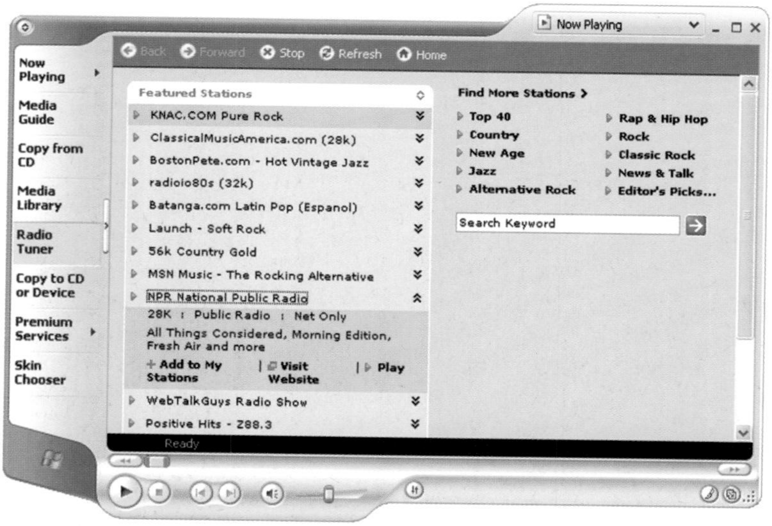
Now Playing
Back
Forward
Stop
Refresh
Home
Now Playing
Media Guide
Copy from CD
Media Library
Radio Tuner
Copy to CD or Device
Premium Services
Skin Chooser
Featured Stations
KNAC.COM Pure Rock
ClassicalMusicAmerica.com (28k)
BostonPete.com - Hot Vintage Jazz
radioio80s (32k)
Batanga.com Latin Pop (Espanol)
Launch - Soft Rock
56k Country Gold
MSN Music - The Rocking Alternative
NPR National Public Radio
28K : Public Radio : Net Only
All Things Considered, Morning Edition, Fresh Air and more
Add to My Stations
Visit Website
Play
WebTalkGuys Radio Show
Positive Hits - Z88.3
Find More Stations
Top 40
Country
New Age
Jazz
Alternative Rock
Rap & Hip Hop
Rock
Classic Rock
News & Talk
Editor's Picks...
Search Keyword
Ready

3. When you find a station you like, click the station name to display more information and listening options.
4. Some stations can be listened to from within Windows Media Player. For these stations, click **Play** to begin listening. The player shows a buffering activity while it pre-loads the first part of the streamed media. Other stations require you to visit their Web sites to listen. For these stations, click the **Visit Website** link, and follow the playback instructions on the site.

> **More About . . . Streaming Audio and Firewalls**
>
> If you want to listen to Internet radio at work, you may experience some difficulties. That's because many corporate networks use firewalls to protect against unwanted intrusions. (A firewall is a software program that blocks certain types of Internet traffic.) Unfortunately, firewalls can also block streaming-audio and streaming-video Web casts. If you find that Internet radio broadcasts are blocked, check with your network administrator to see if the firewall can be configured to allow streaming media to be received.

Internet Radio Sites

Several Web sites offer Internet radio broadcasts. Some of these sites offer Web casts of traditional radio stations, whereas others offer Web-specific content. Yahoo! LAUNCHCast is just one of those sites. Many Internet radio sites, such as LAUNCHCast, enable you to create your own custom "stations" based on your listening preferences. New guests to this particular site are offered fewer channels and features, and more commercials. However, with a small fee, an upgrade to LAUNCHCast Plus gets you commercial-free music and access to many attractive features, such as your own custom station. For how-to information, check the site's help system.

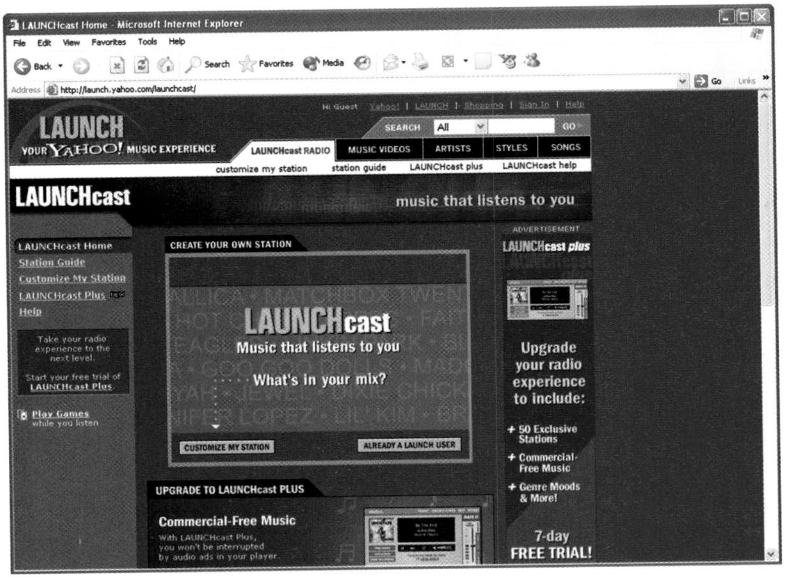

LAUNCHcast Home - Microsoft Internet Explorer
http://launch.yahoo.com/launchcast/
LAUNCH
YOUR YAHOO! MUSIC EXPERIENCE
LAUNCHcast RADIO
MUSIC VIDEOS
ARTISTS
STYLES
SONGS
customize my station
station guide
LAUNCHcast plus
LAUNCHcast help
LAUNCHcast
music that listens to you
LAUNCHcast Home
Station Guide
Customize My Station
LAUNCHcast Plus
Help
CREATE YOUR OWN STATION
LAUNCHcast
Music that listens to you
What's in your mix?
CUSTOMIZE MY STATION
ALREADY A LAUNCH USER
UPGRADE TO LAUNCHcast PLUS
Commercial-Free Music
LAUNCHcast plus
Upgrade your radio experience to include:
+ 50 Exclusive Stations
+ Commercial-Free Music
+ Genre Moods & More!
7-day FREE TRIAL!

Due to the ever-changing nature of the Internet, we cannot guarantee the accuracy or safety of any particular Web site, but we will direct you only to ones we have found have a good reputation in these areas.

Internet radio is a great way to listen to news, sports, or a variety of songs in your favorite genre. However, if you are looking for a specific title to listen to on-demand, you'll find many resources in the Internet designed for this purpose, which we'll talk about next.

Searching for Music Online

The Internet is a vast network of computers that stores billions and billions of files. And chances are, one of those computers houses the very music file you need to complete your collection. The burning question is, how do you find that computer?

In this section, you'll learn about several music Web sites that you can visit to search for your favorite digital music. Some sites, called digital audio archives, offer lots of music for free. Other sites, called subscription music services, charge a monthly fee. Still others (discussed later in this chapter) enable you to connect with other users to swap your own personal files.

 Remember to add any music sites you like to your Web browser's Favorites list for easy access in the future.

Each online site differs in the way it enables you to search for music. That is, you perform a specific set of steps to locate music on one site, and a completely different set of steps to find music on another. We suggest that you consult each site's online help information for specific information about locating the music you want.

> ### More About . . . Digital Audio Archives
> One source of online digital music is at one of the many online digital audio archives. These sites typically offer large databases of music files (most in MP3 format) contributed by other site visitors. In most cases, you can search these digital audio archive sites by artist, song title, or by genre. Some sites, such as Musicseek.com, also function as search engines for music stored on other sites.

Using Online Databases

When you play music using your digital music player, you typically see information about the song displayed somewhere in the player window. Typically, that information comes from an online database, which is a collection of information (in this case, CD information) stored on the Internet.

Most digital music players obtain this data from one of two online databases: CDDB® (Compact Disc Database) or AMG (All-Music Guide). Both databases contain all sorts of information about compact-disc music, such as the artist, CD title, song tracks, and so on. When you access a CD (or certain MP3 files) using a digital music player, the player connects to the Internet and pulls song, artist, and album information from one of the online databases, which the player then displays.

Digital music players will search online CD databases when you insert a custom-made audio CD, but they won't display or find any information. The search is successful usually only for commercially produced audio CDs. In addition, if you're not currently connected to the Internet, most music players will attempt to launch your connection software and establish a connection with your Internet service provider or online service.

CDDB

Gracenote's CDDB® is the world's largest database of audio CD and song titles and is accessed by more than 28 million users each month. Several major subscription music services and many digital music players license CDDB for use with their services or software.

You can also access the CDDB database (www.gracenote.com) on your own to locate information about an artist, album, or song. Simply use your Web browser to open the site. Then, type the name of an artist, album, or song you want to research in the Search box and click Search or press ENTER. CDDB returns a list of matching CDs. Click a title to see the CD's track listing.

Gracenote: Search CDDB - Microsoft Internet Explorer
File Edit View Favorites Tools Help
Back Search Favorites Media
Address http://www.gracenote.com/music/
Go Links
gracenote
CompuServe BASIC only $9.95 a month.
For a 30-day FREE trial, CLICK HERE
HOME COMPANY INFO GRACENOTE PRODUCTS POWERED by GRACENOTE DEVELOPER ZONE SEARCH CDDB
Gracenote's signature CDDB® service is the industry standard for music recognition services. The largest online database of music information in the world, CDDB® is used by over 30 million people in over 130 countries every month.
Search CDDB®
Digital Top Ten Index
How Does It Work
Products with CDDB®
2,198,833 CDs
28,085,827 Songs
CURRENT CDDB® CATALOG
shop now
CDDB® MUSIC SEARCH
Find in any field:
Artist: Exact Phrase
Album: Exact Phrase
THE DIGITAL TOP TEN™
Artist : Album
1 Evanescence : Fallen
2 Norah Jones : Come Away With Me
3 Eminem : The Eminem Show
4 50 Cent : Get Rich Or Die Tryin'
5 Coldplay : A Rush Of Blood To The Head
Internet

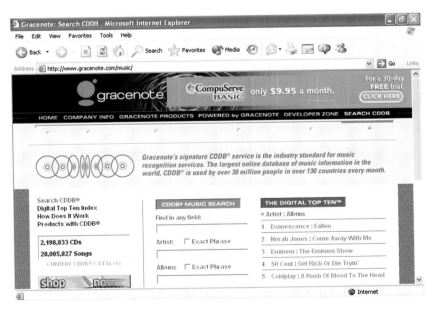

AMG

CDDB's chief competitor is the AMG (All Music Guide), which collected information about recorded music and published it in book form long before the Internet was around. As with CDDB, many major subscription music services, as well as several digital music players, license AMG for use with their services or software. In fact, because the information in the AMG database is typically more comprehensive than that in the CDDB database, some services license with both CDDB and AMG to provide information to their users.

Not surprisingly, you can also access AMG using your Web browser. Once there, you can search the 500,000+ albums in AMG's database by artist, album, song, genre, or record label. Results include album information, track information, and even detailed personnel listings.

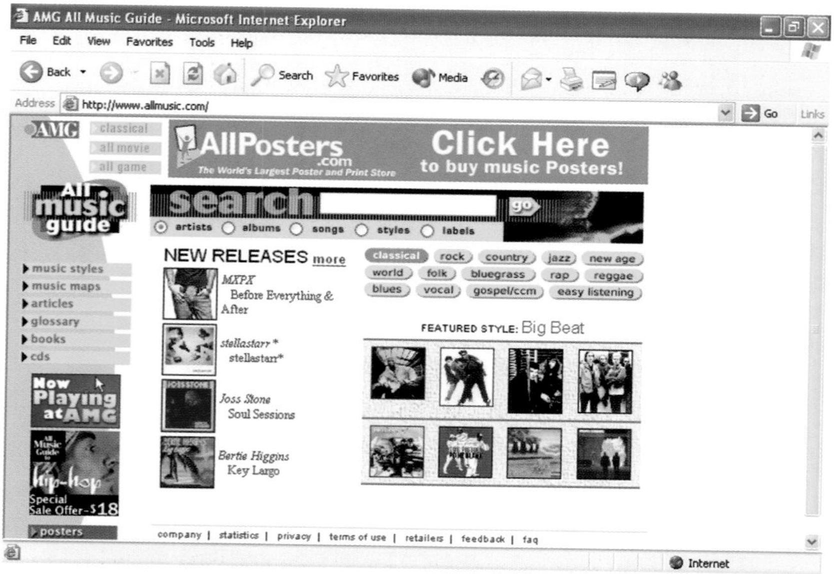
AMG All Music Guide - Microsoft Internet Explorer
File Edit View Favorites Tools Help
Back Search Favorites Media
Address http://www.allmusic.com/
Go Links
AMG
classical
all movie
all game
AllPosters.com
The World's Largest Poster and Print Store
Click Here
to buy music Posters!
All music guide
search
go
artists albums songs styles labels
NEW RELEASES more
MXPX
Before Everything & After
stellastarr*
stellastarr*
Joss Stone
Soul Sessions
Bertie Higgins
Key Largo
classical rock country jazz new age
world folk bluegrass rap reggae
blues vocal gospel/ccm easy listening
FEATURED STYLE: Big Beat
music styles
music maps
articles
glossary
books
cds
Now Playing at AMG
Special Sale Offer-$18
posters
company | statistics | privacy | terms of use | retailers | feedback | faq
Internet

AMG provides similar databases for movies (All Movie Guide) and videogames (All Game Guide). You can access these sites from the main All Music Guide site. See the table at the end of this chapter to find out how to access the site.

Using Subscription Music Services

Understandably, record companies and their artists want to get paid for the music they provide. For this reason, they license their music to Web sites that collect money from users who download it. These Web sites are called subscription music services. In most cases, users who subscribe to such services pay a monthly fee in exchange for the right to download a certain number of songs each month to their computer. In addition, some free downloads, typically for promotional purposes, may also be available.

 If you decide to subscribe to a music service, be sure you carefully read the membership agreement first. As mentioned, some services limit how many files you can download each month. In addition, you may be limited in what you can do with those files. For example, some sites won't let you burn their downloaded files to CD. Finally, be aware that most music subscription sites distribute music using file formats other than MP3, which is very versatile. For example, WMA files, which have built-in licensing features, are commonly used. Make sure your computer's digital music player or portable player can handle the file format used by the subscription service. Windows Media Player, for example, currently handles the following music file formats: Music CD Playback (cda), AIFF, Windows Media audio (asf, wma and others), Windows audio (avi, wav), MPEG, MIDI, AU (au, snd), and MP3.

These subscription sites are, in general, very easy to use, and often carry music from multiple record companies. However, not every subscription site has access to music from every record label, so if you're a real music junkie, you might want to subscribe to more than one service. Subscription services offer high quality digital music for download or over streaming digital radio. Most also offer the ability to create playlists and organize a custom music library. You can usually enroll in a short-term free trial to decide if a particular service fits your needs. There are many to choose from; read on for information about the following subscription services:

- ✦ EMusic

- ✦ RHAPSODY

- ✦ Pressplay

 Because the Internet is a constantly evolving environment, some of the sites we discuss in the following section may change.

EMusic

Unlike most subscription services, which limit the number of downloads you can perform each month, subscribing to the EMusic service affords you unlimited MP3 file downloads for a single monthly fee. This service, which features known artists from more than 900 independent record labels, offers more than 250,000 music files in its database.

EMusic - MP3 Subscription Service. Free MP3 trial - Microsoft Internet Explorer
http://www.emusic.com/pitch.html
emusic
musical styles »
Rock/Pop Jazz Electronic Urban/Hip Hop World/Reggae Alternative/Punk
Country/Folk Blues Classical New Age Inspirational Soundtracks/Other
Home | New | Charts | Sneak Previews | Artists | Labels
Artist Search
Returning Users: Click Here To Log In.
UNLIMITED MP3S - ONE LOW MONTHLY PRICE
ARTISTS GENRES SNEAK PREVIEW NEW
DOWNLOAD
Full Length Tracks
Complete Albums
Unlimited Access
PLAY
Download Once, Play Anywhere
On Your Computer
On Your Portable Player
On any MP3 or CD Player
BURN
Create and Mix your own CDs
No Limits!
Burn as much as you want
Hot releases from over 950 labels, including these:
Epitaph
Get 50 FREE MP3s
START YOUR FREE TRIAL!
JOIN NOW!
Internet

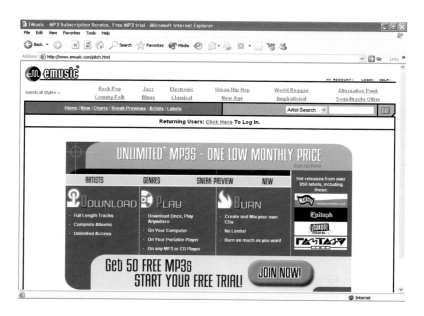

Using the service, you can download either individual songs or complete albums. You can also burn songs directly to CD or download to a portable player. Finding the songs you want is simple. You can search by title or artist, or you can browse through music by category.

RHAPSODY

RHAPSODY is what they call a "Celestial Jukebox" that brings together a collection of thousands of albums, Internet radio, and flexible, legal CD burning. What's unique about RHAPSODY is that you don't download the music. Instead, with an active subscription, you have access to their entire collection of music through an "on-demand streaming service." Any time you want to listen, you can log on and either search through their collection, or you can play tracks from your own custom music library or a custom playlist. Tracks can be

RHAPSODY - The Premier Digital Music Service - Microsoft Internet Explorer
http://www.listen.com/rhap_about.jsp?sect=main
listen.com a subsidiary of RealNetworks.
Home About RHAPSODY The Music Wireless FAQs & Help About Listen.com
The Celestial Jukebox Subscription Plan Details Features & Requirements Tools & Tips Reviews
RHAPSODY brings the "Celestial Jukebox" to life.
RHAPSODY is the celestial jukebox that gives you unlimited access to thousands of albums right from your PC. Only RHAPSODY brings together the largest legal collection of digital music in the world, the Internet's best radio, flexible CD burning, and detailed music information - all in one easy-to-use service.
Click & drag magnifying glass to see the player up close
Get the 7-Day FREE Trial!
START HERE
Get Unlimited, On-Demand Access to a Megastore of Music
More than 20,000 albums at your fingertips
The biggest artists in every imaginable musical style
Listen to complete albums, create custom playlists
CD quality sound - instantly
No viruses or spyware
Play as much music as you like, no meters or limits
Internet

burned directly to a CD, at a set price per track, and you'll soon also be able to copy songs directly to a portable player.

Because Listen's service is based on streaming audio, they strongly recommend a broadband connection, though service is available for dial-up users who can expect periodic interruptions due to Internet congestion.

Pressplay

The Pressplay service is a joint venture between the world's two largest music companies, Sony Music and Universal Music, and it offers a subscription music service featuring artists from all of the five major labels and over 20 independents. Pressplay co-brands the service with its distribution partners. Therefore, you can download the client software at sites such as Yahoo! and MP3.com as well as pressplay.com.

Try pressplay digital music service's free trial and start to stream, download and burn today! - Microsoft Intern...
File Edit View Favorites Tools Help
Back Search Favorites Media
Address http://www.pressplay.com/
Go Links
I am already a member!
pressplay
PRESSPLAY HOME THE SERVICE FAQs / HELP THE MUSIC ABOUT US PRESSROOM
Willie Nelson Coldplay Christina Aguilera Nelly PJ Harvey Fatboy Slim
take a tour CLICK HERE
stream download burn transfer
"For the full-range of features, pressplay is the hands-down winner." - BusinessWeek.com
• Unlimited Access to over 300,000 Songs
• Exclusive Tracks • Commercial-free Radio
Start Your FREE Trial Today!
Start Now!
In the News:
Click here to see why BusinessWeek.com calls pressplay "the hands-down winner."
Internet

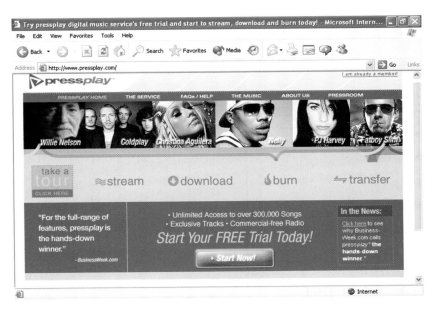

Pressplay offers digital music for downloading, streaming audio, burning, and transfer to portable music players. Subscriptions range from Unlimited to Annual Plus. The different subscription levels determine how many Portable Downloads (downloads that can be burned to CD or transferred to portable players) a member receives on a monthly basis. All plans include the ability to buy as many Portable Downloads as the member wants, for just under a dollar a track.

If you normally buy several CDs a month, you should consider signing up for the higher levels of service at any of these subscriptions services. Also, you might consider signing up for several subscription services for access to a diverse selection of music.

Pressplay offers unlimited access to over 300,000 songs, the ability to burn songs to CDs, to transfer songs to a portable music player, or to listen to music on or offline (a great option for dial-up users). In addition, Pressplay offers commercial-free radio and the option to exclude titles containing explicit lyrics.

Joining a Subscription Music Service

It only takes a minute or two to subscribe to an Internet music service, and usually, after the short enrollment process, you'll have full access to the service's music library. These short subscription forms usually ask for your name, address, and credit card number. Service plans range from several day trial periods to year-long subscriptions, and they usually cost about ten to twenty dollars a month, depending on the length of the subscription and the level of access you want for downloads, CD burning, etc. Let's take a quick look at one subscription music service to illustrate a real world enrollment process.

Generally, subscribing to a subscription service is a quick and easy process. Visit the site of the music service you want to subscribe to and click "Join Now," "Become a Member," or a similar invitation. This link is usually clearly marked. On most sites, you can also opt for a free trial membership that only lasts a few days to explore the service before you buy.

 Most subscription sites still require a credit card number for a free trial. If you enroll in a free trial, be sure to read the corresponding agreement.

You'll then fill out a general information form. Usually, this includes an e-mail address, name, and mailing address. You'll then be asked to enter your credit card information and specify the service plan you desire (if the site offers multiple service plans).

 If you are leery of entering your credit card information, make sure you read the Terms and Conditions. Most subscription sites invest heavily in security, but you'll always want to read any agreements before giving out this valuable information.

On some sites, you'll then be prompted to download a Download Manager, which provides convenience while downloading, such as placing multiple files in a queue. If this is the case, you can download the file to your computer like any other file, and then open it to install the software. When you have completed the subscription, you'll be welcomed to the site and usually have access to music immediately.

Now, you can search for music by artist, title, track, or label. For example, on EMusic's site, choose one of these options from the drop-down menu in the upper right of the screen, and then type who or what you're looking for in the text box, as shown in Figure 7-2. Click **Go** to start the search. Remember, the music available depends on the labels held by each subscription service, so no one service will carry every title.

Search text box
Begin search
Category menu

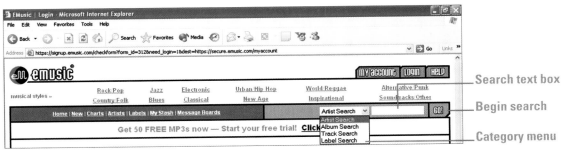

Figure 7-2 Easily search for music using the subscription music service's search engine.

EMusic's search results appear categorized into albums. From here you can download specific tracks or an entire album to your computer.

Once you've found the music you want, downloading it is easy. We'll explain more about downloading music from a subscription service later in this chapter.

EMusic: For The Good Times - Microsoft Internet Explorer
Artist: Kenny Rogers
Album: For The Good Times
Label: Cleopatra Records
Genre: Contemporary: Country
Currently available in 128k MP3 only.

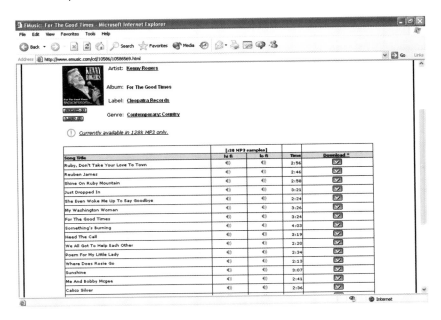

Much effort has gone into creating Internet music services that compensate those who are responsible for the music itself. A portion of the price you pay for your subscription goes to the service's respective artists and record companies. History has shown, however, that the power of the Internet, and its ability to transfer quality recordings quickly and easily, has brought about some major conflicts with those holding the copyrights to this music. In fact, subscription services themselves arose in the wake of another type of music service less capable of rewarding artists and record companies, known as peer-to-peer file sharing.

 While filling out forms online that require a credit card number, look for a lock icon in the lower right of your browser window. This lock indicates SSL (Secure Socket Layer) encryption, which protects you from unauthorized access to this valuable information. Also, to avoid programs that monitor your computer without your permission, called spyware, only download accessories necessary to using the subscription service. We'll talk more about spyware later in this chapter.

Downloading Digital Music Files

Once you've found the song you want, downloading it to your computer is the next step. When you download a digital music file, you simply copy it to your computer from another computer on the Web. When your computer receives the file, it stores it on your hard disk. Once the file is there, you can listen to it anytime you want.

The specific instructions for downloading audio files differ from site to site, but most sites prominently display a Download (or similarly named) link or button alongside when you locate a music file on the site. Simply click this button, specify where on your hard disk you want to store the downloaded file, and then click Save. (If your computer uses a 56.6 Kbps modem to connect to the Internet, downloading a typical 3-minute song in the MP3 format takes about 10 to 15 minutes. The same file downloads in only a minute or two if you have a cable or DSL connection.)

For our example, we're going to download a file from www.gateway.com/mp3downloads using Internet Explorer on Windows XP. To download and play one of the songs on this site, follow these steps:

1. Click start and select Internet to open your browser.
2. Type this URL into the Address field: www.gateway.com/mp3downloads.

3 Click Go or press ENTER. The download music site opens.

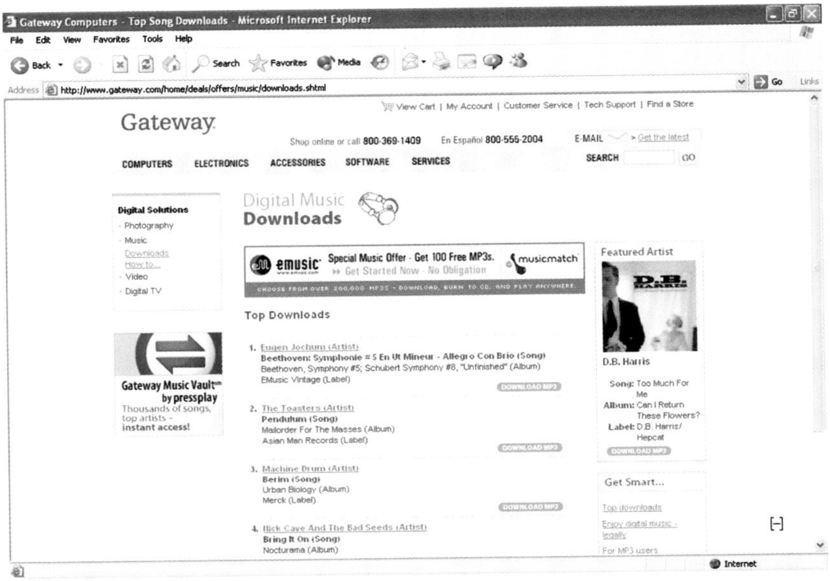
Gateway Computers - Top Song Downloads - Microsoft Internet Explorer
File Edit View Favorites Tools Help
Back Search Favorites Media
Address http://www.gateway.com/home/deals/offers/music/downloads.shtml
Go Links
View Cart | My Account | Customer Service | Tech Support | Find a Store
Gateway
Shop online or call 800-369-1409 En Español 800-555-2004
E-MAIL
SEARCH GO
COMPUTERS ELECTRONICS ACCESSORIES SOFTWARE SERVICES
Digital Solutions
Photography
Music
Downloads
How to...
Video
Digital TV
Digital Music Downloads
emusic Special Music Offer - Get 100 Free MP3s.
Get Started Now · No Obligation
musicmatch
Featured Artist
Top Downloads
1. Eugen Jochum (Artist)
Beethoven: Symphonie # 5 En Ut Mineur - Allegro Con Brio (Song)
Beethoven, Symphony #5; Schubert Symphony #8, "Unfinished" (Album)
EMusic Vintage (Label)
DOWNLOAD MP3
2. The Toasters (Artist)
Pendulum (Song)
Mailorder For The Masses (Album)
Asian Man Records (Label)
DOWNLOAD MP3
3. Machine Drum (Artist)
Berim (Song)
Urban Biology (Album)
Merck (Label)
DOWNLOAD MP3
4. Nick Cave And The Bad Seeds (Artist)
Bring It On (Song)
Nocturama (Album)
Gateway Music Vault℠ by pressplay
Thousands of songs, top artists - instant access!
D.B. Harris
Song: Too Much For Me
Album: Can I Return These Flowers?
Label: D.B. Harris/ Hepcat
DOWNLOAD MP3
Get Smart...
Top downloads
Enjoy digital music - legally
For MP3 users
Internet

4 Right-click the Download MP3 button to the right of one of the available titles, and choose Save Target As.

5 The Save As dialog box opens. Use this dialog box to select the destination download folder. You can also elect to change the file name of the audio file being downloaded.

6 Click Save to initiate the download to the designated folder. A common download destination folder is the My Music folder located within My Documents. Be sure you pick a destination folder that you will remember.

After you download the file, you use a digital music player—such as Windows Media Player or MusicMatch Jukebox—to play the music through your computer. (Review Chapter 6 for information about playing music files.)

It's also possible to download audio files using Windows Media Player. By selecting the Media Guide button, the WindowsMedia.com Web site is displayed within the Windows Media Player. Navigating this content is the same as navigating a Web browser. If you find something that interests you, just click to watch it streaming over the Internet or to download it to your computer.

When you click on a link and hear music immediately or after a few seconds, you're initiating a stream of the music instead of a download.

Downloading From a Subscription Music Service

Downloading music with a subscription music service is very easy. In general, the process involves using the service's search utility to find the song you want to download, and then double-clicking the song to begin the download. Then, you can usually find a window that displays the downloads in progress (or queue), and then relax while your computer downloads all of these files. We'll use the EMusic service again to demonstrate how to download music from a subscription service. You will need to have a subscription to the site to use it. See the "Joining a Subscription Music Service" section earlier in this chapter.

1. In your Web browser, open the service's Web site, and log in using your e-mail address (or user name) and password.
2. Use the site's search engine to find the music you want to download. In this case, choose the criteria from the drop-down list in the upper right, and then type the artist, album, track, or label in the corresponding text box.

Artist Search
GO!

3. Click **Go**. EMusic searches its database based on your query.
4. You may see multiple results. Click the link that corresponds to the artist, album, track, or label you're looking for.

> You may see a heading labeled "Music Like." If EMusic doesn't carry what you are looking for, it will recommend similar music.

5. Navigate through the search process until you've narrowed your search to the track you are looking for. You may find complete albums available for download or compilations created by EMusic.

EMusic: For The Good Times - Microsoft Internet Explorer
File Edit View Favorites Tools Help
Back Search Favorites Media
Address http://www.emusic.com/cd/10586/10586569.html
Go Links
Artist: Kenny Rogers
Album: For The Good Times
Label: Cleopatra Records
Genre: Contemporary Country
Currently available in 128k MP3 only.
[:30 MP3 samples]
Song Title hi fi lo fi Time Download
Ruby, Don't Take Your Love To Town 2:56
Reuben James 2:46
Shine On Ruby Mountain 2:58
Just Dropped In 3:21
She Even Woke Me Up To Say Goodbye 2:24
My Washington Woman 3:26
For The Good Times 3:24
Something's Burning 4:03
Heed The Call 3:19
We All Got To Help Each Other 2:20
Poem For My Little Lady 2:34
Where Does Rosie Go 2:13
Sunshine 3:07
Me And Bobby Mcgee 2:41
Calico Silver 2:36
Internet

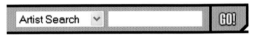

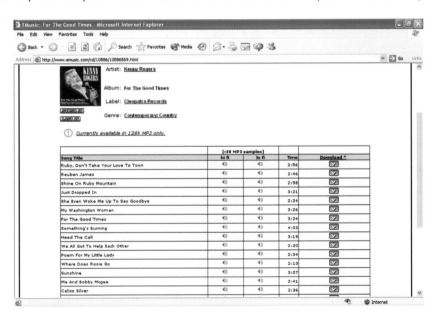

⑥ Click the speaker icon under lo-fi or hi-fi to hear a short, streaming sample of any song on the album. To download a track, click the green button on the right. You can also choose to download the entire album from the link at the bottom right. EMusic's Download Manager appears and displays the song(s) you have chosen to download.

⑦ The download manager lists all the songs you have chosen in a queue. Each of these will be downloaded in turn. You can right-click a track to Cancel, Pause, or Resume the download. Or, choose Clear Completed to remove tracks from the queue that are finished downloading. By default, the music is saved to a folder on your desktop named "My EMusic."

 To specify a folder to save downloaded files, choose Options from the View menu.

Now you can launch your music player and listen to your new tunes. Downloads from EMusic are regular MP3 files that can be burned to a CD or copied to a portable device for personal use without restriction.

Internet Safety

Whether you prefer digital audio archives, subscription music services, or peer-to-peer sharing services, downloading music can be a lot of fun. It can also, however, pose some security hazards to your computer system. Specifically, if your computer is configured improperly, other users could gain access to confidential information on your hard drive. In addition, downloading files over the Internet can put you at greater risk of infecting your system with a virus. Finally, in the course of installing the software you need to download or share music, you may inadvertently download spyware or adware to your system. These programs occasionally display advertisements or upload information about your surfing habits to a central server without your knowledge.

7

What Not to Download

While it is unlikely for a music file to infect your system with a computer virus, it is possible for you to inadvertently download another file type that contains a computer virus. For this reason, you must be absolutely certain when downloading digital music that the file you're downloading is, in fact, a digital audio file. You can tell by checking the file's extension—that is, the three letters appended to the end of the file's name. For example, files whose names end in ".mp3" are MP3 files. Likewise, files whose names end in ".wma" are WMA files.

You especially want to be careful when downloading files that are executable programs—typically, files with ".exe," ".pif," ".bat," or ".vbs" extensions. When launched, these types of files, unlike music files, can infect your computer with a computer virus. It's sometimes necessary to download and install these types of files; however, these extensions are not music file formats. Therefore, if you think you're downloading a song and it has one of these extensions, simply delete it from your hard disk.

In rare cases, MP3s and other audio files can contain a macro virus, which can disrupt the performance of your media player. To repel the possibility of a macro virus, set your player's security features to high (if available), and update anti-virus software on your computer regularly. We'll talk more about anti-virus software next.

 Don't be tricked by users adding a fake ".mp3" file extension to EXE files, like this: myfile.mp3.exe. The expectation is that you won't notice the ".exe" extension and will think you've downloaded a regular MP3 file. When you try to play the file, you instead launch a program, which typically contains a virus. You should always take caution when downloading any file from the Internet. Always make sure your anti-virus software has scanned a file before you open it.

Use Anti-virus Software

The best way to protect your system against unwanted viruses is to use an anti-virus software program. Anti-virus programs continually scan your system for any sign of infection. They also scan each file you download to make sure it's clean. The two most poplar anti-virus programs are Norton AntiVirus® (shown here) and McAfee VirusScan®. Both do a good job scanning for infecting files and disinfecting or deleting any infected files they find.

Norton AntiVirus
LiveUpdate
Options
Help
Norton AntiVirus
Status
Scan for Viruses
Reports
System Status: OK
Security Scanning Features
Auto-Protect On
Email Scanning On
Script Blocking On
Full System Scan 9/27/2003
Virus Definition Service
Virus Definitions 9/24/2003
Subscription Service 12/18/2003
Automatic LiveUpdate On
Item Details
The items marked in red need your attention.
Please select an item by clicking on the item at left in order to get more information and take the necessary action.
symantec.
Norton AntiVirus™ 2003

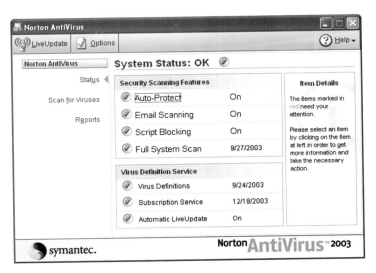

Avoiding Spyware

Although spyware, also called adware, is not a virus, it is, in most cases, a program that is downloaded to your system inadvertently when you download certain file-sharing services. These programs compromise your privacy, lurking in the background whenever you're connected to the P2P network, occasionally popping up advertisements, and, more insidiously, tracking your surfing habits. For example, spyware tracks the URLs visited by the user and sends that data to the host computer—without the user's knowledge or consent.

You can avoid installing spyware on your system by carefully watching your screen when you install file-sharing programs on your computer. Most installation routines ask you whether you want to install these additional programs (although they may disguise their true nature); simply choose not to install any program other than the main file-sharing program. Also, read the license agreement thoroughly before accepting it to ensure you are not granting permission to install unwanted programs that can be embedded in the main program installation.

Satellite Radio

In a world where your entire music collection fits in your pocket, and all your songs are available in your car at the push of a button, is there any need for radio anymore? For many, there certainly is. Even if your catalog of three thousand songs is set on shuffle all the time, there's something exciting about hearing a great song on the radio—perhaps even a new one yet to be added to your collection. In addition, your recordings don't broadcast live news, sports, or radio shows. In the past, listeners have had a choice of two bands, AM and FM, and usually a dozen or so stations to choose from. Now, the digital age has brought us satellite radio, which offers a whole new range of listening enjoyment. With a compatible receiver, your car can link up to a hundred stations—from just about any type of music, to live news, to sports and talk shows—uninterrupted, across an entire continent.

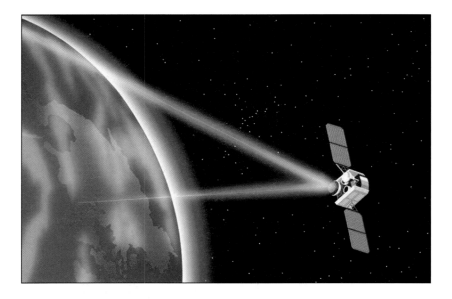

Satellite radio has been in the making for over ten years. In 1992, the FCC allocated a spectrum in the "S" band (2.3Ghz) for nationwide broadcasting of satellite-based Digital Audio Radio Service (DARS). Since then, several companies have applied for licenses to transmit streaming digital radio using a portion of the "S" band. Today, there are three satellite radio services: XM Satellite Radio Service, Sirius, and WorldSpace. Each of these services has its own broadcasting system, but all use the following in their basic network structure.

- ✦ Broadcasting station
- ✦ Ground repeaters
- ✦ Satellites
- ✦ Radio receivers

The basic framework employed by satellite radio services is pretty straightforward. First, a central station transmits the broadcast to powerful satellites. These satellites beam the digital signal to receivers in cars, homes, or portable radios. To increase the range of this signal, repeaters on the ground relay the signal to hard-to-reach places, such as urban canyons where tall buildings can block the signal. Radio receivers are programmed to descramble the digital data, which contains up to 100 channels of digital audio. The transmission also contains other data, including the title, artist, and genre, which appear on the receiver's LCD display. Figure 7-3 illustrates how satellite radio works.

SATELLiTE RADiO
Two Boeing 702 Satellites beam XM directly to listeners
ROCK
ROLL
Terrestrial Repeater
XM Headquarters 1500 Eckington Place NE, Washington, DC 20002
Choose up to 100 channels of programming
AM/FM/XM radios and small antenna receive XM seamlessly from coast to coast
© 2001 XM Satellite Radio Inc. All rights reserved.
From its state-of-the-art studios and uplink facility in the Washington, DC area, XM Satellite Radio will beam up to 100 channels of digital quality music, news and entertainment directly from two powerful satellites to cars and homes coast to coast.
A small antenna and AM/FM/XM car radio, home audio system or transportable radio will receive the signal.
SATELLiTE RADiO
© 2001 XM Satellite Radio Inc. All rights reserved.

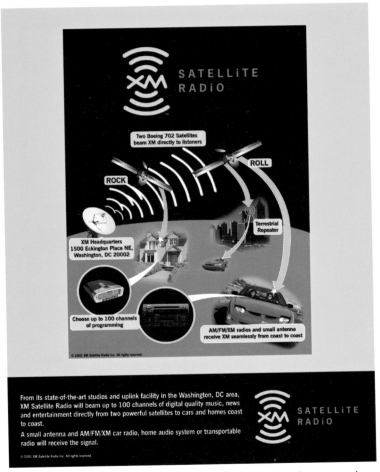

Figure 7-3 Satellites, repeaters, and receivers are used to transmit a digital signal over a wide area.

Setting up a complex network such as this wasn't easy, and millions of dollars in financing has gone into it. With so many resources going into providing such a service, there's also a lot you can get out of it.

The Benefits of Satellite Radio

There are many benefits to satellite radio over traditional AM and FM radio:

- Satellite radio offers improved sound quality compared to its AM and FM counterparts. In addition to eliminating the static that invades at the fringe of a traditional station's range, the digital signal delivers near-CD quality sound, with a highly defined low, mid, and high range when compared side-by-side with FM. Since the digital signal relies on line-of-sight, however, reception can sometimes fade among tall buildings of an urban area, but repeaters have been installed in such areas to minimize this inconvenience as much as possible.

- The diversity of satellite radio caters to a variety of listeners that local stations simply cannot accommodate. For example, there aren't enough Reggae listeners in Minot, North Dakota to support an all-Reggae station there—unfortunate for all of Minot's Reggae enthusiasts. There are, however, enough Reggae listeners across the continent to support such a station, and satellite radio can deliver this service to them. Music in genres economically impossible before are now available 24-7. On the other hand, satellite radio doesn't broadcast local stations. So hearing about your local high school's performance in the regional finals will still require AM or FM, but you will be able to hear news and a variety of channels brought from other providers, such as CNN and the BBC.

- Fewer commercials! Most FM music stations play 18 to 22 minutes of commercials per hour, and some up to 24 minutes. If you've ever flipped through every available channel in search of music, any music at all, satellite radio will come as a refreshing relief. Because satellite radio is offered as a subscription service, many channels do not run commercials at all. In this way, it's somewhat like cable TV. At most, some channels run about six minutes of ads an hour, and one satellite radio provider offers commercial-free broadcasting for all sixty of its music channels.

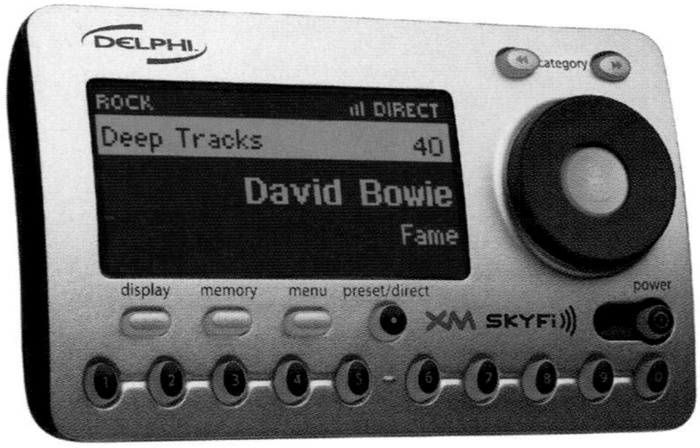
DELPHI
category
ROCK
DIRECT
Deep Tracks
40
David Bowie
Fame
display
memory
menu
preset/direct
XM SKYFi
power

✦ If you're cruising to your favorite FM radio station and hear a new tune you love, you might never know the artist or song title. Or, how many times have you heard the same great song over and over and wondered, "Who the heck is this?" If the DJ doesn't mention the artist or title, you have no way of knowing. With satellite radio, the title and artist of the song playing displays right on the LCD display, so you'll know exactly where to look when it's time to visit the record store or download the tune from your subscription music service.

Finally, the price of satellite receivers has gone down recently, bringing this technology into the affordable range for many consumers. These days you can get an in-dash, satellite-ready unit for about the price of an average mid-range receiver. Sony, Alpine, Pioneer, Delphi Delco, and many others offer car decks with satellite radio capability. Also, many auto manufacturers, including Ford and GM, offer satellite-ready stereos as an option in new car models. As satellite radio becomes more and more popular, chances are, prices will continue to drop.

7

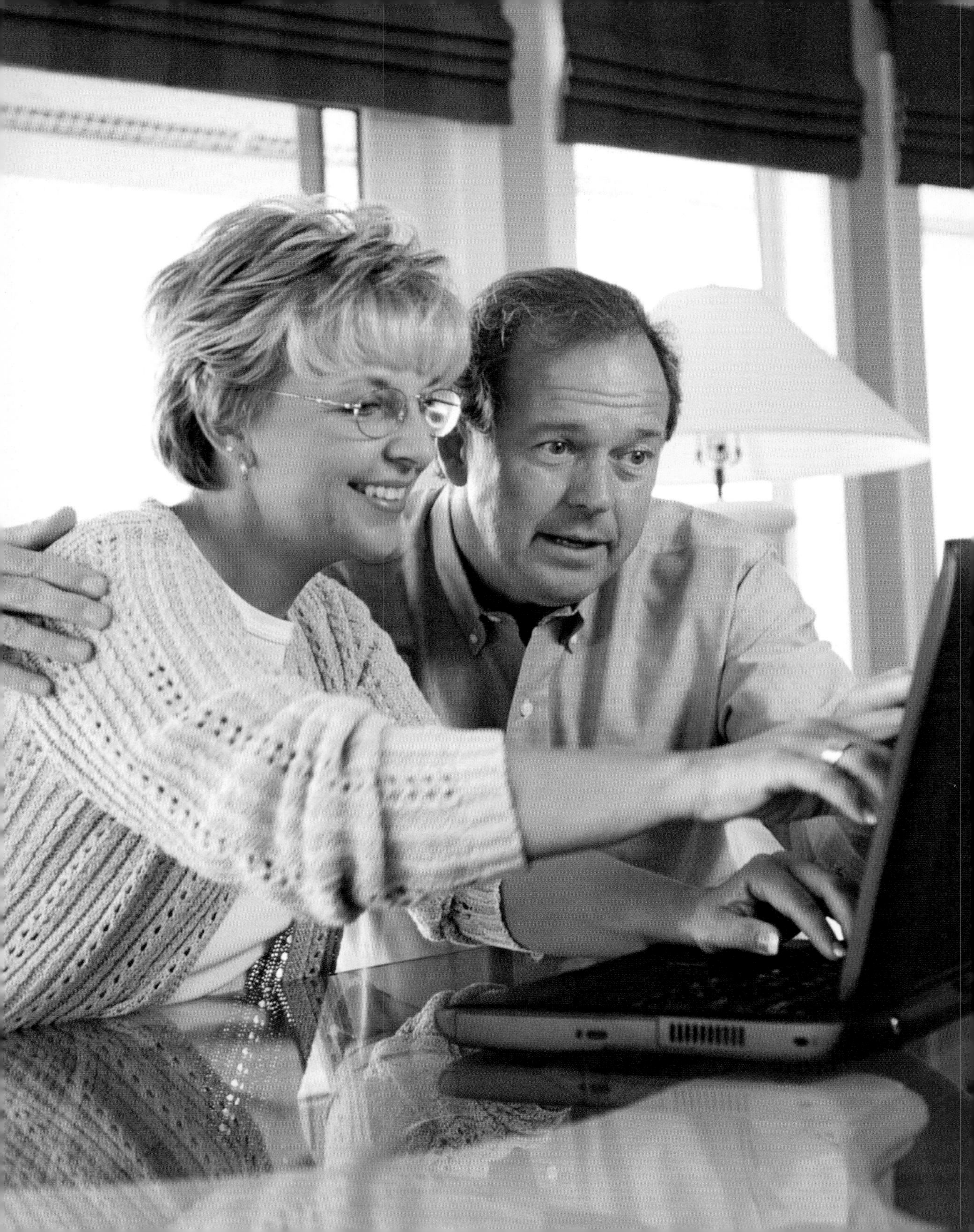

Work with Digital Music

You obviously take your music seriously. Just like you would organize and care for your albums, tapes, and CDs, you need to care for your digital music as well. When the files are stored on a huge hard drive, it's easy to lose track of your digital music. By using Windows XP folders, playlists, and utilities that accompany your digital music player, you can organize the music files on your computer, making each music file easy to locate.

But your computer is not the only place you can listen to your digital music. By burning your own CDs, you can make your music portable. Listen anywhere you have a CD or MP3 portable player. In this chapter, you'll learn how to organize and transport your favorite audio files.

Using Windows to Store Your Music

When you download a music file, most online music sites enable you to specify where on your hard drive the file should be saved. In most cases, the default location is the My Music folder. Likewise, if you use a digital music player to record files from a CD, the player probably copies them to the My Music folder by default. Some programs and sites, however, save files to their own special directories.

 When you copy an entire CD to the My Music folder, the CD cover art is also copied. As a result, when you open the My Music folder, you see the cover art for each CD in the folder.

The My Music folder is a good location to store your digital music files for a couple reasons. First, a lot of programs look in the My Music folder for music files by default. Second, Windows XP provides some useful digital music file-management tools in this folder in the Music Tasks pane. For example, you can play all the songs in a folder by clicking **Play All** in the Music Tasks pane, as shown in Figure 8-1. Alternatively, to launch your digital music player and play individual songs directly from the My Music folder, just double-click the file you want to hear.

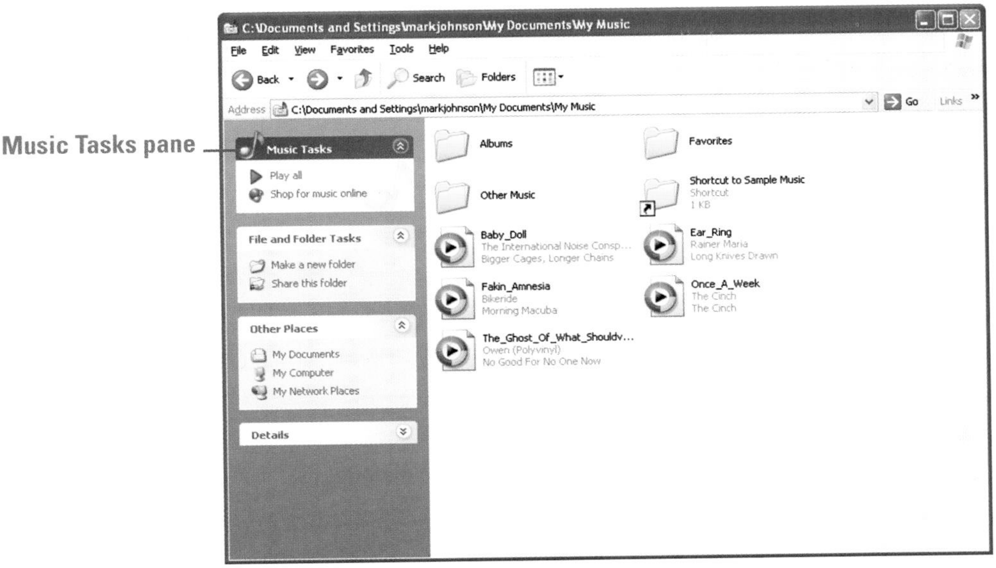
Music Tasks pane
C:\Documents and Settings\markjohnson\My Documents\My Music
File Edit View Favorites Tools Help
Back Search Folders
Address C:\Documents and Settings\markjohnson\My Documents\My Music
Go Links
Music Tasks
Play all
Shop for music online
File and Folder Tasks
Make a new folder
Share this folder
Other Places
My Documents
My Computer
My Network Places
Details
Albums
Favorites
Other Music
Shortcut to Sample Music
Shortcut
1 KB
Baby_Doll
The International Noise Consp...
Bigger Cages, Longer Chains
Ear_Ring
Rainer Maria
Long Knives Drawn
Fakin_Amnesia
Bikeride
Morning Macuba
Once_A_Week
The Cinch
The Cinch
The_Ghost_Of_What_Shouldv...
Owen (Polyvinyl)
No Good For No One Now

Figure 8-1 Click Play all in the Music Tasks pane of the My Music folder to play the music stored there.

Of course, you can create subfolders in the My Music folder to better organize the files you download. For example, some users create subfolders for specific artists, albums, genres, or compilations.

If you can't fit all your digital music files on your hard disk because it isn't large enough, you can store your files on removable Zip or Jaz drives, or on recordable CDs.

Creating and Working with Playlists

If you're like most people, you enjoy several different kinds of music. For example, you might listen to jazz when you're feeling mellow, blues when you're feeling down, or rock and roll when you're feeling energized. You'll probably have your music stored in your My Music organized by genre, artist, and/or album using folders. But what if you want to play one song from one album, two from another, and then three from another genre?

Well, that's where playlists come in. After your player has gathered the track information and indexed your music, you can use this index to add songs to a playlist. Playlists can be created from any song in your media library, and the same song can appear in multiple playlists. They can also be saved and played on demand at any point in the future.

A playlist is an ordered listing of songs that you want to play (see Figure 8-2). It's a bit like creating a custom tape or CD that only includes your favorite songs. For example, you might place all your music files that contain songs from your youth into a playlist called "songs from the past." That way, when you want to play all those songs, you need not load each one individually. Instead, you simply load the playlist.

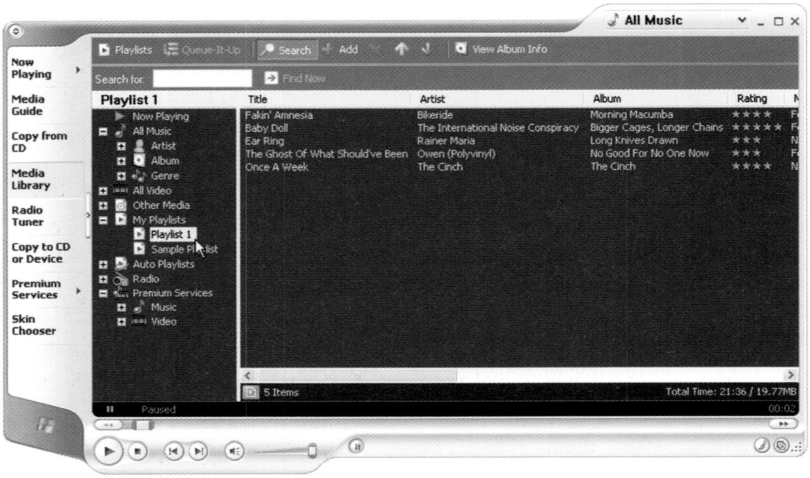
All Music
Playlists
Queue-It-Up
Search
Add
View Album Info
Search for:
Find Now
Now Playing
Media Guide
Copy from CD
Media Library
Radio Tuner
Copy to CD or Device
Premium Services
Skin Chooser
Playlist 1
Now Playing
All Music
Artist
Album
Genre
All Video
Other Media
My Playlists
Playlist 1
Sample Playlist
Auto Playlists
Radio
Premium Services
Music
Video
Title
Artist
Album
Rating
Fakin' Amnesia
Baby Doll
Ear Ring
The Ghost Of What Should've Been
Once A Week
Bikeride
The International Noise Conspiracy
Rainer Maria
Owen (Polyvinyl)
The Cinch
Morning Macumba
Bigger Cages, Longer Chains
Long Knives Drawn
No Good For No One Now
The Cinch
5 Items
Total Time: 21:36 / 19.77MB
Paused
00:02

Figure 8-2 Playlists can include any number of songs, in any order.

Creating a Playlist

Playlists enable you to organize your music files into customized groups, much the same way you would on a cassette tape or CD compilation. You can add as many tracks to a playlist as you like. Then, you can opt to play the files in the playlist either in the order in which they're listed or randomly.

Creating a new playlist couldn't be simpler. Just do the following:

1. Click the **Playlists** button in the upper-left corner of the Media Library window and select **New Playlist.**

2. The New Playlist dialog box opens, as shown in Figure 8-3. Type a name for the playlist.
3. Double-click tracks on the left side of this window to add them to the playlist. Use the drop-down menu under View Media Library by to sort tracks and find them more easily. After adding a track to the list, you can move it up or down by selecting it and using the up and down arrows at the bottom. Click **OK** to return to the Media Library.

New Playlist
Click an item from your Media Library to add it to the playlist. To change the way items are sorted in the Media Library list, click view Media Library by:
View Media Library by:
Playlist Name:
Artist \ Album
New Playlist
Bikeride
Bob Marley
Marc Seales, composer. New Stories. Ernie Watt
Owen (Polyvinyl)
Rainer Maria
The Cinch
The International Noise Conspiracy
0 Items
Total Time: 0:00
OK
Cancel

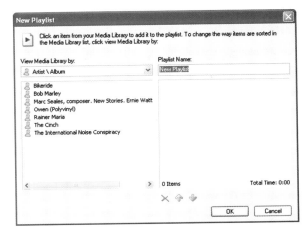

Figure 8-3 Name and create new playlists in the New Playlist dialog box.

After you create a playlist, click **My Playlists** on the left side of the Media Library to choose it. After you've created a playlist, you can easily add more files to it without leaving the Media Library. Here's how:

1. In the Media Library window, click a file you want to add to your playlist to select it.

   In Windows Media Player, as in most music players, to select non-adjacent files, hold down the **CTRL** key as you click. Hold down **SHIFT** and drag to select adjacent files.

2. Drag the file(s) to the desired playlist under My Playlists on the left side of your Media Library window, as shown in Figure 8-4.

All Music
Now Playing
Media Guide
Copy from CD
Media Library
Radio Tuner
Copy to CD or Device
Premium Services
Skin Chooser
Playlists
Queue-It-Up
Search
Add
View Album Info
Search for:
Find Now
All Music
Title
Artist
Album
Rating
Now Playing
All Music
Artist
Album
Genre
All Video
Other Media
My Playlists
New Playlist
Playlist 1
Sample Playlist
Auto Playlists
Radio
Premium Services
Music
Video
Baby Doll
Ear Ring
Fakin' Amnesia
The Ghost Of What Should've Been
Once A Week
The International Noise Conspiracy
Rainer Maria
Bikeride
Owen (Polyvinyl)
The Cinch
Bigger Cages, Longer Chains
Long Knives Drawn
Morning Macumba
No Good For No One Now
The Cinch
5 Items
Total Time: 21:36 / 19.77MB
Paused

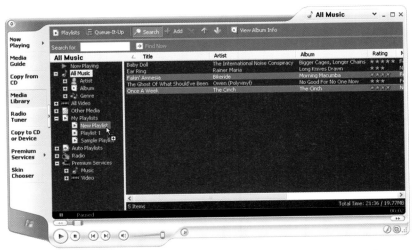

Figure 8-4 Easily add new tracks to a playlist by dragging them from the track list in the Media Library.

3. To change the order, click a track and drag up or down. When the gray line appears between the desired tracks, release the mouse button. You can also highlight a track, and use the blue arrows at the top-middle of the player window to move the track up or down in the list.

To listen to an entire playlist, simply double-click it under My Playlists on the left side of your Media Library window. The songs in the Playlist play in order by default. To shuffle them—that is, play them in a random order—click the **Turn Shuffle On** button.

Ready
Turn shuffle on or off button

Auto Playlists

Sometimes, you might not want to spend time creating a new playlist or can't decide between the ones you've already saved. If this is the case, you can have Windows Media Player create one for you automatically using specific criteria, such as fresh tracks recently added to the library, or tracks you have given a high rating. These are called Auto Playlists.

To use an Auto Playlist:

1. Click **Auto Playlists** on the left side of the Media Library window. A list of options appears on the right, as shown in Figure 8-5.

All Music
Now Playing
Media Guide
Copy from CD
Media Library
Radio Tuner
Copy to CD or Device
Premium Services
Skin Chooser
Playlists
Queue-It-Up
Search
Add
View Album Info
Search for:
Find Now
Auto Playlists
File Name
Favorites -- 4 and 5 star rated
Favorites -- Have not heard of recent
Favorites -- Have not heard recently
Favorites -- Listen to at night
Favorites -- Listen to on Weekdays
Favorites -- Listen to on Weekends
Favorites -- One Audio CD worth
Favorites -- One Data CD-R worth
Fresh tracks
Fresh tracks -- yet to be played
Fresh tracks -- yet to be rated
High bitrate media in my library
Low bitrate media in my library
Music tracks I dislike
Music tracks I have not rated
Music tracks with content protection
Paused
00:02

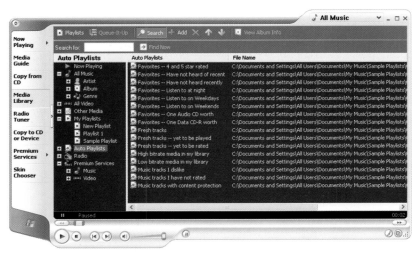

Figure 8-5 With Auto Playlists, compile a list of tracks to be played automatically.

2. Double-click one of the Auto Playlists. A list of tracks appears based on your selection and begins playing automatically.

If you like the compilation that was created, you can save it as a new playlist. To do this, right-click the Auto Playlist on the left and choose **Save as New Playlist**. The New dialog box appears, as shown in Figure 8-6. Name the playlist and click **OK**. Now, the new playlist appears under the My Playlists category on the left side of the Media Library.

New Playlist

Enter the new playlist name:

Songs rated 4 or 5 stars

OK   Cancel

Figure 8-6 While saving an Auto Playlist as a regular playlist, specify a new name in the New Playlist dialog box.

 Some Auto Playlists depend on a track rating. To give a track your own personal rating, move your mouse over the stars under the Rating column in the Media Library, and click to specify the number of stars. One star is the lowest rating; five stars is the highest. By default, all music is given a three-star rating.

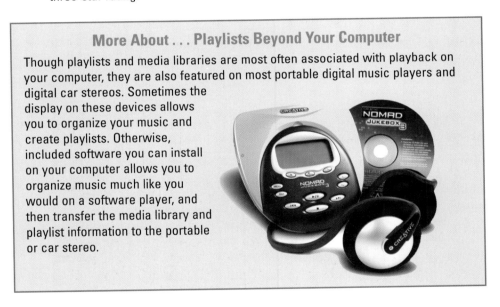

More About . . . Playlists Beyond Your Computer

Though playlists and media libraries are most often associated with playback on your computer, they are also featured on most portable digital music players and digital car stereos. Sometimes the display on these devices allows you to organize your music and create playlists. Otherwise, included software you can install on your computer allows you to organize music much like you would on a software player, and then transfer the media library and playlist information to the portable or car stereo.

8

Understanding CD Formats and Media

Everything you do to care for your normal audio CDs (and a little more) applies to CD-R and CD-RW. That's because recordable and rewritable CDs are more susceptible to sunlight, heat, and humidity than normal CDs. CD-Rs and CD-RWs are more vulnerable because the disc's recording layer has to be sensitive enough for a CD burner's low-powered laser to burn it. To ensure long disc life:

✦ Avoid scratching the disc surface or spilling liquids on the disc.

✦ Avoid leaving the CD in direct sunlight or hot cars.

✦ You can write on or label the top of the disc, but don't write or put labels on the bottom side, because that's the music side.

✦ When it's not being used, always put your CD in a sleeve or jewel case (a plastic case with a special tray for holding the CD).

When you buy an audio CD at the music store, it comes in a jewel case or other sturdy packaging, along with an insert displaying cover art and artist information, such as a song list and lyrics. To keep your personal audio CDs clean and scratch-free, it's a good idea to buy jewel cases for them—just like the pros. You can buy empty jewel cases separately, or purchase them as part of a bundle including both the recordable CDs and cases.

 CD-Rs and CD-RWs sold without jewel cases, usually packaged on a spindle, are significantly less expensive than those sold with jewel cases.

Burning Your Own CDs

Okay. You've organized your music files and built playlists that would make even the most seasoned DJ weep. There's just one problem. The only way you've managed to enjoy this dazzling array of music is by parking yourself in front of the computer.

Fortunately, you can easily transfer music files on your computer to a CD—a process called burning. If your system has a recordable CD drive and runs Windows XP, you already have the software you need to record your own CDs.

CD-burning technology on the average home computer is faster and more flexible than ever before, but you need to understand the different CD formats so you can select the one best for your needs.

Blank compact discs come in two different formats: CD-R (compact disc-recordable) and CD-RW (compact disc-rewritable). CD-R discs are "write once, read many," because you can record music or data on a disc only once, but you can play the disc as many times as you want. Once you've recorded music (or data) onto a CD-R, it's done; you can't go back and re-record over it.

CD-R

There are two different kinds of blank CD-R discs: one for audio recording and one for general data recording. Both types of CD-Rs can be used to record an audio CD, but the ones designated for audio recording provide a little higher quality.

Any time you create an audio CD, you should use CD-R format blank discs. That's because nearly all CD players and CD drives can read this format. CD-R is the most common type of blank compact disc. CD-R discs are "write once, read many," because you can record music on a single disc only once, but you can play the disc as many times as you want. Once a CD-R has been written to (that is, once you've recorded music or some other type of data on it), it becomes a CD-ROM. The ROM in CD-ROM stands for Read Only Memory, meaning that unlike a CD-R, which can be read and written to, you can only read from a CD-ROM.

Once you've recorded music (or data) onto a CD-R, it's done; you can't go back and re-record over it. If you don't like what you recorded or if an error occurred, simply throw the disc away and burn a new one.

If you plan to record a CD using a home CD recorder (that is, one connected to your home stereo rather than on your computer), you must use the special audio CD-Rs. General-purpose CD-Rs will not work.

CD-RW

If you want to add data to a CD over a period of days or even weeks, or if you want to record over previously recorded material, you want a rewriteable CD: CD-RW. Rewritable CDs—which cost more than CD-Rs—let you write over existing data over and over. In other words, it's a "write many, read many" format. CD-RW discs are most useful for recording text data as opposed to audio because many audio CD and players also can't read CD-RW discs. For these reasons (and the added expense of buying blank discs), you shouldn't use the CD-RW format for recording audio CDs. CD-RWs are also better for text data because they provide an easy way to frequently update data on the CD.

Choosing CD Burning Software

Before you fire up your computer recording studio, you should know that standard audio CD players and computers differ in how they store and play audio clips. Most audio CDs store clips in the Red Book format. Computers, on the other hand, store audio clips in various formats, including MP3 and WMA.

For this reason, to record CDs, your computer must have special CD-recording software that can convert the files stored on your computer into a format that standard CD players can read. In addition, this software organizes the songs you want to record and burns those songs onto a blank CD-R disc.

Many digital music players offer CD-burning features. Depending on what type of player is installed on your machine, it may do the trick. If not, or if you want to use a more full-featured program, there are several free-standing CD-recording programs on the market.

Since opinions vary on which CD-recording program is the best, try downloading a shareware version of a program and using it for a while before purchasing the full version. First, however, check your own computer to see if the manufacturer installed a CD-recording program.

Digital music players that you can use to burn your own CDs include:

- Windows Media Player
- MusicMatch Jukebox
- Liquid Player

Later in this chapter, you'll learn how to burn CDs using Windows Media Player. Since the Windows XP operating system includes Windows Media Player, it's a popular choice for burning audio CDs.

As mentioned, free-standing CD-recording programs may be more full-featured than the CD-recording software found with digital music players. For example, in addition to enabling users to burn CDs, many free-standing programs include the functionality to create CD labels and jewel case inserts.

Popular free-standing CD-recording programs include:

- **Easy CD & DVD Creator.** This program by Roxio is a popular choice, because it's often preinstalled on new computers. Easy CD & DVD Creator can do more than record CDs. It can also copy songs from other CDs directly to your new audio CD and combine digital audio files and tracks from CDs in the same new CD. This program also supports DVD burning.

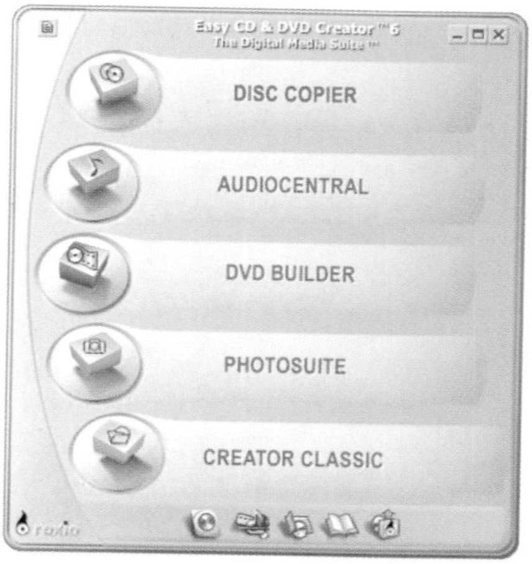
DISC COPIER
AUDIOCENTRAL
DVD BUILDER
PHOTOSUITE
CREATOR CLASSIC

- **Nero Burning ROM.** In addition to burning audio CDs, this program also supports DVD recording and both track-at-once and disc-at-once recording. It supports all major models of CD-R and CD-RW drives.

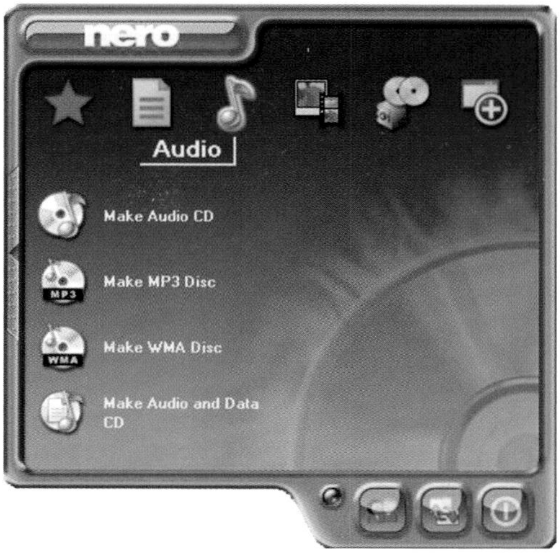

nero
Audio
Make Audio CD
Make MP3 Disc
Make WMA Disc
Make Audio and Data CD

- **Click 'N' Burn Pro.** This program offers the basic tools for duplicating CDs, backing up data, and creating custom audio CDs, as well as a full complement of features that appeal to high-end users. If you're a musician, for example, and need to make multiple copies of CDs for distribution, you'll appreciate Click 'N' Burn's ability to support as many as four CD burners. Click 'N' Burn also uses BurnProof technology, giving you more trouble-free recordings.
- **MP3 CD Maker.** This program enables direct MP3-to-CD burning, with no interim WAV files involved. It also includes the ability to print CD covers and automatic volume normalization (so that songs recorded at different volumes will play back at a similar volume).
- **RecordNow MAX.** This program also offers DVD recording, as well as a series of Burning Wizards that lead you through any type of recording with a series of simple questions and answers.

If you decide to purchase CD-recording software instead of using software that's already installed on your system, you'll need to install it yourself. (In some cases, you may need to download the software from the Internet first.)

Burning a CD

Once CD-recording software is installed on your computer, you're ready to begin burning your own CDs. Before you do, however, you'll need to decide what type of CD you want to burn:

✦ A CD that can be played in any audio CD player

✦ A CD that can be played by an MP3 CD player

This section has step-by-step instructions for recording both types of CDs, as well as information about recording an entire CD already in your collection. You'll even learn how to record music from albums and cassette tapes that you have in your "pre-digital" music library, including cleaning up the notorious pops and clicks on old vinyl records and the hiss from audio tapes. Before you begin recording, however, you should take a few steps to prepare your system and configure your recording options.

Preparing Your System for Burning

Copying large audio files from your hard drive to a blank CD-R requires tremendous processing power. For this reason, you should exit all other open programs, including your e-mail software, Web browser, even your system's screen saver and programs running in the background to ensure that they don't consume processing power better used by your recording program. Otherwise, the recording process may be interrupted by activity in one of these programs. If the recording process is interrupted in any way, the file you're recording might be damaged—or the recording process itself might be halted and an error message displayed. More importantly, you've wasted a CD-R, and possibly a CD-RW.

CD Burning Methods

Depending on what type of CD-burning software you use, you may be able to configure various recording methods to suit the type of recording you want to make. For example, you may be able to configure any of the following settings:

✦ **Multi-session CDs.** A multi-session CD includes both audio and computer data. If you select this option, you'll only be able to play the CD in a computer CD player.

✦ **Track-by-track recording.** When you record track-by-track, the CD burner turns off its laser between tracks and places a standard two-second blank space between each song on your CD. In most cases, you'll want to select this option for creating audio CDs that can be played on any CD player.

- **Entire-disc recording.** If you want to eliminate the two-second gap between songs, you can opt to record the entire disc at once. Not all CD players can play a CD burned using entire-disc recording.
- **Test recording.** Most CD-recorder programs give you the option to create a "test write" before the actual CD-recording process begins. This test steps you through the entire burning process, but with the recording laser turned off.

You should choose a test recording the first few times you make CDs to get the hang of it or if you think there might be some problems with the recording process. Otherwise, you can skip the test and go right to the burning.

Burning an Audio CD

As mentioned previously, you can use your computer to burn two types of CDs: those playable by any standard CD player and those playable by MP3 players. In this section, you'll learn how to create the former using Windows Media Player.

When you create a CD playable by any standard CD player, your CD-recording software converts the MP3, WMA, and other similar music files on your computer to adhere to the CDA format used by standard audio CDs. Although the specific instructions for recording a CD differ from program to program, the general process follows these steps (see Figure 8-7):

1. Using a playlist, you assemble and organize the digital music files you want to burn to a CD.
2. The software converts the files (typically in MP3 or WMA format) to WAV-format files.
3. The software copies the WAV-format files to CDA-format files on the CD-R disc.
4. The software "closes" the CD so no other files can be recorded on it.

8

MP3
DECODER SOFTWARE
WAV

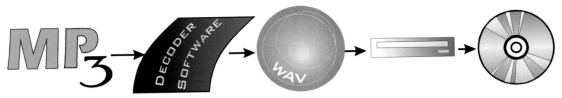

Figure 8-7 Several steps are required to copy digital music from your computer to an audio CD.

Windows Media Player is a popular choice for burning audio CDs because this capability is included with the Windows XP operating system. If you use Windows Media Player for organizing your music and creating playlists, burning CDs is a snap. You won't need to launch a separate CD burning application or move your files around to different folders.

Whatever program you use to organize your music is probably the best for burning CDs (if the player supports burning), since your music is already consolidated and available from the player interface.

To burn an audio CD using Windows Media Player, do the following:

1. Click **start**, point to **All Programs**, and select **Windows Media Player**.
2. In the Windows Media Player window, click the **Media Library** button in the taskbar on the left side of the program window.
3. Click the **Playlists** button located near the top and choose **New Playlist**.
4. Type a name for this playlist, like "Copying Music," and click **OK**.
5. Highlight the tracks you want to record, and drag them to the new playlist.
6. Select the playlist, and then organize the tracks in the playlist so they appear in the order you want them recorded on the CD. To do so, drag tracks up or down the list and drop them where you want them. See Figure 8-8.

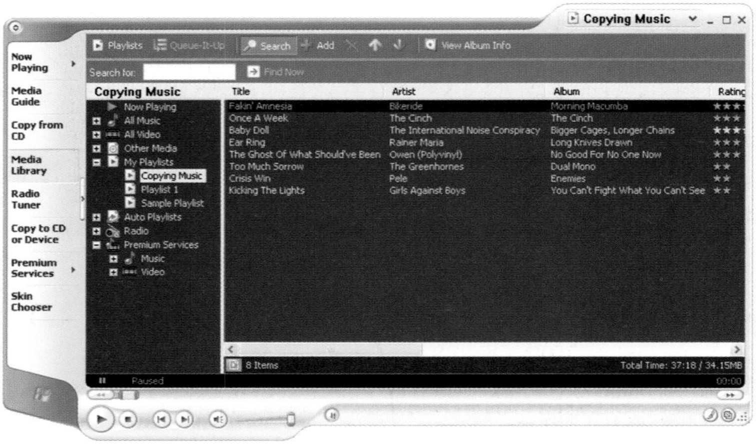
Copying Music
Now Playing
Media Guide
Copy from CD
Media Library
Radio Tuner
Copy to CD or Device
Premium Services
Skin Chooser
Playlists
Search
Add
View Album Info
Search for:
Find Now
Copying Music
Title
Artist
Album
Now Playing
All Music
All Video
Other Media
My Playlists
Copying Music
Playlist 1
Sample Playlist
Auto Playlists
Radio
Premium Services
Music
Video
Fakin' Amnesia
Bikeride
Morning Macumba
Once A Week
The Cinch
The Cinch
Baby Doll
The International Noise Conspiracy
Bigger Cages, Longer Chains
Ear Ring
Rainer Maria
Long Knives Drawn
The Ghost Of What Should've Been
Owen (Polyvinyl)
No Good For No One Now
Too Much Sorrow
The Greenhornes
Dual Mono
Crisis Win
Pele
Enemies
Kicking The Lights
Girls Against Boys
You Can't Fight What You Can't See
8 Items
Total Time: 37:18 / 34.15MB
Paused
00:00

Figure 8-8 Organize music in a playlist in preparation for burning to an audio CD.

As you add songs to the playlist for your CD, note the total time for the playlist in the lower-right corner, below the song list. This time must not exceed 74 minutes; otherwise, the playlist won't fit on a standard CD-R disc. In fact, it's a good idea to keep the total time a minute or two shorter than that to leave time for spaces between songs.

7. In the Windows Media Player window, click the **Copy to CD or Device** button in the taskbar.

8. In the **Items to Copy** list, select the tracks from the playlist that you want to copy. Windows Media Player assumes you want to record all the tracks in the list to a blank CD. To prevent Windows Media Player from copying a particular track in the list, clear the check box next to the track to deselect it.

Status
Minutes free
Copying Music
Copy "All Music" to "CD Drive (E:) - Audio CD"
Copy
Now Playing
Media Guide
Copy from CD
Media Library
Radio Tuner
Copy to CD or Device
Premium Services
Skin Chooser
Items to Copy
Edit Playlist
Items on Device
All Music
CD Drive (E:) - Audio CD
Title
Status
Length
Size
There are no items on the CD or device.
Fakin' Amnesia Ready to copy 3:15 2.98MB
Once A Week Ready to copy 4:11 3.83MB
Kicking The Lights Ready to copy 3:39 3.34MB
Too Much Sorrow Ready to copy 4:07 3.77MB
Baby Doll Ready to copy 5:17 4.83MB
Ear Ring Ready to copy 3:43 3.41MB
The Ghost Of What Should've Been Ready to copy 5:08 4.70MB
Crisis Win Ready to copy 7:55 7.25MB
8 Item(s), Total Time: 38 Minutes
75 Minutes Free
Ready

9. Insert a blank CD-R disc in your computer's CD-recorder drive. If a dialog box appears asking what you want to do with the disc, click **Cancel**.
10. If your recordable CD drive is not already selected in the **Items On Device** list (in the right-hand pane), click it to select it.
11. Click the **Copy** button in the upper-right corner of the window. Windows Media Player converts each track to WAV format, then to CDA format, and then copies them to your blank CD-R disc.

Progress bar
Copying Music
Copy "All Music" to "CD Drive (E:) - Audio CD"
Stop Copy
Items to Copy
Edit Playlist
Items on Device
Copy in progress
Overall 7% complete, estimated time remaining: 14 minute(s)
Title
Status
Length
Size
Fakin' Amnesia Complete 3:15 2.98MB
Once A Week Complete 4:11 3.83MB
Kicking The Lights Copying to CD (64%) 3:39 3.34MB
Too Much Sorrow Converted 4:07 3.77MB
Baby Doll Converted 5:17 4.83MB
Ear Ring Converted 3:43 3.41MB
The Ghost Of What Should've Been Converted 5:08 4.70MB
Crisis Win Converted 7:55 7.25MB
Overall 46% complete, estimated time remaining: 8 minute(s)
75 Minutes Free
Ready

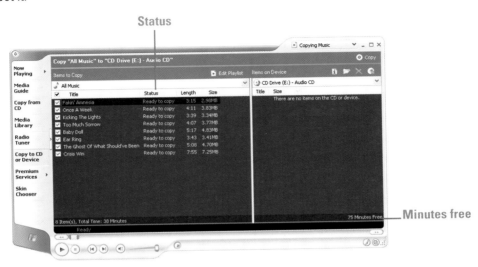

8

This operation can take several minutes, depending on the length of the selected tracks, the speed of your computer, and the transfer rate of your CD burner.

If you try to copy too much music to the CD-R disc, Windows Media Player displays a "May Not Fit" message. If you see this message, you'll need to rethink your playlist and burn another disc.

12 When Windows Media Player finishes the burning process, it displays a Closing Disc message, a Complete message, and then displays the contents of the CD in the Items on Device pane.

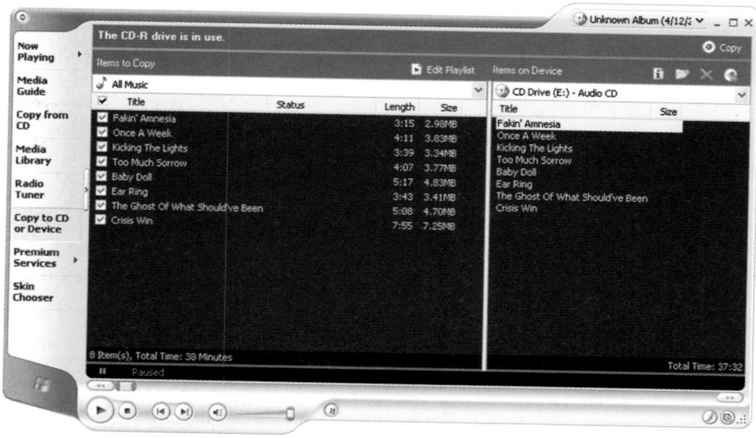

Unknown Album (4/12/2
The CD-R drive is in use.
Copy
Now Playing
Media Guide
Copy from CD
Media Library
Radio Tuner
Copy to CD or Device
Premium Services
Skin Chooser
Items to Copy
Edit Playlist
Items on Device
All Music
CD Drive (E:) - Audio CD
Title
Status
Length
Size
Fakin' Amnesia 3:15 2.98MB
Once A Week 4:11 3.83MB
Kicking The Lights 3:39 3.34MB
Too Much Sorrow 4:07 3.77MB
Baby Doll 5:17 4.83MB
Ear Ring 3:43 3.41MB
The Ghost Of What Should've Been 5:08 4.70MB
Crisis Win 7:55 7.25MB
8 Item(s), Total Time: 38 Minutes
Paused
Total Time: 37:32

> **More About . . . Burning Audio CDs**
>
> You can also use a number of other programs to burn music from your computer to audio CDs. For example, MusicMatch Jukebox includes a utility called Burner Plus, which you can use to burn a CD from your favorite MP3, WMA, or WAV files. Nero Burning ROM and Roxio Easy CD and DVD Creator are both free-standing CD burning programs and are both designed to offer easy and intuitive creation of CDs. Simply insert a recordable CD into your CD recorder drive, add tracks to the burner program project window, and start burning. You'll find detailed instructions in each program's help documentation.
>
> You can also use Nero and Roxio to copy songs from other CDs directly to your new audio CD. Just insert the CD with the songs to copy into your CD-ROM drive, and then, while adding files, navigate to the CD-ROM drive where you can select the track(s) you want to copy. This adds the selected song(s) to your new music project. You can also combine digital audio files and tracks from CDs on the same CD; Nero will prompt you when to insert and remove the audio CD and the blank CD.

Copying LPs and Cassettes to CD

If you're a true audiophile, there's a good chance you have an extensive collection of pre-digital music—that is, vinyl records and audio cassettes. You can even convert 8-tracks if you want. If so, you can transfer the albums in your aging collection to digital format and burn them onto CDs. You'll get the portability, easy access, and flexibility benefits from the digital audio format—after all, it's a lot easier to listen to an audio or MP3 CD on the go than it is to lug around boxes of albums and a turntable. As an added bonus, your new digital files should last many times longer than aging albums and tapes.

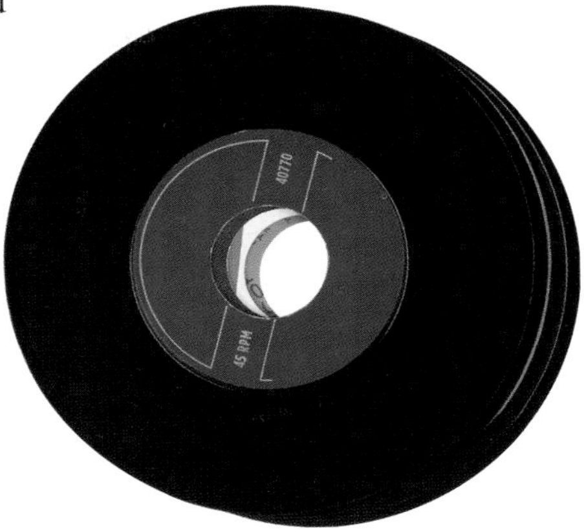
40770
45 RPM

Because albums and cassettes are analog media, converting them to CD is a much slower process than ripping tracks from a CD. That's because you record these analog media at the same speed they play.

To make a CD copy of a vinyl record or cassette tape, you need the same equipment you use to burn a CD from any other source—namely, a computer with a sound card installed, a recordable CD drive, and CD-burner software. In addition, you'll need a few extra components connected to your computer:

- A turntable or cassette tape deck
- Audio amplifier or receiver
- Stereo cable

8

To connect these components to your computer, do the following:

1. Connect your turntable or cassette deck to the receiver/amplifier in your home audio system.

   Although it's not recommended, you can connect a cassette deck directly to your computer. You cannot, however, connect a turntable in this fashion. Your turntable must be connected through a receiver to achieve the correct sound levels for recording.

2. Run a stereo cable from the line out jacks on the receiver/amplifier's back to the line in jacks on the back of your computer.

   If you only have a single line in jack on your computer, you'll need an adapter cable that goes from separate right and left jacks to a single stereo plug.

After you've connected these components to your computer, you're almost ready to go. First, however, you need to install some special software on your computer to handle the recording process. This software converts the audio signal sent from your turntable or cassette deck to a WAV-format digital audio format. This WAV file can then be burned to a blank CD-R disc.

You can also convert the WAV file to an MP3 or WMA file using your digital music player. These files consume less hard disk space and can be used with portable MP3 players.

When it comes to software for converting vinyl records or cassettes to digital music files, you have several choices, including Windows Sound Recorder, already available on all Windows computers.

You can record all the songs on a vinyl record or cassette tape as separate files, or you can record the entire side of an LP or tape as one large file. Although you might like the convenience of recording one large file, recording separate files provides more flexibility when you burn the songs to CD or play individual songs from your music library with your digital music player.

Recording Analog Sounds

The sounds on vinyl records and cassettes aren't the only analog sounds you can record to your computer. In fact, if you have a microphone and your sound card has a microphone in port, you can record just about any sound you like! You can then convert this sound to digital format using Windows Sound Recorder. To do so, follow these steps:

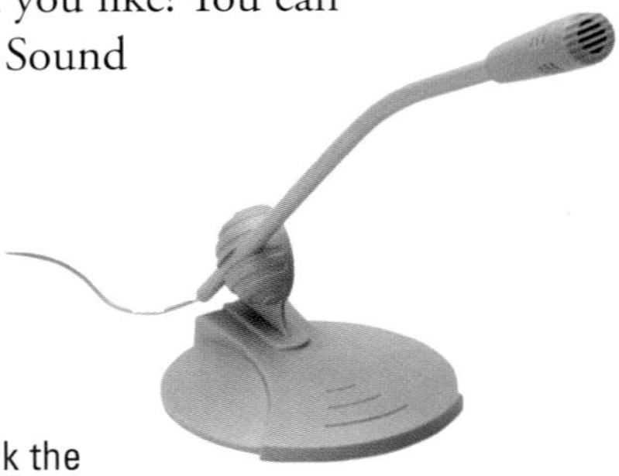

1. Click **start**, point to **All Programs**, **Accessories**, **Entertainment**, and select **Sound Recorder**.
2. Plug an input device, such as a microphone, into the input port on your sound card.
3. The buttons you use to control Sound Recorder are similar to those on VCRs or cassette recorders. To begin recording, click the **Record** button.

Sound - Sound Recorder
File Edit Effects Help
Position:
57.00 sec.
Length:
77.50 sec.
Recorded Sound Wave
Rewind
Record
Fast Forward
Play
Stop

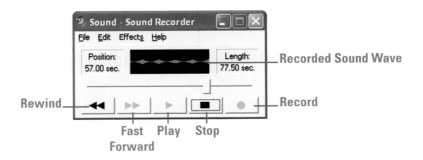

④ Speak or sing into the microphone. As you record, the sound recorder window displays a graph of the incoming sound wave.

⑤ When you've captured the sound you want to save, click **Stop**.

⑥ To save the file, click **File**, and then choose **Save**.

⑦ Specify the folder in which you want to save the file, and type a descriptive name for the file.

⑧ Click **Save**.

 One of Sound Recorder's limitations is that it only reads and writes WAV files. If you want to save your file in a different format, you must use another software program to record it. Alternatively, you can use another program like MusicMatch Jukebox to convert the sound to another format after recording it with Sound Recorder.

Syncing Your Portable Player with Your Computer

Moving music from your computer to your portable player is generally easy. You typically connect the two machines using USB or FireWire (IEEE 1394) ports. Sometimes a cradle is included, which acts as both a battery charger and USB adapter. In any case, once a portable digital music player is connected to your computer, it usually appears as a removable storage device similar to a floppy or a CD-RW.

8

 The following instructions apply to media card players and hard drive players. To play digital music from your computer on a dual-mode MP3/CD player, you need to first burn an MP3 CD.

Copying Music to Your Portable Player with Windows XP

Copying music to your portable player is as simple as moving files to the drive representing the player. To load music into a portable digital music player using Windows XP, follow these steps:

1. Using the included cable, plug the player into the computer's USB or FireWire port. With some smaller players, the player itself can be plugged into the slot without needing a cable. Windows XP recognizes the player as a removable storage device automatically. To confirm Windows "sees" the player, simply open **My Computer**.

My Computer
File Edit View Favorites Tools Help
Back Search Folders
Address My Computer
Go Links
System Tasks
View system information
Add or remove programs
Change a setting
Other Places
My Network Places
My Documents
Control Panel
Details
My Computer
System Folder
Name Type Total Size Free Space Comments
Hard Disk Drives
Local Disk (C:) Local Disk 9.30 GB 353 MB
Devices with Removable Storage
3½ Floppy (A:) 3½-Inch Floppy Disk
CD Drive (D:) CD Drive
MP3 PLAYER (E:) Removable Disk
Portable Digital Music Player

If you are using a version of Windows prior to XP, you may need to install drivers before your computer recognizes the player as a storage device. If this is the case, follow instructions included with the player to install the appropriate drivers. A CD containing the necessary drivers is included in the portable player package. Usually drivers can also be downloaded from the manufacturer's Web site.

2. Navigate to the folder containing the music you want to copy to the portable player, and highlight the files you want to copy (CTRL-click to select non-adjacent files).

C:\Documents and Settings\Tom\My Documents\My Music
File Edit View Favorites Tools Help
Back Search Folders
Address C:\Documents and Settings\Tom\My Documents\My Music
Go Links
Music Tasks
File and Folder Tasks
Move the selected items
Copy the selected items
E-mail the selected items
Delete the selected items
Other Places
My Music
My Computer
My Network Places
Details
8 items selected.
Total File Size: 34.1 MB
Name Size
Baby_Doll 4,957 KB
Crisis_Win 7,426 KB
Ear_Ring 3,497 KB
Fakin_Amnesia 3,056 KB
Kicking_The_Lights 3,432 KB
Once_A_Week 3,930 KB
The_Ghost_Of_What_Should... 4,818 KB
Too_Much_Sorrow 3,867 KB

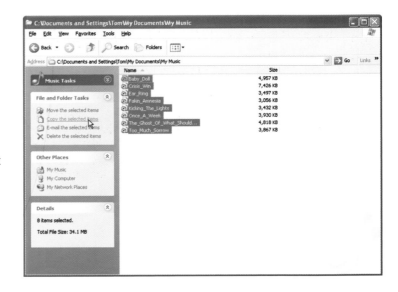

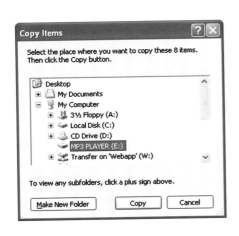

Copy Items
Select the place where you want to copy these 8 items.
Then click the Copy button.
Desktop
My Documents
My Computer
3½ Floppy (A:)
Local Disk (C:)
CD Drive (D:)
MP3 PLAYER (E:)
Transfer on 'Webapp' (W:)
To view any subfolders, click a plus sign above.
Make New Folder
Copy
Cancel

3. On the left, under File and Folder Tasks, select **Copy the selected items**. The Copy Items dialog box appears.

4. Select the portable player drive, often labeled "MP3 Player." Click **Copy** and you're done. The music copies to your portable player. This process may take several minutes, depending on the player, the number of songs copied, and the type of connection.

Copying...
Baby_Doll.mp3
From 'Favorites' to 'E:\'
Cancel
20 Seconds Remaining

Some portable players connect to a computer using a FireWire connection, which is capable of transferring files to and from your computer faster than a USB connection. To connect a player to your computer via FireWire requires a computer with a FireWire port and compatible player.

Some players even have a transfer button you can use to control the copying from the player instead of the computer. When you're ready to listen to your music through the player, simply disconnect it, attach the headphones, and use the player's playback controls to play your music.

In addition to music, you can use portable players to listen to other types of digital audio media. For example, Audible's Otis digital player is specifically designed to play back audio books and other spoken-word media. With a subscription to the Audible Web site's library you can browse through thousands of spoken audio files including books, magazines, and newspapers. Then download the files you want to hear, load them to the player, and start listening. Controls on the Otis player provide easy access to the portions you want to hear.

Copying Music to a Portable Device with Your Digital Music Player

Most digital music player programs on your computer are also capable of transferring music directly to a portable digital audio player. If all of your music is neatly organized in Windows Media Player, or MusicMatch Jukebox for example, this option is the most convenient way to transfer your files because you won't have to rummage through your computer to find the tracks you want to move.

To copy music from Windows Media Player to a portable device, do the following:

1. Click the **Copy to CD or Device** button in the taskbar on the left side of the player.

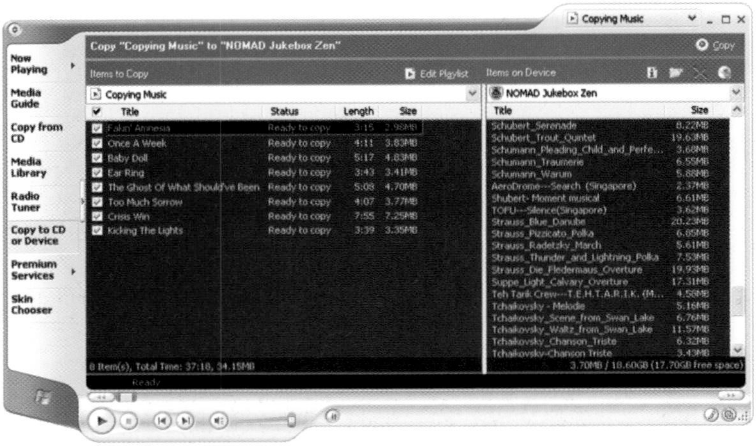

Copying Music
Copy "Copying Music" to "NOMAD Jukebox Zen"
Copy
Now Playing
Media Guide
Copy from CD
Media Library
Radio Tuner
Copy to CD or Device
Premium Services
Skin Chooser
Items to Copy
Edit Playlist
Items on Device
Copying Music
NOMAD Jukebox Zen
Title Status Length Size
Once A Week Ready to copy 4:11 3.83MB
Baby Doll Ready to copy 5:17 4.83MB
Ear Ring Ready to copy 3:43 3.41MB
The Ghost Of What Should've Been Ready to copy 5:08 4.70MB
Too Much Sorrow Ready to copy 4:07 3.77MB
Crisis Win Ready to copy 7:55 7.25MB
Kicking The Lights Ready to copy 3:39 3.35MB
Title Size
Schubert_Serenade 8.22MB
Schubert_Trout_Quintet 19.63MB
Schumann_Pleading_Child_and_Perfe... 3.68MB
Schumann_Traumerie 6.55MB
Schumann_Warum 5.88MB
AeroDrome---Search (Singapore) 2.37MB
Shubert- Moment musical 6.61MB
TOFU---Silence(Singapore) 3.62MB
Strauss_Blue_Danube 20.23MB
Strauss_Pizzicato_Polka 6.85MB
Strauss_Radetzky_March 5.61MB
Strauss_Thunder_and_Lightning_Polka 7.53MB
Strauss_Die_Fledermaus_Overture 19.93MB
Suppe_Light_Calvary_Overture 17.31MB
Teh Tarik Crew---T.E.H.T.A.R.I.K. (M... 4.58MB
Tchaikovsky - Melodie 5.16MB
Tchaikovsky_Scene_from_Swan_Lake 6.76MB
Tchaikovsky_Waltz_from_Swan_Lake 11.57MB
Tchaikovsky_Chanson_Triste 6.32MB
Tchaikovsky-Chanson Triste 3.43MB
3.70MB / 18.60GB (17.70GB free space)

2. Under Items to Copy, click the drop-down menu and choose **All Music**, or a playlist containing the tracks you want to move. Any playlist compilation you have already created in Windows Media Player can be copied easily to a portable device by choosing it here.

> In addition to Windows Media Player, other software players such as MusicMatch Jukebox and RealOne offer the ability to copy entire playlists you have already created directly to a portable device.

3. Under Items on Device, click the drop-down menu and choose the portable player.
4. Highlight the desired tracks from the list on the left.
5. Click the **Copy** button in the upper right. The music transfers to the portable device.

Sending a Playlist to a Portable Device

Given their small size, the LCD display and controls featured on many portable players isn't the most convenient way to manage large numbers of tracks and create playlists. Some player packages include software you can install on your computer to browse your hard drive for music, organize playlists, edit track data, and transfer the information and music to the portable device. Usually players with hard drives that store large amounts of music come with accompanying software of this kind. For example, Creative PlayCenter, shown in Figure 8-9, comes with the Nomad Jukebox player, and can, among other things, be used to organize music into playlists. These playlists can be transferred to the player, where they can be browsed through and played.

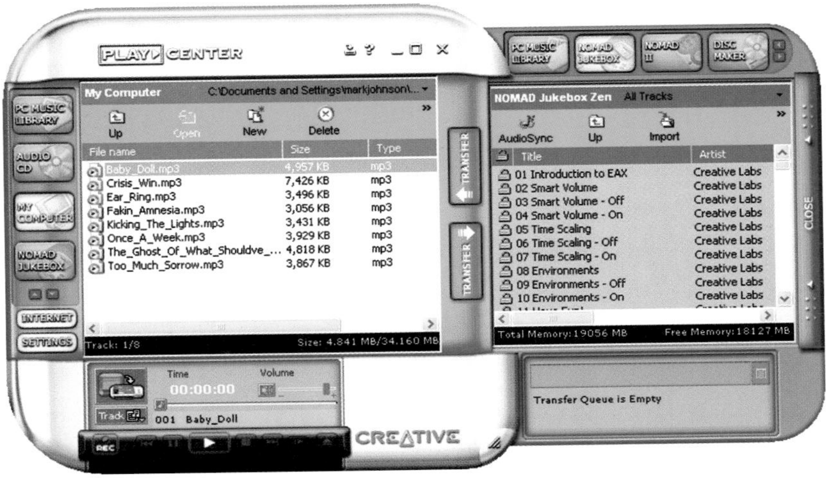
PLAY CENTER
PC MUSIC LIBRARY
NOMAD JUKEBOX
NOMAD III
DISC MAKER
My Computer
C:\Documents and Settings\markjohnson\...
Up
Open
New
Delete
File name
Size
Type
Baby_Doll.mp3 4,957 KB mp3
Crisis_Win.mp3 7,426 KB mp3
Ear_Ring.mp3 3,496 KB mp3
Fakin_Amnesia.mp3 3,056 KB mp3
Kicking_The_Lights.mp3 3,431 KB mp3
Once_A_Week.mp3 3,929 KB mp3
The_Ghost_Of_What_Shouldve_... 4,818 KB mp3
Too_Much_Sorrow.mp3 3,867 KB mp3
PC MUSIC LIBRARY
AUDIO CD
MY COMPUTER
NOMAD JUKEBOX
INTERNET
SETTINGS
Track: 1/8
Size: 4.841 MB/34.160 MB
TRANSFER
TRANSFER
NOMAD Jukebox Zen
All Tracks
AudioSync
Up
Import
Title
Artist
01 Introduction to EAX Creative Labs
02 Smart Volume Creative Labs
03 Smart Volume - Off Creative Labs
04 Smart Volume - On Creative Labs
05 Time Scaling Creative Labs
06 Time Scaling - Off Creative Labs
07 Time Scaling - On Creative Labs
08 Environments Creative Labs
09 Environments - Off Creative Labs
10 Environments - On Creative Labs
Total Memory: 19056 MB
Free Memory: 18127 MB
CLOSE
Time
Volume
00:00:00
Track
001 Baby_Doll
REC
Transfer Queue is Empty
CREATIVE

Figure 8-9 Creative PlayCenter, which accompanies the Nomad Jukebox, can be used to organize files and create playlists to be sent to the player.

Programs like Creative PlayCenter can also be used for general organization and playback on your computer as well. If you plan to use your portable player as your primary playback device, you might consider using the software that came with your portable player to manage your computer's digital music library.

More About . . . Portable Players and Digital Media

Though portable digital music players are designed and marketed to store and play back audio files, many are also capable of storing digital media in other formats as well. Hard drive and media card players use the same type of hardware for file storage you'll find in your computer; Windows XP even recognizes these players as general mass storage devices automatically when you connect them to your computer. Therefore, copying a doctoral thesis or photo gallery to a portable device is as easy as dragging these files to the portable player drive listed in My Computer. Then, you can connect the device to another computer and navigate to the drive to retrieve your files. In this way, your portable digital player can double as a regular portable storage device and be used much like a floppy or Zip disk. Note that you won't be able to view documents, pictures, or other media with a portable digital music player because they are only designed to recognize digital audio files.

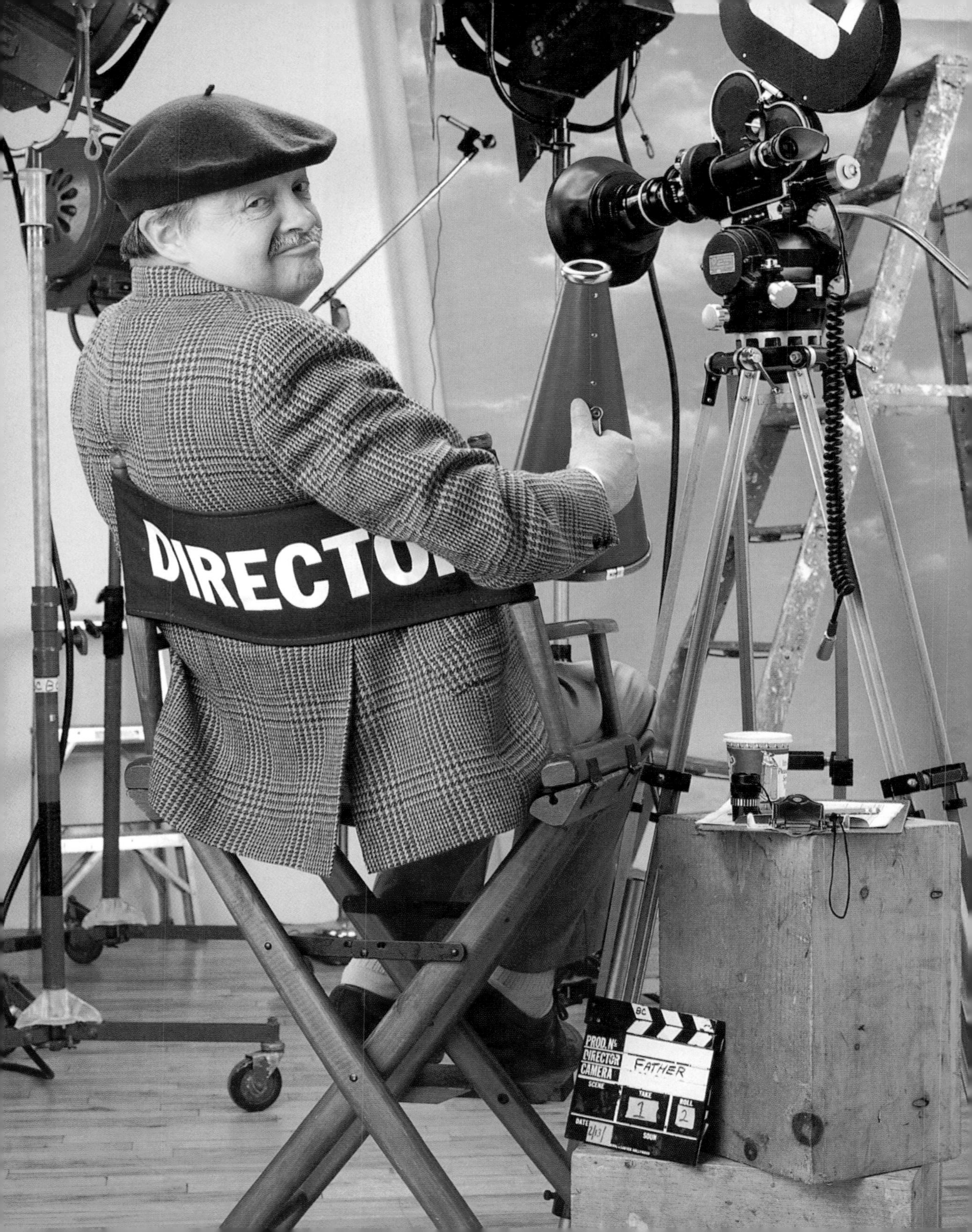
DIRECTO
BC
PROD. No
DIRECTOR
CAMERA
FATHER
SCENE
TAKE
1
ROLL
2
DATE
2/13/

Work with Digital Video

You just took some wonderful video of your granddaughter playing with her new puppy, and you'd like to transfer it from your camcorder to your computer so you can watch it whenever you want; maybe even share it with your sister who lives in another state. The ability to get your video from the camcorder to the computer is a critical step toward creating a video project. This process is called "capturing," and in concept, is almost as easy as it sounds. Almost. You will need to make sure the video feed is making its way to your capturing program and know how best to capture your raw video footage, including which formats and compression to use.

In this chapter, you will discover the video transfer process. By walking through the process step-by-step, you will learn about uptake speed, dropped frames, and other factors that indicate video transfer quality. Your transfer settings will be determined by your creative goals. Do you want to make a video CD, DVD, or video for the Web? Or do you want to just edit, and then transfer the video back to your camcorder? You will know how to choose transfer options with those choices in mind.

Video compression options are also discussed. It's because of video compression that we have the ability to transfer and export video, and you will learn the type and degree of compression suitable for your project. You will also discover how to transfer video to your computer from an analog source, such as VHS tape or analog video camcorder. When you've applied the skills discussed in this chapter, you will be ready for computer video editing.

Transferring Video to Your Computer

To transfer digital video, you will need a digital video camcorder with a FireWire port, (all DV camcorders have them), a FireWire card in your computer, and a cable. With a FireWire card installed on your computer and video footage on a MiniDV tape in your camcorder, you are ready to move your video from camcorder to computer. You will use the video capture capabilities of your video editing software package.

 We'll use Pinnacle Studio 8 in this chapter, but you could also work with Windows Movie Maker (included with Windows XP), Ulead VideoStudio, or other video software.

Video Capture Overview

To move digital video from your camcorder to computer requires video capture software installed on your computer. However, note that video capture is one component in a video editing program. You will not have to purchase separate capture software. Capturing is usually presented as "Step 1" in a menu of editing tasks. Every video capture program has common methods and goals. They are the following:

- Transfers video from your MiniDV tape (or MiniDisc) and saves it on your computer's hard drive. A workspace with VCR-like controls so you can play, rewind, and fast-forward through your footage without having to physically touch your camcorder.

- Divides your movie into scenes, or segments. Once your video is captured, these scenes automatically appear in the program's video editing workspace, where they can be moved around, deleted, or otherwise edited.

- Allows you to determine the video's format, frame size, and compression amount. This is important because you don't want "too much" video to work with. Too large a file will slow down your computer and makes each editing step into a major chore. On the other hand, if you choose a small frame size and high compression, you will have "too little" video to work with. The resulting movie will have a low-quality picture and be too small on the screen.

- Monitors the recording process. As you transfer video, you will want to keep track of elapsed time, hard drive usage, and number of dropped frames. That way, if any of these factors go awry, you can stop the process, tend to the error, and again begin to transfer.

 Previewing your video before transferring is important because since movies take up so much hard drive space, you will want to avoid transferring segments that will be of no use to you.

Before moving through the steps to capturing your video, here are important settings you want to note or modify before you begin:

- **Dropped Frames.** Most capture programs let you specify that recording should automatically stop if too many frames have been dropped. That's because dropped frames indicate that your computer cannot keep up with the recording. You can specify that if a certain percentage of frames have been dropped, recording should cease.

- **Time.** Some capture programs let you limit how many seconds of video are filmed at once. This is a great safeguard. For example, if the phone rings while

9

you are recording and you get sidetracked, having this feature engaged could avoid inadvertently filling your entire hard drive with a single video.

- **Disk Space.** A safety feature similar to the above, filming stops after the movie has reached a specified file size. Use this setting to keep your movie segments manageable and easy to edit.
- **Automatic Scene Detection.** Some programs automatically divide your movie into scenes as soon as capture is completed. You will know this is happening when you notice the video program's workspace gradually filling up with thumbnail views of your movie, broken into segments.
- **Compression.** All video capture programs present you with several compression choices before recording.

Video Capture: Basic Steps

Below is an overview of the steps involved in capturing video to your computer. Although the feature names and exact process will vary from program to program, the following steps will provide a guide to let you know what's involved.

1. Turn on your camcorder. Choose Play/VCR, rather than Record (Figure 9-1). This is the setting for playing back previously recorded footage.

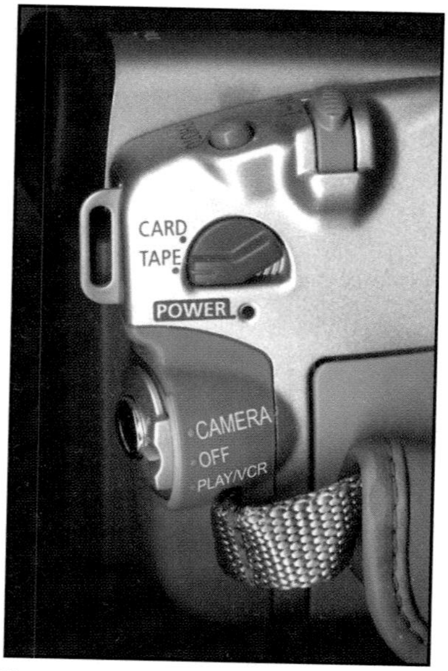
CARD
TAPE
POWER
CAMERA
OFF
PLAY/VCR

Figure 9-1 The camcorder button for switching between Record and Play (VCR) mode.

Since video transfer can involve a few false starts and take a little more time than intended, make sure your camcorder has lots of battery life left, or that your camcorder is plugged into a power source.

2. Position computer and camcorder near each other, and plug the FireWire cable into computer and camcorder.
3. At this point, the video editing program installed on your computer may open immediately and display the Capture screen. If not, open the program and display video capture options.
4. When the program first starts, note that it recognizes your digital camcorder model and displays information about your computer. You will be informed how much video footage your hard drive is able to save.
5. Using the VCR-like controls on the Capture screen (Figure 9-2), locate the first few frames of the video you want to upload. The computer can control camcorder playback options without you having to touch the camcorder.

Pinnacle Studio - Untitled.stu *
File Edit View Album Toolbox Setup Help
1 Capture
2 Edit
3 Make Movie
PINNACLE STUDIO 8
(Ready to capture)
Captured:
0:00:00.00
Frames dropped:
0
Drive (Z:)
Free 48322.1 MB
Used 29826.0 MB
Full-quality capture
Preview-quality capture
Start Capture
Settings...

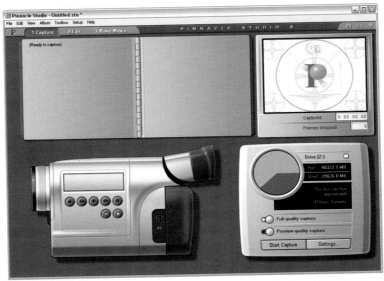

Figure 9-2 The Pinnacle 8 Video Capture screen displays VCR-like buttons for remotely controlling your camcorder.

6. Review the segment you want to transfer to your computer. Make a mental note of "In" and "Out" points so that you don't inadvertently record much more than intended. Some programs let you set "In" and "Out" points, and will begin and end transfer according to your selections.

There may be Dropped Frame and Timer options to choose, and these options vary somewhat from program to program (Figure 9-3). Settings for these options let you control the amount of footage saved onto your computer during transfer and the number of dropped frames you will tolerate. Settings for controlling the amount of footage will typically be called File Size, Time Limit, or something similar. Settings for dealing with dropped frames will be similar to Error Tolerance or Frame Drop Percentage.

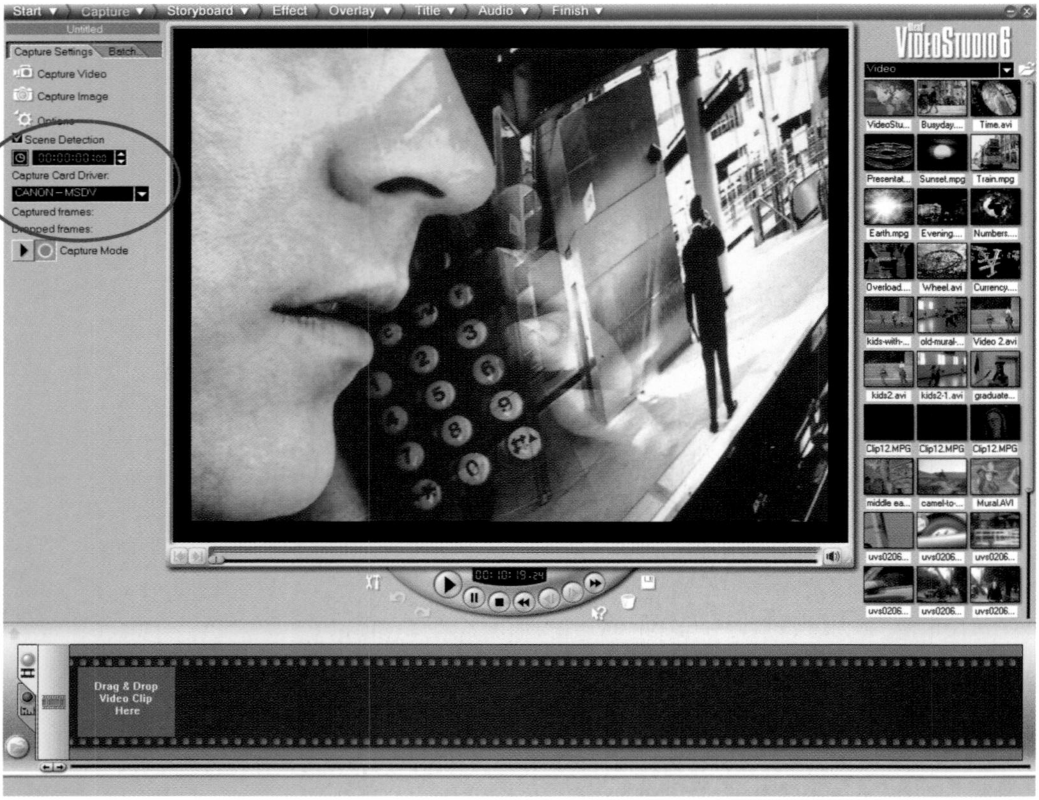
Start
Capture
Storyboard
Effect
Overlay
Title
Audio
Finish
Untitled
Capture Settings
Batch
Capture Video
Capture Image
Scene Detection
Capture Card Driver:
CANON – MSDV
Captured frames:
Capture Mode
Video
Drag & Drop Video Clip Here

Figure 9-3 The Ulead VideoStudio 6 video capture screen displays dropped frames and elapsed time.

7. The capture program will display the folder where your video is being saved. You may or may not be given an option to change this.
8. Set compression options. These options determine frame rate, movie dimensions, audio quality, and other options.
9. As you begin recording, the capture screen may display file size, elapsed time, and dropped frame rate. Keep an eye on this information, if available, as well as when in your video you want the recording to stop.

⑩ When finished, press **Stop**. Note that the movie has already been transferred to your computer. There may appear a Save Movie dialog box so you can name your movie, but the actual transfer has taken place.

⑪ More than likely, it is your saved movie that now appears in the preview screen, not the video from your camcorder. You can safely disconnect your camcorder, turn it off, and put it away.

Your capture program may be busy detecting scenes, or may have already placed your video clip in the program's editing area so you can begin building your video project (Figure 9-4). If scene detection did not take place automatically (if your video appears as one single thumbnail, not broken into segments), you may need to locate the Scene Detection option in a menu, and start it manually.

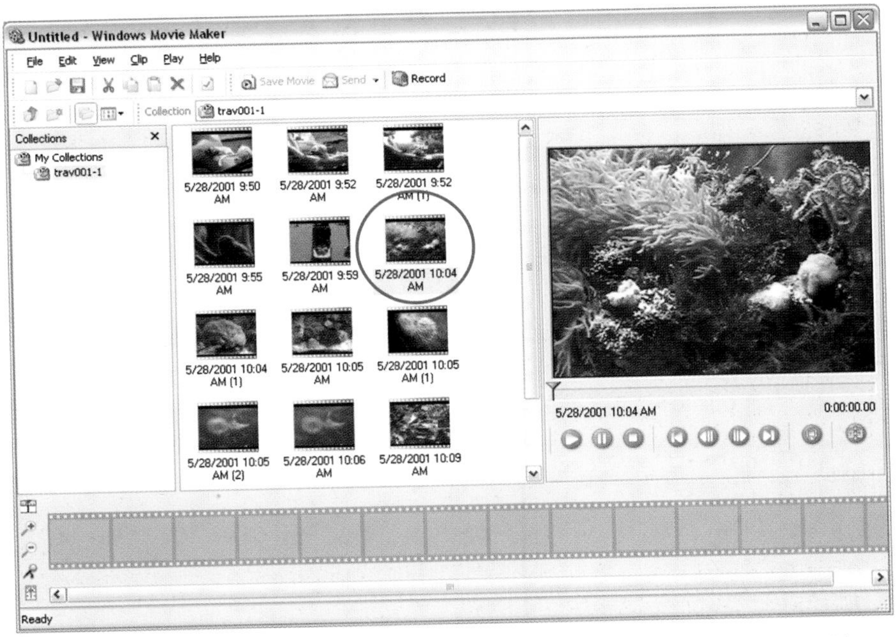
Untitled - Windows Movie Maker
File Edit View Clip Play Help
Save Movie Send Record
Collection trav001-1
Collections
My Collections
trav001-1
5/28/2001 9:50 AM
5/28/2001 9:52 AM
5/28/2001 9:52 AM (1)
5/28/2001 9:55 AM
5/28/2001 9:59 AM
5/28/2001 10:04 AM
5/28/2001 10:04 AM (1)
5/28/2001 10:05 AM
5/28/2001 10:05 AM (1)
5/28/2001 10:05 AM (2)
5/28/2001 10:06 AM
5/28/2001 10:09 AM
5/28/2001 10:04 AM
0:00:00.00
Ready

Figure 9-4 After capturing video with Windows Movie Maker, the captured video appears divided into scenes, ready for editing.

Frame Dimension

You may want to specify a frame dimension for your project. Here are some examples:

- ✦ If your video is destined for DVD or VHS, you can create a Wide Screen Format movie. Keep your video at 748×480 pixels, or see if you have a 16:9 dimension option available.
- ✦ Video that will be viewed mostly on a PC looks good at 640×480 pixels.

- If you are creating video for 56kbps Internet connection or slower, your movie should be about 120×160 pixels, almost the smallest size possible.
- Movies for CD distribution are generally 320×240 pixels.

Keep in mind that you cannot go from small to big. If you choose to transfer your video using a small frame size, you will want to avoid enlarging it. For example, if you import your video at 120×160, and try to enlarge it later, the quality will be poor:

> A 120×160 pixel movie is very tiny. Movies with detail and lots of subtle nuances will not look their best at this speed.

Frames Per Second

Another significant setting is frames per second (fps). Playback devices differ in how many frames of video they can smoothly display in any given second. Specifying an appropriate fps setting for your playback device is essential for smooth video playback. Figure 9-5 shows Pinnacle Studio 8's compression options, which include frames per second (fps) settings.

Studio Setup Options
Capture source
Capture format
Edit
CD and Voice-over
Presets
Custom-quality preview
Choose your own custom settings for preview capture.
Video settings
List all codecs
Options...
Compression:
Indeo® video 5.10
Width:
Height:
Framerate
720
480
29.97
Quality
Data rate
Percent
100
Audio settings
Include audio
Options...
Compression:
PCM
Channels
16-bit stereo
Sample rate
48 kHz
OK
Cancel
Help

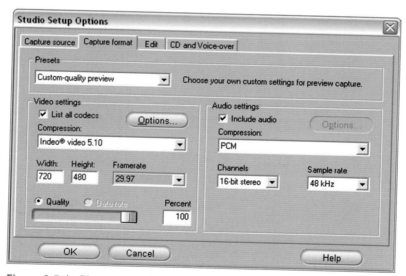

Figure 9-5 In Pinnacle Studio 8, selecting compression options includes fps settings (Framerate).

- If your video will be played back from a computer hard drive, DVD, or MiniDV tape, choose 30 fps. These mediums can accommodate fast video uptake.

- For video distributed in Europe (using the PAL standard), choose 25 fps.

- For CD or VCD distribution, choose 15 fps. To avoid jerky video, you will want to choose this slower speed for this slower medium.

- Video on the Web moves between 6 and 12 fps.

Keep in mind that if you capture video at a slower speed, you will not be able to bump up the frame rate later. So, if you are creating a CD-based project, but you think there's a possibility you may create a VHS tape from it as well, go ahead and capture the video at the higher, 30 fps rate. You can always export your completed project at the slower rate, but you will not be able to go back to the faster speed to accommodate a faster output need.

Video Data Rate

Data Rate targets your video for specific transfer capabilities. For example, online video projects require a low data rate, since even DSL or other high-speed Internet options cannot support full-quality high-speed video transfer. CD-ROM-based projects also require a relatively low data rate (1100 to 1600 kilobytes per second). For VCR or broadcast video, data rate should be very high to ensure the highest possible quality.

> ### More About . . . Compression
>
> Your choice of video compression is one of the most significant decisions you will make at upload time. Too much compression, and your video quality suffers. Too little, and your computer chokes every time you try to make a simple edit. It's a bit like crumpling up paper into a ball. The tighter the ball, the harder it is to read the writing when you uncrumple it. Always go for the smallest amount of compression your system can handle without editing becoming a chore. When you're ready to distribute your video later on, you can decide to compress more.

9

Video Capture with Pinnacle Studio 8

Pinnacle Studio 8 is a digital video editing program suite that offers all editing tools in one common interface. You capture, edit, and distribute video from one program. Before stepping through the capturing process, you should be familiar with the highlights of Studio 8's capture workspace, called Capture Mode. Much of your work will be completed there. Capture Mode has four sections (Figure 9-6).

Album
Player
Camcorder Controller
Diskometer
Pinnacle Studio - Untitled.stu *
1 Capture
2 Edit
3 Make Movie
PINNACLE STUDIO 8
Captured:
Frames dropped:
Full-quality capture
Preview-quality capture
Stop Capture

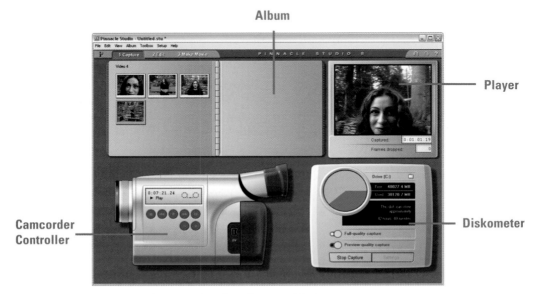

Figure 9-6 Pinnacle Studio 8 Capture Mode.

- The Album, on the upper left, will display your video clips as you capture them.
- On the upper right is the Player, which displays both the video in your camcorder before you transfer it and the same video once it has been uploaded to your computer. Once capture has begun, the Player displays the number of frames captured and frames dropped.
- On the bottom left is a graphic representation of your camcorder, called the Camcorder Controller. It displays your camcorder's current mode of operation. Rather than reach for your camcorder, you can click the screen controls to operate it
- A control panel, dubbed the Diskometer, lets you view available hard drive space for video capture and control video transfer settings. Located on the lower right, the Start Capture and Stop Capture buttons are found here.

Before you get started capturing, one of the sections above bears more explanation. In the Diskometer, the Settings button—also accessible via the menu by clicking **Setup, Capture Source** or **Setup, Capture Format**—contains a number of important features to help you determine your capture source and capture format.

Video File Types

When video is digitized and stored on your computer, it carries information about its frame speed and size, color mode, operating system compatibility, and other playback data—in addition to the actual video data itself. These characteristics, along with the way in which the video data is arranged and stored, make up a video file format. You will know video formats by their filename. Here are the most common digital video formats:

AVI. Audio Video Interleave (.AVI) is the standard Windows movie format. Figure 9-7 shows an .AVI video file in a hard drive folder. Most any .AVI movie can be played on a Windows computer.

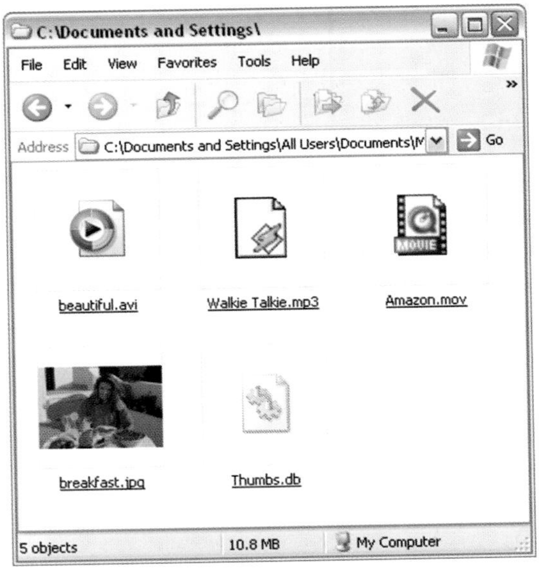
C:\Documents and Settings\
File Edit View Favorites Tools Help
Address C:\Documents and Settings\All Users\Documents\M
Go
beautiful.avi
Walkie Talkie.mp3
Amazon.mov
MOVIE
breakfast.jpg
Thumbs.db
5 objects
10.8 MB
My Computer

Figure 9-7 An AVI video file in a Windows folder.

The advantage to .AVI is that it is not highly compressed, so the quality is fairly high. You can transfer your movie from camcorder to computer as .AVI, then save it to a more portable format for output, such as MPEG or one of the Web-friendly streaming formats such as ASF or WMA.

9

QuickTime. QuickTime is the Apple video and media format. QuickTime movies can be played on the Web, Macs, and PCs (Figure 9-8). Recognized by the .MOV file extension, QuickTime movies are efficiently compressed, look very good, and are compatible with a number of screen dimensions, frame, and data rates. QuickTime is an ideal format for sharing movies across the Internet or computer-based playback. The only downside is the viewer must have the QuickTime movie viewer installed.

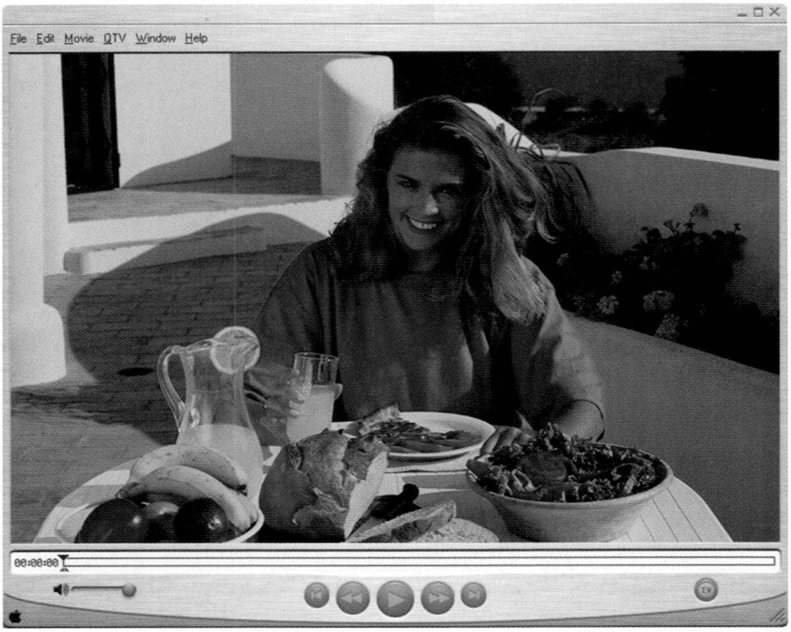
File Edit Movie QTV Window Help
00:00:00

Figure 9-8 A movie in QuickTime.

DVD. You will use MPEG-2 compression to create DVDs, and your DVD movie creation program will walk you through the steps of preparing your movie for DVD formatting.

VCD. VCD is a CD-friendly video format that uses MPEG-1 compression to create a movie that will look good and play back smoothly on most any CD-ROM drive, 8X speed, or higher. VCD easily facilitates cataloging still images onto the CD as well as video, so you can include digital photo albums along with your movie.

SVCD. SVCD allows DVD-ready movies formatted with MPEG-2 compression to be saved onto standard CDs. Many DVD players will also play SVCD-formatted CDs. SVCD movies require fast CD-ROM drives with Pentium III computers or higher.

Video Compression and Codecs

Video compression is the science of making video files smaller by removing non-essential information. Compression is a necessary element to video editing. The goal of the technology is to provide you with a movie that is easily transportable, but still looks good. It does this by meeting other needs as well:

+ Video compression is designed to accommodate a number of format requirements. For example, if your original video is 740×480, at 30 frames per minute, you may want to maintain that specification even after your movie is compressed, and not have to reduce your movie frame size.

+ Compression is flexible. At times, you will need to reduce your movie's frame size significantly, as well as its frame rate.

+ Compression allows you to choose your own tradeoff between file size and movie quality. For example, a movie to be viewed on the Web must be small in every way and accommodate a slow frame rate. It will, thus, have to be very compressed. A DVD movie can be much larger. Compression schemes let you choose the amount of compression based on your needs.

Video compression comes in many types, each using differing algorithms to remove data that affects your viewing experience as little as possible. However a compression scheme requires two components to work: First, the video is compressed. Then, when preparing to be viewed, it must be decompressed. Compression schemes are referred to as codecs, (Compression/Decompression). When saving your movie for output, you will see many codec choices. Below are the codecs most significant to non-professional videographers:

MPEG. MPEG is unique in that it compresses video by comparing each frame of video to its neighbor and throwing away redundant information. MPEG only recompresses the new information between each frame. The result is a very efficient compression and good-looking movie. Currently, MPEG-1 and MPEG-2 compression are in high use, as described below:

+ MPEG-1, generally used for 352×240 pixel movies 15 to 30 fps (frames per second) MPEG-1 is the best choice for CD-ROM movies and small clips to be downloaded from the Web or Intranet. Because MPEG works by comparing video information from frame to frame, you should choose MPEG-1 compression after you've edited your video, not before. That's because part of the editing process is making frame cuts, which is not a tidy process on MPEG-1 video. If MPEG-1 is required, it's best to choose that option at output time, not when transferring video from camcorder to computer.

9

✦ MPEG-2 is the compression used for creating DVDs and is becoming the standard broadcast compression for High Definition TV and other digital broadcast requirements. The picture is large (720×480 at a possible 60 fields per second), looks good (Figure 9-9), and the compression is very efficient. Beyond use of DVDs and broadcast, you should only use MPEG-2 compression if the viewers will have Pentium II computers or above, or high-powered Macs.

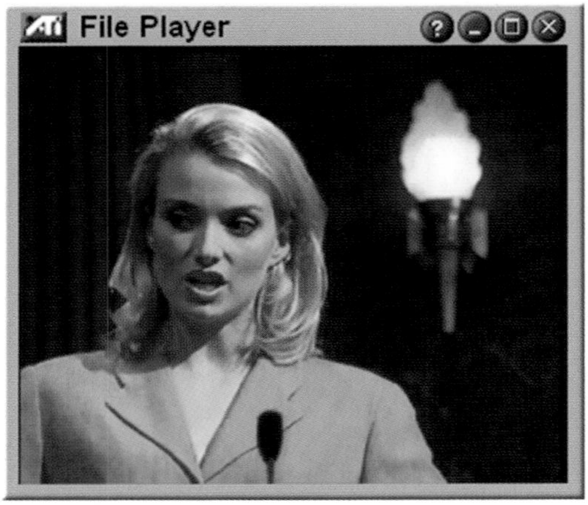
File Player

Figure 9-9 An MPEG movie in an MPEG viewer.

Sorenson. Sorenson works well with 320×240-pixel footage when played back from a hard drive or Internet connection faster than a dial-up, such as DSL or ISDN. It is not a preferred method for compressing video for CD-ROM drives. One issue with Sorenson is it takes a long time to encode. That means if you select Sorenson as your output choice, you will be waiting a long time for the job to complete.

Intel Indeo 4 and 5. The Intel Indeo codecs produces high-quality .AVI video with decent compression rates for fairly fast computers. With Indeo-coded .AVI movies, if the viewer does not have the correct codec installed, the program playing back the movie will try to open an Internet connection and download it. .AVI with Indeo is a good choice for transferring video to your computer from your camcorder. You can edit your .AVI file, then choose a more portable, highly compressed option for your final output.

Cinipak. If your movie will be played back on older computers or older CD-ROM drives, choose the Cinepak codec. It is already installed on most machines. Cinipak can be used efficiently for movies 320×240 pixels or smaller. Its real value is its usability on even old 486 computers. There's no real reason to choose this codec if all your viewers will be playing your movie on computers that are less than five years old.

Capturing Analog Video

You can use your digital camcorder to facilitate digitizing older movies. Your old VHS, Super 8, and other analog tapes can be made digital, and they can be edited and archived just like other digital movies.

Many digital camcorders—the Canon ZR45 and ZR50, for instance—provide an S-Video input, and some provide a complete set of analog line-in and line-out connections. Also, many newer VCRs and analog camcorders have S-Video connections. Using these, you can transfer your movie to digital camcorder MiniDV tape, or directly to your computer. These are used to digitize movies from your analog tapes, such as VHS or Super 8. If you have movies on VHS that you want to make more permanent, you can make digital copies by plugging a cable into the Analog Line-In connection of your camcorder. This option requires that your output device (VCR or analog camcorder) have an S-Video connection. After doing this, you have a choice.

You can record the VHS data onto a MiniDV tape. To do this, simply have a tape in the camcorder and press record as you begin playing back the VHS tape. Once you have your digital MiniDV master, you can then send it to your computer via FireWire for editing, if you desire.

The other option is to save your VHS data directly onto your PC, essentially using the camcorder as a digital converter. The Canon camcorders mentioned here have this capability. Two cables are required, one from the VHS to the camcorder, and the other from the camcorder to the computer. The camcorder-to-computer cable would be FireWire. You would then capture the video via FireWire card using the same tools and methods previously described. You would press Play on your VCR, and press Record on your video capture program on your computer. The camcorder would simply allow the data to pass through.

9

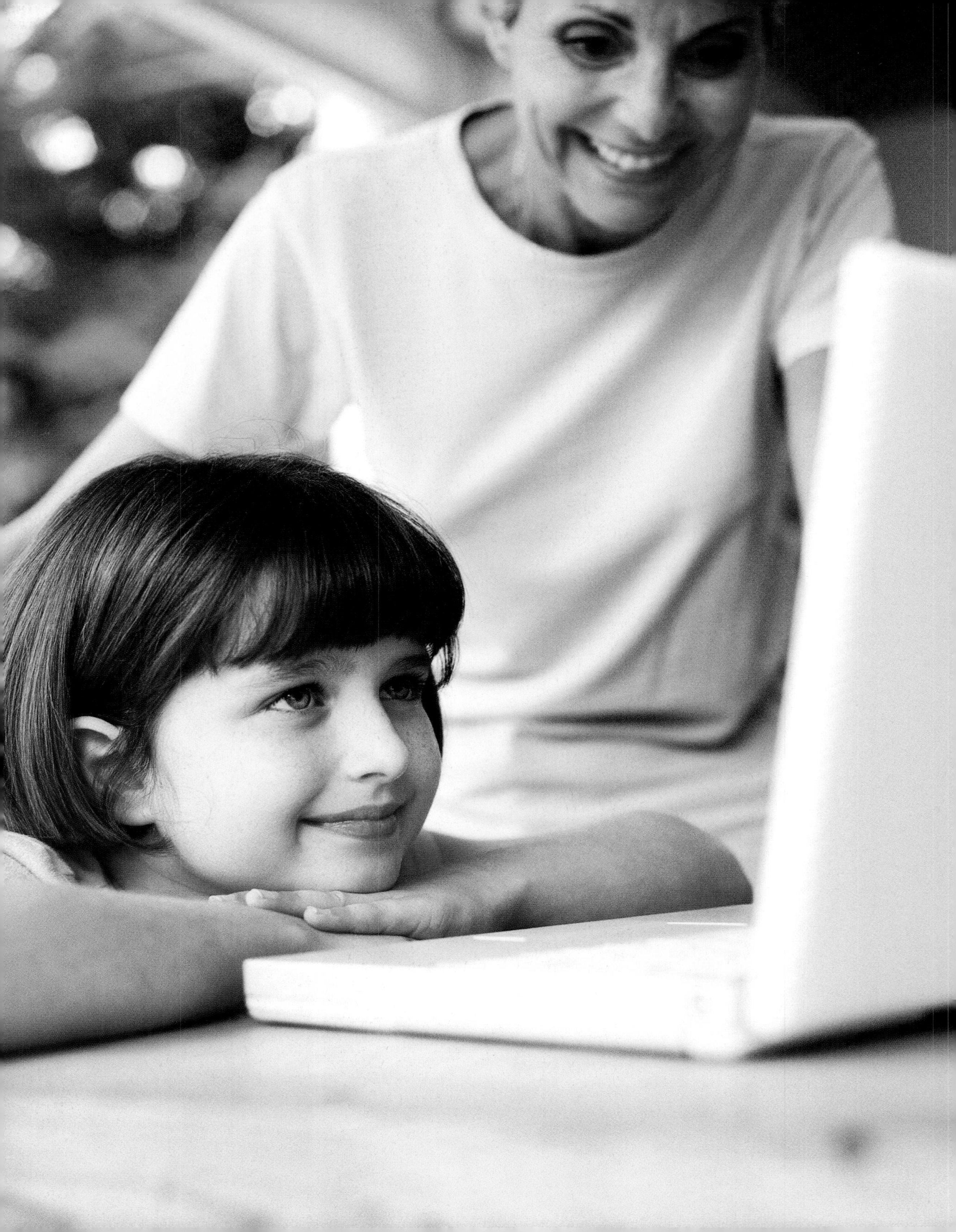

Manage Your Video Projects

B asic video editing is the first step toward building a complete video project. Including text, backgrounds, and transitional effects with your video all provide a contrast to video motion. This chapter shows you how to work with your video-editing software to provide the elements to make a good video.

Additionally, when it comes to video, the medium really is the message. For example, if you post a large, uncompressed video file on the Web and expect users to download it over a 56 Kbps modem, your movie will probably never be seen. After a few minutes of waiting and frustration, your potential viewer will be gone and probably won't be back. Likewise, if your movie is headed for DVD playback, no one will suffer through it if you render it as a tiny, postage stamp-sized movie with maximum compression.

In this chapter, you will learn how to choose the right format for the right audience, as well as what your file format and compression options are. You will also learn various techniques and options for optimizing video performance. For instance, while most video-editing programs provide presets for different viewing environments, there are times when you may want to make some additional choices, like selecting a larger frame size or a slower data rate. This chapter will arm you with a variety of output choices and show you when and why to use them.

Digital Video-Editing Software– A First Look

You may have heard that digital video editing is "non-linear." In a very real sense, this is true, since, unlike the days before digital editing, you do not have to physically cut and splice film or tape from beginning to end.

In another sense, video editing is still very much a linear process. From a creative standpoint, most good videos have something resembling a beginning, middle, and end. This is also true on a practical level, where you will take the same steps time and time again on the road to a completed project. The fundamental steps to editing any video project are:

1. Gather video files for your project.
2. Assemble video clips on a video-editing storyboard or timeline.
3. Cut away undesirable footage.
4. Position repeating segments.
5. Add transitions.

These steps are covered in detail in this chapter using three popular and easy-to-use video-editing programs.

Essential Definitions

Before diving into the process of video editing, let's review some important terms you will need to know:

✦ **Video clip.** A video clip is the source video, or raw video footage, that you will use in your video project. Though most of your raw footage will likely be video you've captured using your camcorder, you can also use video clips from other sources. Nature videos, footage of historical events, or video captured from broadcast are examples.

Before using video from another source, always obtain permission to use it from the owner of the video.

✦ **Video scene.** A video clip is divided into many video scenes. A video scene is the small snippet of film you drag from a video library, album, or collection in your editing program and add to your presentation. How do you get scenes? When you capture video, your video-capturing program looks for natural divisions in the video clip and divides it there. These divisions are determined either by sensing at what points the camera was turned on and off during filming or just based on where the content appears to shift.

✦ **Movie.** A movie is your final video output—your finished production. It is what you save and share with your friends, family—even the world—when you have finished editing your project. You can output your project in several ways. For example, you might make a copy of your movie on DVD, and viewers could simply pop it into their DVD player and see your work. You could spin the same project into a Web-based movie, optimized exclusively for Web viewing.

✦ **Video project.** A video project is the collection of all your video and media elements in one place. You assemble, edit, and archive your video clips, scenes, and movies using your video-editing program and a little imagination.

The Basic Video-Editing Workspace

A common element of a video project is an editing workspace, which typically gives you two views of your video clips. These views provide the ability to add or delete video clips, text, images, sounds, and special effects. Think of the workspace as the factory floor, where all the assembly, building, and inspection of your video takes place. A workspace includes several elements:

✦ A preview or playback window for viewing individual video clips or project playback (Figure 10-1)

10

- A control panel with VCR-style controls for playing, rendering, fast-forwarding, and rewinding video playback, including "one-frame-at-a-time" controls (also shown in Figure 10-1)
- A library or resource area to display video clips, images, transitions, and special effects (Figure 10-2)
- An editing area where you will sequence, trim, and combine your video clips, and build your project (Figure 10-3)

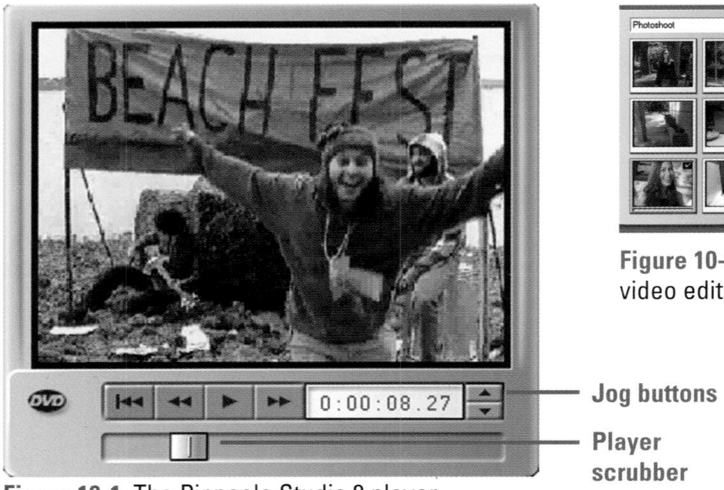
BEACH FEST
DVD
0:00:08.27
Jog buttons
Player scrubber
Figure 10-1 The Pinnacle Studio 8 player.

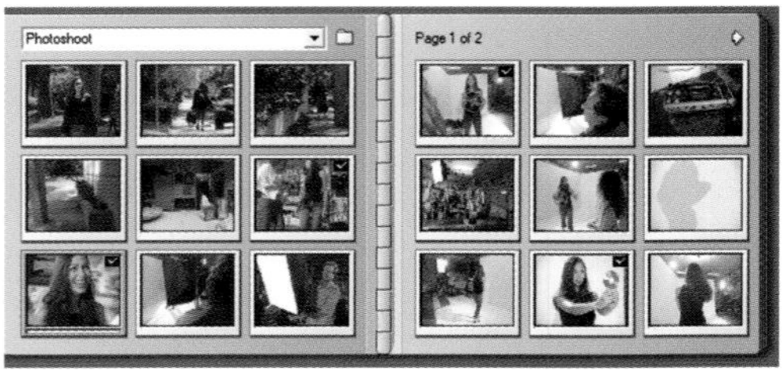
Photoshoot
Page 1 of 2
Figure 10-2 The Pinnacle Studio 8 Library for video editing.

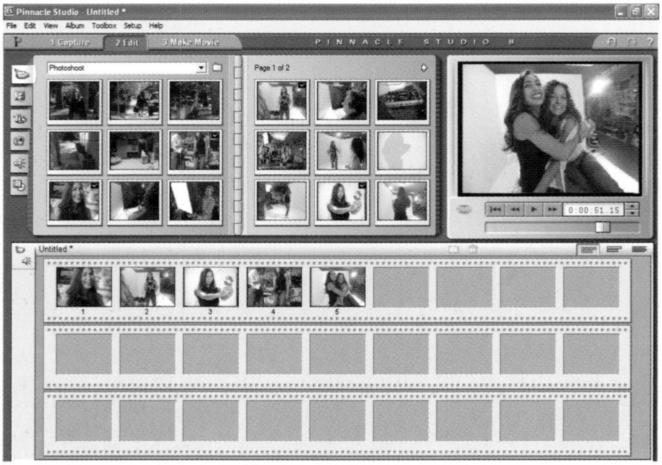
Pinnacle Studio - Untitled *
File Edit View Album Toolbox Setup Help
1 Capture
2 Edit
3 Make Movie
PINNACLE STUDIO 8
Photoshoot
Page 1 of 2
0:00:51.15
Untitled *
Figure 10-3 The Pinnacle Studio 8 workspace.

> ⚠ To avoid losing your work, save your projects frequently. Because video editing programs handle such large files, your computer could reach its memory limit and require an unexpected restart.

The Video Project Working Folder

Most of the files you pick to create your video project are located in what we will call a video project working folder. This folder was probably created automatically when you captured video from your camcorder. In this folder, you will find the following types of files (Figure 10-4):

C:\Documents and Settings\
File Edit View Favorites Tools Help
Address
d Settings\protools\My Documents\My Videos\My Videos
Go
HelenasArms.jpg
Werewolf.vsp
Werewolf.mpg
werewolf.avi
Thumbs.db
first-cut.wav
6 objects
13.2 MB
My Computer

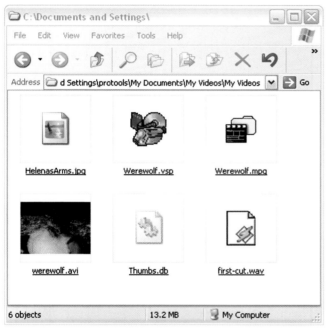

Figure 10-4 A folder with files for a video-editing project.

- **Captured video footage.** These files, produced by your camcorder, will be large. They will probably have a .AVI or .MPG file extension, depending on what type of file you created when you captured your video.
- **Edited video.** Most editing software will create a copy of your video and edit that copy, leaving your original footage safe.
- **Project file.** When you open a video-editing program and develop a project, it creates a file that keeps track of all your edits, where you want the video cut, where you want music added, transitions added, etc. This is the file you click on in order to edit your project, and it's this file that you save in order to keep all your changes intact and available for further editing later.
- **Output file.** You will not see the output file until you are done editing and are ready to create your movie. An output file is your completed work. It will probably have a .MPG, .AVI, or .MOV file extension. This is the file you are sharing with the world, and it will be compressed—smaller than your original video footage, perhaps much smaller depending on the options you choose.

Basic Video Editing

You will now learn basic video editing tasks using two different video-editing programs: Microsoft® Windows Movie Maker and Pinnacle Studio 8. Video editing is where you'll spend the bulk of your time developing your project, and while each program performs similar functions, each does so uniquely. By taking a look at these two programs, you will get a better understanding of the overall editing process and will learn how to use each program's editing features.

Other types of video-editing software, such as Ulead, work similarly to Pinnacle and Windows Movie Maker. What you learn in this chapter can be applied to other similar applications.

Basic Video Editing with Windows Movie Maker

Windows Movie Maker is a basic video-editing package. Though it doesn't offer some of the frills and thrills of programs like Pinnacle Studio 8 and Ulead VideoStudio 6, you can use Movie Maker to record both audio and video source material, import source files, then edit and arrange your video clips to create movies. Best of all, Movie Maker is included with Windows XP and has a stable and well-designed interface, which is divided into three main areas (Figure 10-5):

Collection
Monitor
Workspace
Untitled - Windows Movie Maker
Collection: Windows Movie Maker 2 Sample File
Drag a clip and drop it on the storyboard below.
Show Timeline
Drag media to the storyboard to begin making a movie.

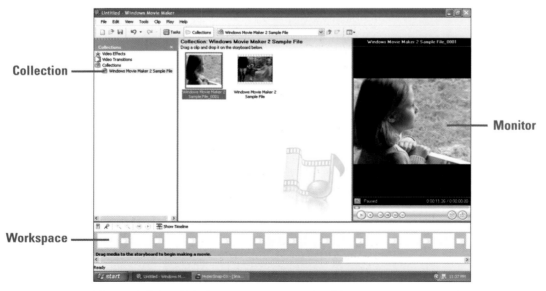

Figure 10-5 The Windows Movie Maker GUI (Graphic User Interface).

+ **Monitor.** A playback or preview screen where editing is monitored.
+ **Collection/Collections area.** An album or library of videos, images, or other media such as audio, to be used in your project.
+ **Workspace.** An assembly area where clips and scenes are edited, and elements such as text overlays or special effects are added.

The Monitor

The Monitor (Figure 10-6), displays a video clip as you are previewing it. After you've added a video clip, the monitor also shows where the clip appears as part of the project. Below the monitor is the Seek Bar that tells you the current playback position. To the right of the Seek Bar is a clip counter. It counts time as you play back the clip.

If you drag the Seek Bar along the length of the clip, you will see the counter change. Use the counter to note exactly where you are in a clip, down to the hundredth of a second. This is important, because you ideally want to trim or cut a video clip at a point where the subjects are not in mid-movement, so having a very accurate clip counter helps you keep your cuts precise.

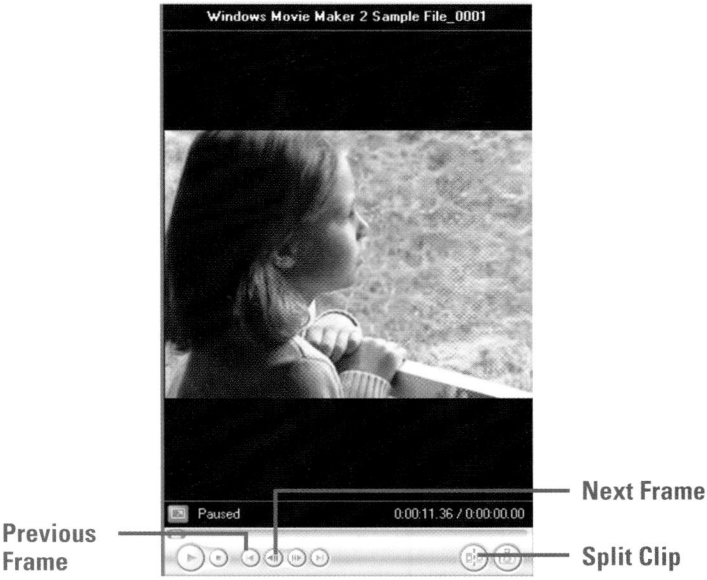
Windows Movie Maker 2 Sample File_0001
Paused
0:00:11.36 / 0:00:00.00
Previous Frame
Next Frame
Split Clip

Figure 10-6 The Movie Maker Monitor used to preview video.

10

The Collections Area

Movie Maker organizes your video, images, and sounds into a Collection, which is a Windows Explorer-like interface including a folder view and the Collections area, which allows you to view your source media in thumbnail, list, and detail views.

To add new media to your project, right-click the folder view on the left-hand side of Movie Maker, choose Import, and locate a folder on your hard drive that contains videos, images, sounds, or any other media you want to add to your project. Alternately, you can simply drag-and-drop the media to the Collections area. To actually add a video clip or other media type to your project, just drag it to the storyboard at the bottom of the screen.

The Storyboard/Timeline View

At the bottom of the screen is where your project is assembled. In Movie Maker, this is called the Workspace. There are two project views: Storyboard and Timeline. You can switch between views by clicking the button at the upper left of the storyboard (Figure 10-7).

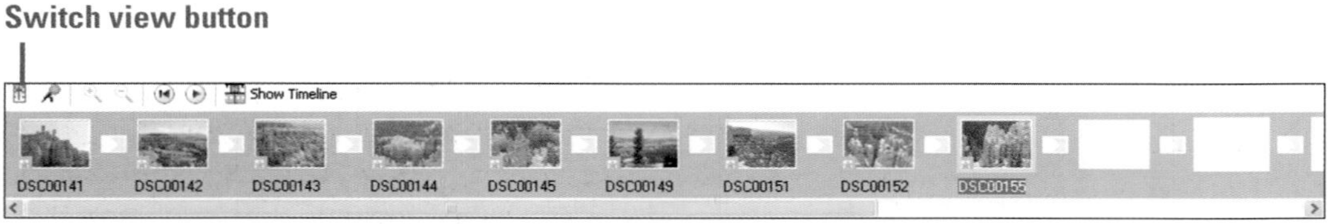
Switch view button
Show Timeline
DSC00141
DSC00142
DSC00143
DSC00144
DSC00145
DSC00149
DSC00151
DSC00152
DSC00155

Figure 10-7 The Movie Maker Storyboard/Timeline workspace.

The Storyboard View

The Storyboard view shows you each video or still image in your project as a thumbnail. Viewing from left to right, you can see the order in which your video project's components will be played back. In Figure 10-8, you can see nine media items on the Storyboard.

While in Storyboard view, you can drag a clip in between other clips. To do so, just select the clip and drag it to the space between the two clips already in the Storyboard.

When you click on a thumbnail on the Storyboard, it appears in the monitor. You can then drag the Seek Bar to any location in the clip for trimming or editing. Click another thumbnail on the Storyboard, and that clip will appear in the monitor.

Untitled - Windows Movie Maker
File Edit View Tools Clip Play Help
Tasks
Collections
Windows Movie Maker 2 Sample File
Collection: Windows Movie Maker 2 Sample File
Drag a clip and drop it on the storyboard below.
Video Effects
Video Transitions
Collections
Windows Movie Maker 2 Sample File
DSC00141
DSC00142
DSC00143
DSC00144
DSC00145
DSC00146
DSC00147
DSC00148
DSC00149
Paused
Show Timeline
DSC00151
DSC00152
Ready

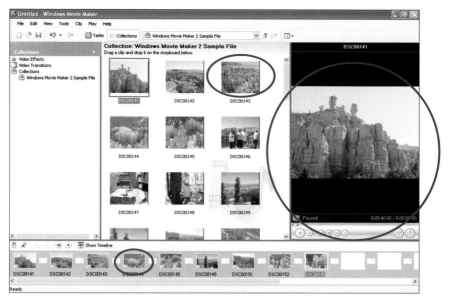

Figure 10-8 A work in progress in the Movie Maker Storyboard view.

The Timeline View

To see more of a frame-by-frame view of your project, use the Timeline view (Figure 10-9). In the Timeline view, your movie is shown right below a time ruler, so you can see exactly how long each clip is. You can then drag the clip to the right or left. Drag from the middle of the clip, and it will be repositioned on the timeline, making playback begin earlier or later. Drag from the clip's edge, and the clip's total playback time will be shortened or lengthened.

First Clip Here
Second Clip Here
Show Storyboard
Video
DS...
DSCO...
DSC...
DSC00143
DSC00148
D...
DSC00185

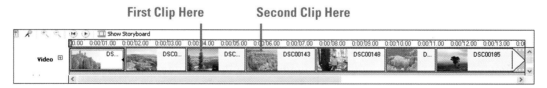

Figure 10-9 The Movie Maker Timeline view.

Basic Video Editing with Pinnacle Studio 8

Pinnacle Studio 8 is a polished and intuitive video-editing application. In fact, after just one editing session, you will find editing with Studio 8 particularly easy, considering the power behind this workhorse of an application.

Video editing using Studio 8 is accomplished by entering Edit mode. To edit a movie in Studio 8, click the Edit tab at the top of the screen. The editing workspace appears, divided into three segments (Figure 10-10). The Album, at the upper left, displays video clips and other media resources, arranged as if in a photo album. The Player is located at the top right, while the storyboard/timeline area—dubbed the Movie Window in Studio 8—is at the bottom.

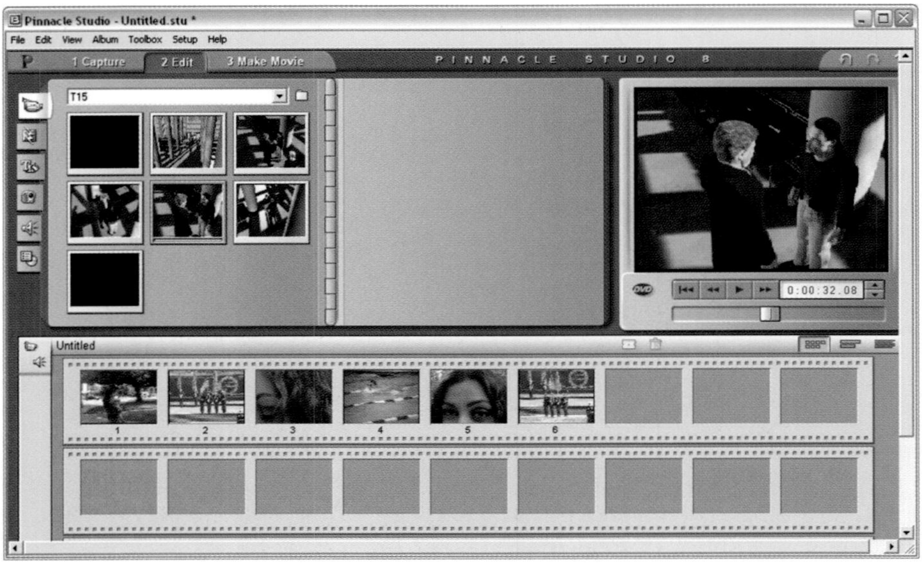

Pinnacle Studio - Untitled.stu *
File Edit View Album Toolbox Setup Help
1 Capture
2 Edit
3 Make Movie
PINNACLE STUDIO 8
T15
0:00:32.08
Untitled
1
2
3
4
5
6

Figure 10-10 Pinnacle Studio 8's Edit mode.

Adding Transitions

A transition blends one video clip into the next, using everything from a simple fade, wipe, or dissolve, to geometric shapes and patterns, special animations, and changing colors and sizes. In fact, there are some transitions that almost defy description. You will discover them for yourself as you browse through the different effects available in Pinnacle Studio 8.

The duration of a transition is important. Though video editing programs apply transitions using a default length, you can edit the duration, creating an instant transition or an extra-long fade. Studio 8 gives you the ability to set up transitions the way you want them.

Transitions are a drag-and-drop affair in Studio 8: You first display the Transition section in the Album, then choose a transition and drag it between two clips. At least one clip must be present in the Movie Window. You can drop transitions between two clips in the Timeline view, but it's a little easier to verify your placement using the Storyboard view. Here's how its done.

1. Click the **Show transitions** tab on the left side of the Album. The Album now displays a page of transitions (Figure 10-11). To see additional pages, click the arrow at the upper right of the album. The drop-down menu at the upper left provides access to many transition types, including **Alpha Magic**, **HFX Wipes and Fades**, and **Hollywood FX** (discussed below).

Pinnacle Studio - Untitled.stu *
File Edit View Album Toolbox Setup Help
1 Capture
2 Edit
3 Make Movie
PINNACLE STUDIO 8
Alpha Magic
Page 1 of 2
0:00:01.07
Untitled *

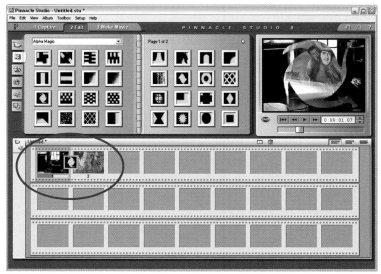

Figure 10-11 The Pinnacle Studio 8 Transition section.

2. You will want to preview the transition to see the type of effect it creates between clips. To do so, double-click it, and the transition alone will appear in the Player. The transition is displayed over what is known as an A/B Roll. As such, the letter "A" represents the first clip, the letter "B" represents the second.
3. To apply a transition between two clips, drag it from the Album to the space between the clips.
4. To preview your transition as it appears with the clips, just click the first clip on the Movie Window, and click **Play**.

10

To delete a transition from a project in Studio 8, click the clip, then click the **Delete Clips** button at the top of the Movie Window.

Studio 8 includes a large group of dramatic transitions, some with complex 3D graphics, called Hollywood FX. These effects work particularly well for opening sequences, sports footage, and music videos. Demo versions of other Hollywood FX effects are also included and are watermarked with a Pinnacle "P." If you like the demos, you can purchase the real versions by clicking the large Pinnacle Hollywood FX button in the Album, which links to the Pinnacle Web site.

Hollywood FX transitions also include a special editor (Figure 10-12), which lets you customize transitions by giving you control over settings like angles, direction, shadows, lighting, and anti-aliasing (edge smoothing). Dubbed the Easy FX editor, you can access it by double-clicking a Hollywood FX transition in the Movie Window, then by clicking the **Edit** button in the Clip properties window.

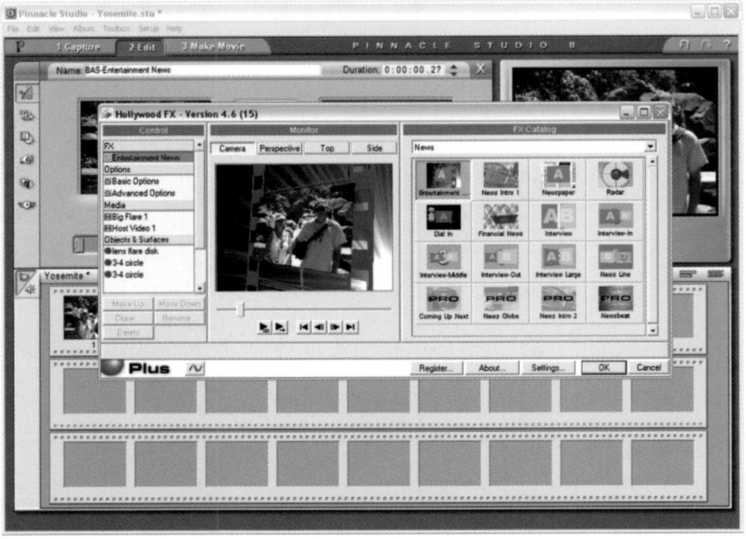
Hollywood FX - Version 4.6 (15)
Plus

Figure 10-12 Pinnacle's EasyFX editor gives you complete control over Hollywood FX transitions.

Adding Text to Your Movie

There are a number of reasons why you may want to add text to your video. Pinnacle Studio 8 will help get you started by providing preset titles, like "Happy New Year" and "My Birthday Party," that you can easily edit to fit your own needs. How and where you use text is then up to you. For example, you could use text overlays to:

- Announce transitions or time jumps in your video, like "Near the End of the Game," or "The Last Day of Our Trip"
- Title your video project, for example: "Zion National Park Trip - 2002"
- Create scrolling credits and list everyone who was involved in your video production (Figure 10-13)
- Create thought bubbles, or exclamatory remarks, as in a comic strip
- Add song lyrics or quotations at key moments in your production

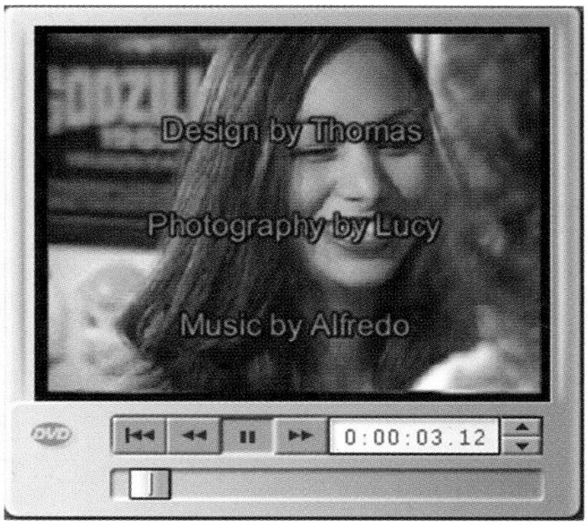
Design by Thomas
Photography by Lucy
Music by Alfredo
0:00:03.12

Figure 10-13 Scrolling credits created in Pinnacle Studio 8.

Creating Titles and Animations

In Pinnacle Studio 8, you can work with text in Storyboard or Timeline view. In either view, Studio 8 processes animation results very quickly and provides 36 editable presets at the click of your mouse. To add text or titles to your video in Pinnacle Studio 8, perform the following steps:

1. Open Studio 8.
2. Make sure you are in Edit mode by clicking the **Edit** tab.
3. If necessary, click the **Show videos** tab in the Album, and add at least one video clip to your project. In Studio 8, the duration for most text animations is set, by default, to four seconds. You may want to add a video clip of at least four seconds in length.

10

Show titles tab
Pinnacle Studio - Untitled.stu *
File Edit View Album Toolbox Setup Help
1 Capture
2 Edit
3 Make Movie
PINNACLE STUDIO 8
Page 1 of 2
Our Summer Vacation
0:00:07.26

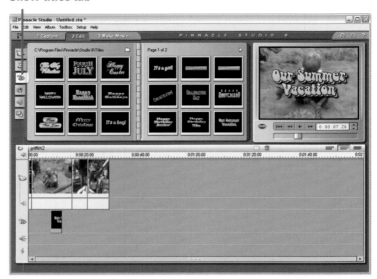

Figure 10-14 The Show titles tab displays Text animations.

4. Click the Album's **Show titles** tab (the third tab down on the left, as shown in Figure 10-14). Animated text titles will appear and the first eighteen preset titles are shown. To view more, turn the "page" by clicking the arrow on the upper right of the Album.

Our Summer Vacation
0:00:15.29
0:00:18.00

Figure 10-15 A new text title appears superimposed over a video clip.

5. To add a title, drag it from the **Album** to the **Movie Window**. Drop it on a video clip, and the title will appear superimposed over the video (Figure 10-15).

> You can also drop the title icon on a blank frame in the Movie Window, or insert the title between two frames. In both of these cases, Studio 8 will automatically create a new clip for the text title.

6. Click the **Play** button under the Player to see the results of your new text title.

Editing Text with the Title Editor

Studio 8 provides a number of text-editing options. Using Studio 8's Title Editor, you can change the text message, font, font size, and color. You can also animate your text, scrolling it either from bottom to top or from right to left, and add shadow, edge, and gradient color effects.

Here's how to edit a title:

1. In either Storyboard or Timeline view, right-click on the video clip for which you have created a title and select **Go to Title/Menu Editor**. The text animation appears in Studio 8's Title Editor, ready for editing (Figure 10-16).

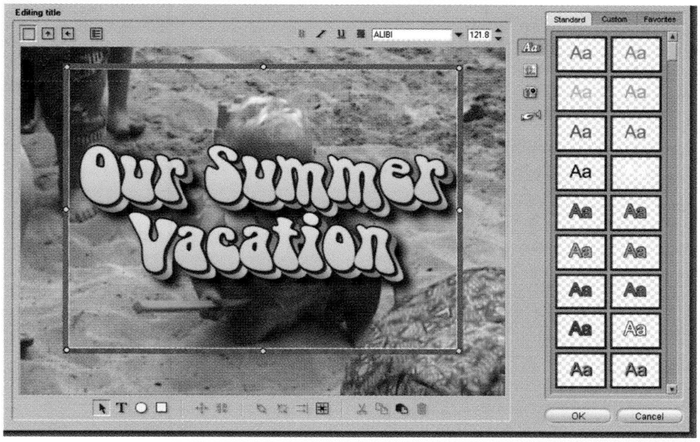

Editing title
Our Summer Vacation
Standard
Custom
Favorites
OK
Cancel

Figure 10-16 A text title is ready for editing.

You can also open Studio 8's Title Editor by clicking on the Video Toolbox button in the upper left of the Movie Window. When the Video Toolbox window appears, simply click the Edit Title button. If you are in Timeline view, double-clicking the title thumbnail will also open the Title Editor.

2. To edit the text, highlight the text you want to edit (Figure 10-17).

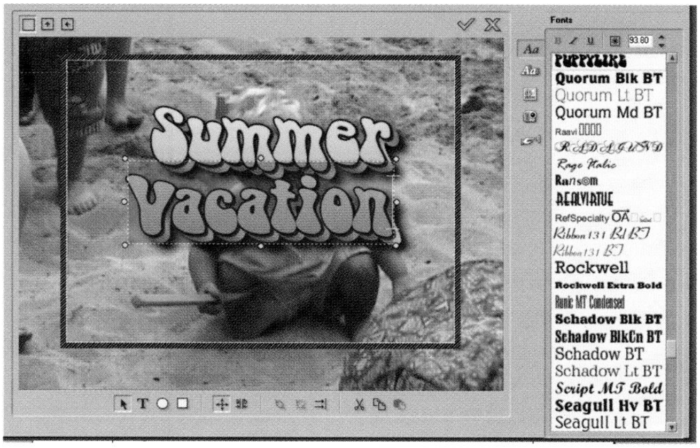

Summer Vacation
Fonts
Quorum Blk BT
Quorum Lt BT
Quorum Md BT
Rockwell
Rockwell Extra Bold
Schadow Blk BT
Schadow BlkCn BT
Schadow BT
Schadow Lt BT
Seagull Hv BT
Seagull Lt BT

Figure 10-17 Selected text will appear bounded in a semi-transparent blue box.

10

❸ To change the font, highlight the text you want to change, then click the **Font drop-down menu** on the top right side of the Title Editor (Figure 10-18). Scroll to find your new font, and click it.

Font drop-down menu
ALIBI
121.8
ALIBI
Allegro BT
Amelia BT
Americana BT
Americana XBd BT
Americana XBdCn BT
AmeriGarmnd BT
AmerType Md BT
Architecture
Arial
Arial Baltic
Arial Black
Arial CE
Arial CYR
Arial Greek
Arial Narrow
Arial TUR
Arriba Arriba LET
AvantGarde Bk BT
AvantGarde Md BT

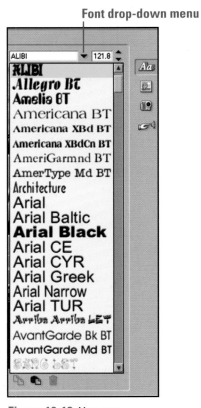

Figure 10-18 You can change fonts using any font installed on your computer.

Studio 8 lets you change fonts for individual letters in any title. If you want to change the font for text you have already typed, you must highlight the text first. If you don't highlight the text you want to change, you will not see any changes on-screen, though you will have set the font for any new text you will add.

❹ To change the font size, click inside the Font size field, to the right of the Font drop-down menu, and type a new font size. Alternately, you can use the small arrows next to the Font size field to increase or decrease the size.

Adding Color Backgrounds to Your Movie

A color background applies frames of single color to your movie. The color will display for a set number of seconds. Color backgrounds can be positioned and inserted in between clips (Figure 10-19) or used to open or close a movie.

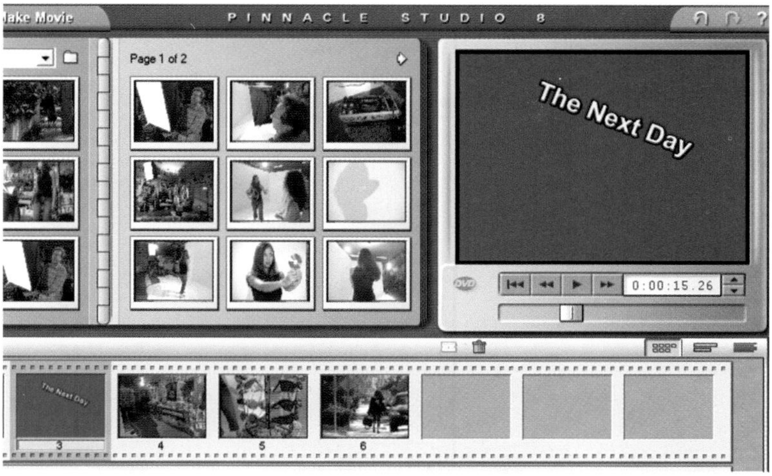

PINNACLE STUDIO 8
Page 1 of 2
The Next Day
0:00:15.26

Figure 10-19 Adding a color background to a movie

There are many uses for color backgrounds. For example, you can apply text to color frames, allowing the text animation to play against the backdrop of a single color, rather than against the video. This can be helpful, since reading text against a background with moving video content can be difficult.

You can also use color backdrops to display a video overlay, which is a video superimposed on another media. For example, a color background can be used as a backdrop while a video clip moves across the screen from one end to the other.

In Pinnacle Studio 8, color backgrounds are added using the Title Editor. To add a color background to your project with Pinnacle Studio 8, do the following:

1. In either Storyboard or Timeline view, right-click on any video clip and select **Go to Title/Menu Editor**.
2. Click the **Backgrounds** button.
3. Click the **Change color** or **Change gradient** option buton at the top right of the Title Editor.
4. To change the selected color, click the color rectangle next to the option button. If you are changing the gradient, click each corner color box that you want to change. The color-picker dialog box will appear.

10

5. Use the color-picker to select or create any color you like. Click **OK** to close the color-picker, and your new color will be applied to the video. If you are creating a gradient, the gradient will not be applied until you click the **X** button in the Change gradient box.

File Saving Options

No matter who your audience is, your ultimate goal is to save your movie in a format optimized for your target playback environment. For example, Figure 10-20 shows four video frames, each optimized for a different audience.

DVD Quality
Web Quality (small but not so compressed)
CD Quality
Web Quality (very compressed)

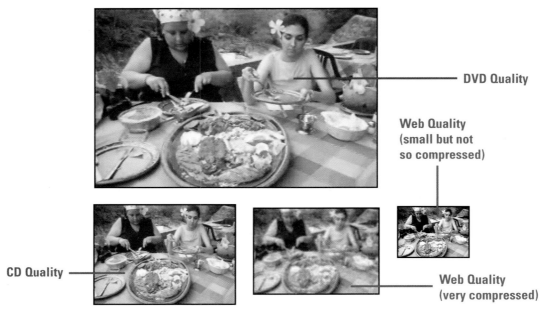

Figure 10-20 Four video frames showing various degrees of compression and frame size.

The first frame is very high-quality and large, suitable for DVD playback, MiniDV tape, or hard disk playback. The second is mid-sized and decent quality, and would work well on a CD or high-speed Internet connection. The third is mid-sized, but the video is highly compressed, which makes it ideal for lower-bandwidth Internet connections. The fourth serves the same audience as the third—low-bandwidth—with a nod toward quality over size.

Achieving these radically different frame sizes and compression rates is accomplished by using different video file formats. There are a number of different formats you can use. Let's focus on practical choices for a variety of playback situations. The video output options listed below are found in Pinnacle Studio 8 as well as other video-editing software.

Export to Web Page. Creates a Web page with a link to a video clip. By uploading both the page and the clip, viewers can visit that page and play back your clip whenever they like.

Export to E-mail. Opens your e-mail program, attaches the selected clip, and includes the video file name in the subject field.

Greeting Card. Lets you position a video clip against a background image of your choice and add a greeting message. Click on this video clip file and playback will begin. This greeting card file can be played back on almost any PC (Figure 10-21).

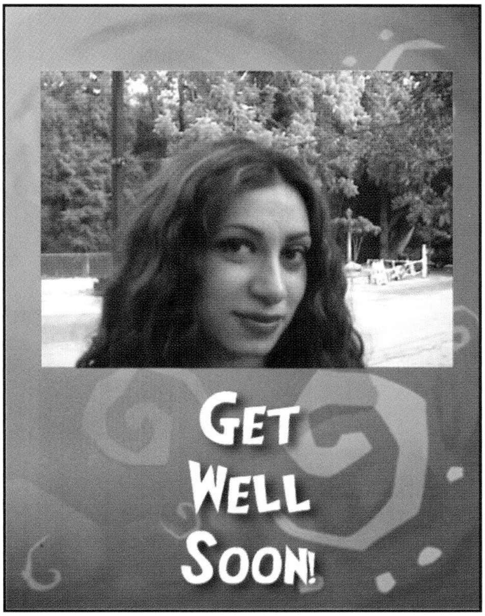
GET
WELL
SOON!

Figure 10-21 A Ulead VideoStudio 6 video Greeting Card.

DVD. Saves your movie for playback on most DVD players. You can divide your movie into chapters and create a menu. Viewers access this menu, fast forward to any chapter, and view from there. Saving to DVD requires a computer with a recordable DVD drive.

SVCD. Creates movies for saving on recordable CDs for playback in a DVD player. Note that many standalone DVD players are not compatible with SVCDs. More than likely, your viewers will need a PC-based DVD player.

VCD. Creates movies for saving on recordable CDs for playback in any 8X or higher CD-ROM drive.

Tape/Project Playback. With your camcorder attached to your computer via FireWire, the movie is played back while the camcorder records it. You can also record your movie directly to VHS using this method.

NTSC DV. Renders your movie in high-quality .AVI format, compatible with saving onto MiniDV tape for playback on TV according to NTSC broadcast standards, as used in North America.

NTSC DVD/SVCD/VCD. Renders your movie in North American TV-compatible format for DVD, SVCD, or VCD, whichever you choose.

PAL DV. Renders your movie in high-quality .AVI format, compatible with saving onto MiniDV tape for playback on TV according to PAL broadcast standards, as used in most of Europe.

PAL DVD/SVCD/VCD. Renders your movie in European TV-compatible format for DVD, SVCD, or VCD.

MPEG-1. Renders your movie for Web-based or CD-based playback. Creates compressed movies that provide options for balancing multiple output requirements.

MPEG-2. Renders your movie for DVD, broadcast, or PC playback. Creates compressed movies that provide options for balancing multiple output requirements.

QuickTime (.MOV). You can view these files in PC and Mac environments. This is a Web-friendly format that provides many quality vs. compression options. QuickTime movies are highly customizable. You can create multiple video layers or add interactivity and links to Web sites. QuickTime is a natural choice for videographers who want to develop video-based applications (Figure 10-22).

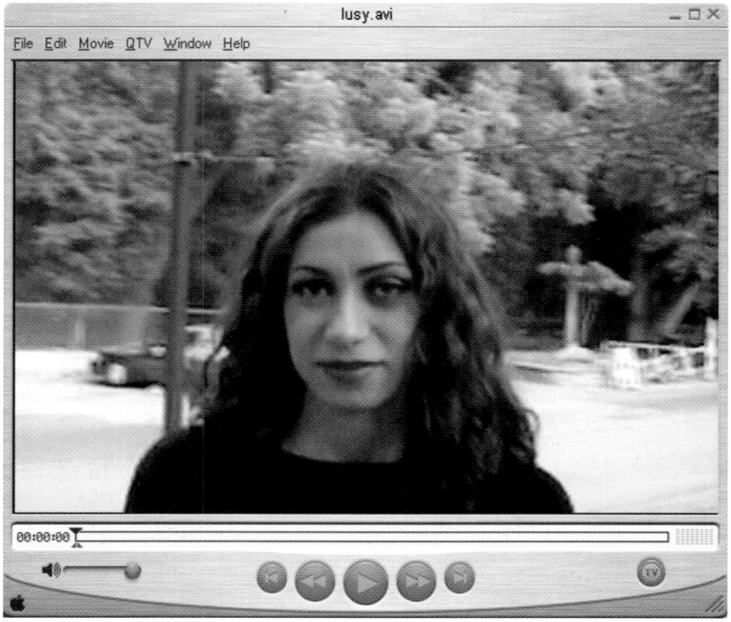
lusy.avi
File Edit Movie QTV Window Help
00:00:00

Figure 10-22 A QuickTime movie.

Video For Windows (.AVI). Universal video format for PCs running some form of the Windows operating system. .AVI movies maintain high quality even when compressed, and they are a preferred format for tape transfer, PC-based viewing, and high-speed Internet and intranet viewing.

Streaming RealVideo (.RM)/Streaming Windows Media (.WMV). Renders your movie in the most Web-efficient format. Unlike other formats, the movie will begin playback before download is complete. This means your viewers are less likely to lose patience and go on to something else before they've enjoyed your show. Allows you to select several playback speeds; for example, one for slower Internet connections and one for faster. Figure 10-23 shows a RealVideo movie.

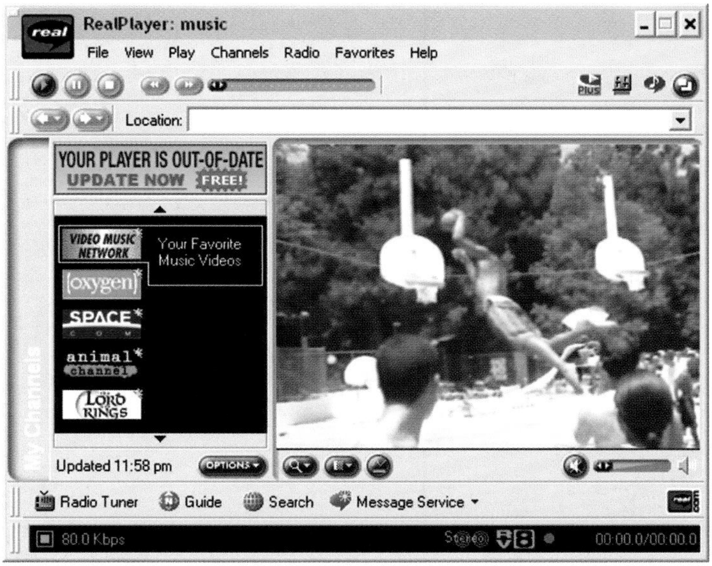
RealPlayer: music
File View Play Channels Radio Favorites Help
Location:
YOUR PLAYER IS OUT-OF-DATE
UPDATE NOW FREE!
VIDEO MUSIC NETWORK
Your Favorite Music Videos
oxygen
SPACE
animal channel
My Channels
Updated 11:58 pm
OPTIONS
Radio Tuner
Guide
Search
Message Service
80.0 Kbps
00:00.0/00:00.0

Figure 10-23 A RealVideo movie.

Customizing Video Output Options

While all video programs provide video export presets that will work fine for most uses, you will eventually find a reason to do a little customization on your own. For example, you can choose a larger frame size, slightly lower data rate, or lower-quality audio. You will make these choices to find the right balance between movie quality on one hand and portability and smooth playback on the other. The list below describes the most common customizable output options.

- **Frame Type.** Choose Frame-based for computer monitor or Digital TV viewing, and choose Field Order A or B (check broadcast specification for which one) for broadcast TV viewing.

- **Video/Audio or Video Only.** To discard all audio, choose Video Only. The results will be a silent movie, and you will save a little on file size.

◆ **Frame Rate.** Higher frames per second (fps) means higher-quality video. However, higher frames per second requires more CPU power and bandwidth.

◆ **Frame Size.** Increasing frame size makes the picture bigger, and thus, more fun to watch. However, file size and bandwidth requirements are increased as well.

◆ **Compression Type.** Some video formats allow you to choose a compression type. Each compression type has a special use, so this feature can be helpful.

◆ **Video Data Rate.** Your video can be optimized for the rate at which the playback device is likely to ask for data. High data rates, such as above 2000 Kbps, are good for high-speed Internet connections or intranet. Low data rates, such as 800 or below, are good for 56 Kbps modems or for viewing your movie during times of heavy Internet traffic.

◆ **Keyframes.** Keyframes are the frames of video that the in-between frames use as their baseline, reproducing only the data that changes in between keyframes. A higher number of keyframes means better-quality video but larger file size.

◆ **Hinted Streaming.** Hinted Streaming is a QuickTime Web video option that lets you specify which segments should be allowed more CPU power for smoother downloading.

◆ **Pad Frames for CD-ROM.** Select this option for more efficient CD-based video playback.

◆ **Interleave Audio and Video.** You can specify how many packets of video information should be stacked together in the video stream before an audio packet is added. If audio playback is particularly important, specify a high audio-to-video ratio.

◆ **Audio Bit Rate.** A high audio bit rate (in Kbps) results in better audio quality. 128 to 256 Kbps supports high-quality audio, but you will need a high-speed Internet connection to deliver it reliably.

◆ **Target Audience.** When creating RealVideo or Windows Media movies for the Web, you can specify the type of Internet connection that your audience will have.

Movie Output Options

As mentioned earlier, several video editing programs have presets that select the best compression, frames size, data rate, and other options for each output situation. The process involves selecting the project you want to export, choosing a format, and noting the location of the resulting files, so you can easily access it. Beyond this, the other requirement is patience, since rendering and exporting a movie can take a while. Let's move through the exporting process for various formats using Pinnacle Studio 8.

Pinnacle Studio 8 provides a single interface for exporting movies. To export a movie, click the **Make Movie** tab at the top of the Studio 8 screen. On the left side of the screen, there are tabs for accessing six format types: Tape, AVI, MPEG, Stream, Share, and Disc.

Tape

To output your movie to MiniDV tape using your camcorder, do the following:

1. Make sure your camcorder is connected via FireWire to your computer. It should be powered on and set to **Play/VCR** mode. Make sure the MiniDV tape currently loaded has enough tape to record your project.
2. Click the **Tape** tab at the top left.
3. Click the **Settings** tab. Make sure DV Camcorder is the selected option.

> To allow Studio 8 to start and stop recording without requiring manual handling of the camcorder, click the **Automatically Stop and Start Recording** check box.

4. Click **OK** to close the dialog box. In the Estimated size field of the Make Movie screen, note the size of your .AVI file (Figure 10-24). After verifying that the settings are correct, you are ready to record to tape.

Tape
AVI
MPEG
Stream
Share
Disc
Status
Click the Create button below to prepare your project for output to tape.
Create
Drive (C:)
Free: 8226 MB
Estimated size
120.6 MB
Video:
Audio: 16-bit stereo, 44.1 kHz
Settings...

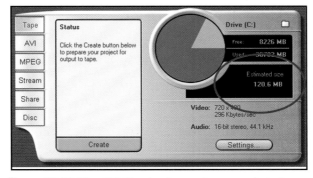

Figure 10-24 The AVI file size for saving a movie to tape should be quite large.

10

5. Click the green **Create** button (Figure 10-25). If you have not already output your project as an .AVI file, Studio 8 will immediately begin rendering the movie first.

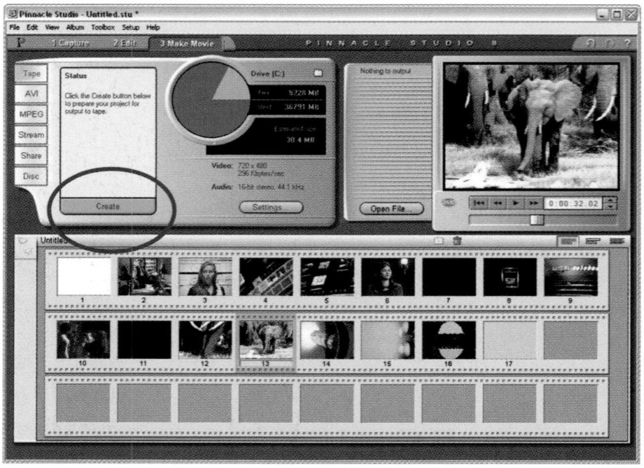

Figure 10-25 Click the Create button to start the process of saving your movie to tape.

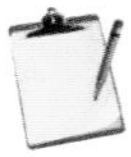

If you intend to return later and output this movie to tape rather than output it now, note the folder where the video is saved. By default, Studio 8 will save .AVI files for Tape output in C:\...\My Documents\Pinnacle Studio\Auxiliary Files.

6. Once your movie is saved as an AVI movie, it can be saved immediately to tape. To do this, just click the **Play** button on the Player. The REC indicator will appear in your camcorder's LCD screen, and you will hear the camcorder's tape transport motor kick in, indicating that tape is moving.
7. To stop recording, use the **Stop** control beneath the Player.
8. After you have played back your project, the camcorder's LCD reads STOP. You're done!

AVI

If you want to create a movie for hard drive playback on a PC-based computer, .AVI is a natural choice. The format is well-supported on most Windows platforms, and Studio 8 provides many .AVI compression options so you can create an .AVI movie for various environments and requirements. In addition, if you create your .AVI file first, it will be pre-rendered and ready to copy your movie to tape, if you so desire, as discussed in the last section.

To render your movie as an .AVI file, do the following:

1. From the Pinnacle 8 Make Movie screen, click the **AVI** tab on the far left.
2. To specify options for your movie, click the **Settings** button. The Pinnacle Studio Setup Options dialog box appears with the Make AVI File tab selected (Figure 10-26).

Pinnacle Studio Setup Options
Make tape
Make AVI File
Make MPEG File
Make RealVideo®
Make Windows Media®
Make disc
Video settings
Include video in AVI file
List all codecs
Options...
Compression:
DVSoft (TM)
Width:
Height:
Frames/second:
352
240
29.97
Percent
Audio settings
Include audio in AVI file
List all codecs
Type:
PCM
Channels:
Sample rate:
16-bit stereo
44.1 kHz
Force settings to be same as current project
Same as Project
OK
Cancel
Help

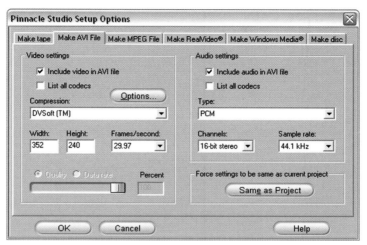

Figure 10-26 Saving a Pinnacle Studio 8 project as an .AVI file.

3. Choose a compression option. If you choose DV Video Encoder or Indeo Video 5.10, your movie will be quite large. If this is not your intention, choose one of the other compression options, such as Cinepak. To create a movie for MiniDV tape, choose DV Video Encoder.

   By default, the Compression drop-down menu does not display all of the available codecs. To see all the codecs installed on your computer, select the **List all codecs** check box.

4. After making any adjustments to your .AVI settings, click **OK**. You are now ready to create an .AVI movie.
5. Click the **Create AVI file** button. A Save As dialog appears, allowing you to specify where your movie will be saved. Note this location; this is your finished product you will be sharing with the world.
6. After clicking **OK**, the .AVI file will begin rendering. Status messages will appear on the screen, indicating when the movie is completed or if there are errors in rendering. You can monitor the rendering progress by watching the progress bar at the bottom of the Player.
7. When the bar has moved across the final scene, rendering is complete.

MPEG

MPEG movies are popular because of their small file size, good quality, and flexible playability. MPEG-2 is used for DVD and HDTV broadcast, and MPEG-1 is popular for the Web and for creating video CDs. To render your movie as an MPEG, do the following:

1. With a video project loaded, click the **Make Movie** tab located at the top of the Studio 8 screen.
2. Click the **MPEG** tab on the far left.
3. Click **Settings** to choose one of the presets or customize your compression and movie output choices. The presets, ranging from Internet Low Bandwidth to DVD Compatible, will suit most needs (Figure 10-27).

Pinnacle Studio Setup Options
Make tape
Make AVI File
Make MPEG File
Make RealVideo®
Make Windows Media®
Make disc
Presets
VideoCD
Internet Low Bandwidth
Internet High Bandwidth
VideoCD
Multimedia
VHS
SVCD Compatible
DVD Compatible
MicroMV Compatible
Custom
352 x 240
44.1 kHz
OK
Cancel
Help

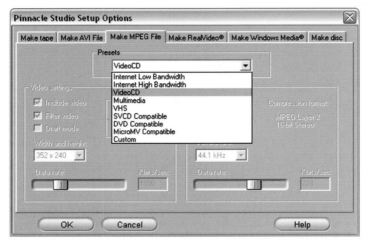

Figure 10-27 The Make MPEG File tab.

4. If you click **Custom** in the Preset list, you can select which MPEG format to use, choose a video dimension, data rate, as well as audio sampling and data rate.
5. When you are happy with your Settings, click **OK** to close the dialog box, and click the **Create MPEG file** button. A Save As menu appears, prompting you to name your movie.
6. Monitor rendering progress by noting the progress bar.
7. When rendering is finished, you can play your movie in any MPEG player, or preview it in Studio 8 by clicking the **Open a file for playback** button.

Sharing Your Movie Online

Movies destined for the Web have special requirements. Before the viewer can watch your movie, they are required to download it (or at least a portion of it), which takes time. Even if you are reasonably certain that the viewer will have a high-speed Internet connection, download speeds will still often vary depending on Internet traffic. This means that your Web-based movie should be as small and compact as possible. In this section, you will learn what makes a good Web-based movie, and how to format and save your movies for viewing on the Web or send as an e-mail attachment. We'll also touch on Internet Streaming technology and how you can create Web movies that play optimally in a number of different online environments.

Before using another's audio in your movie, always obtain permission from the property rights owner.

Making a Good Web Movie

A good Web movie will be short and to the point. You may need to return to the editing screens and remove content that is not essential to your project; for example, scenes where the camera lingers on a single subject for more than a few seconds. You will show mostly close-ups of main subjects. Keep in mind that subtleties tend to get lost in Web-based movies due to the smaller frame size (Figure 10-28 displays a movie in both the Windows Media and RealMovie players, which are both typical Web viewing environments). Also, note that transitions and special effects greatly increase movie download time. So, if you are making a point to edit your project for the Web, consider removing them.

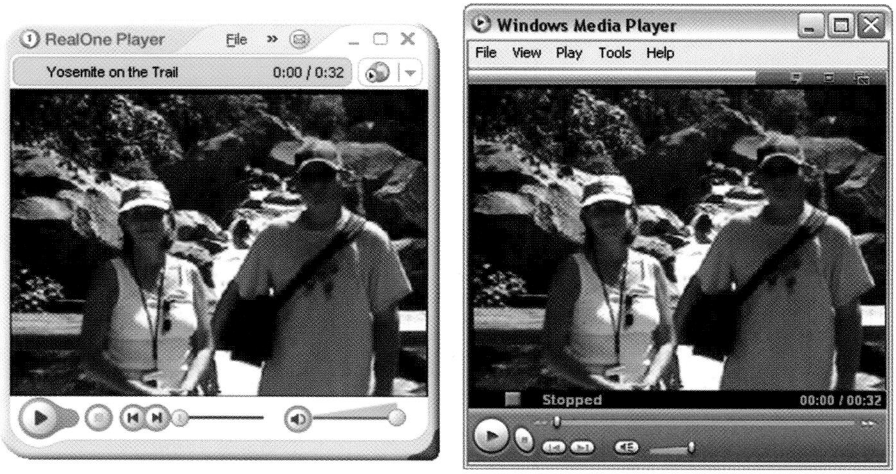
RealOne Player
File
Yosemite on the Trail
0:00 / 0:32
Windows Media Player
File View Play Tools Help
Stopped
00:00 / 00:32

Figure 10-28 A movie clip shown in both RealMovie and Windows Media players.

Let's begin with some general tips for creating Web-based videos:

✦ Before posting your video online, take the time to reduce file size, frame rate, color, and audio depth. Movies designed for 56 Kbps modem download should not be larger than 250 Kb. Movies designed for ISDN, DSL, or cable modems should not be more than about 1.5 MB.

✦ Movies with fewer colors transmit faster than films with detailed, complex images. An ideal Web-based movie shows people talking against a single-color background.

✦ Avoid using transitions. If a movie is destined for the Web, eliminate fades and just use straight cuts.

✦ Use a frame rate somewhere between six and 15 frames per second.

✦ Edit your movie ruthlessly. The Web version of your project will be much shorter in length than movies distributed through other media.

✦ Take time to experiment with audio settings. Unless music plays a huge role in your project, make your tracks mono, 12-bit at 22Hz.

 Video dimensions do not affect download times as negatively as the other factors mentioned. If you have a video at 320 x 240 pixels that you really want to post, but the file size is too large, reducing the dimensions to, say, 160 x 180 won't make much difference.

Pinnacle Studio 8 lets you create a Web-formatted movie with a Web page ready for viewing. It provides a Web site, allowing each Studio 8 owner 10 MB of video space for personal videos. All you must do is provide an e-mail address and choose a username and password. This registers you for your free Web space. Use Pinnacle Studio 8 to create your Web movie using the Share feature; choose a Web page template for your video, allow the program to upload your video, and you are done. You can e-mail the link to your online movie to anyone you wish and it can be viewed at any time.

The following describes how to share your movie online using Pinnacle Studio 8:

❶ With a video project loaded in Studio 8, click the **Make Movie** button at the top of the screen.

❷ Click the **Share** button on the left.

❸ Click the **Share** button that appears in the Status window on the left. Pinnacle will begin creating a Web-formatted movie from your project.

❹ When the movie is completed, Pinnacle will open your browser and visit the Pinnacle Studio Online Web site (You will need an open Internet connection to do this). You will be prompted to register for the site, with no fee. Studio 8 customers are provided 10 MB (about five minutes) of free storage space for movies.

5. After registering, a screen appears prompting you to choose a template for your video. After you choose a template you then see the following screen (Figure 10-29). Here, you can indicate an e-mail recipient. The recipient will get an e-mail providing a link to the movie.

Pinnacle Systems - StudioOnline - Share your Videos!
ONLINE
THE EASIEST WAY TO SHARE MOVIES ON THE INTERNET
Share your videos!
Find Out How!
DV500 PLUS
Real-time where it counts!
MY HOME
MY VIDEOS
MY ACCOUNT
ADDRESS BOOK
CALENDAR
SIGN OUT
Step 2: Personalize your Video
When you share your video with a friend, the video file isn't emailed to him. Instead, your friend will receive an email instructing them how to view your video here at StudioOnline.com
To:
Recipient name:
Recipient email
From:
Your name
Tom
Your email
tom@gway.com
Use Address Book
Notify me of pickup
Yes
No
When do you want your card sent?
Today
Caption:
Type your greeting here
Message:
Type your message here
Preview
Send
Internet

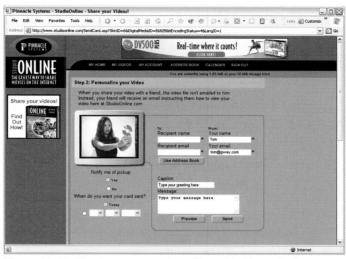

Figure 10-29 Sharing your movie online with Pinnacle Studio 8.

6. Personalize the template by adding a message.
7. Click **OK** and the movie will be uploaded to the site. The e-mail will be sent. You can send that same link to others as well, notifying as many people as you wish about your online movie.

E-mailing Your Movie

In Pinnacle Studio 8, you have the option to e-mail your movie from both the MPEG and Stream tabs under the Make Movie tab. The process is quick and easy:

1. Once your movie has been rendered, you will see a new button to the right of the **Open a file for playback** button—the **Send file by e-mail** button. Clicking it will open a dialog where you can select your new movie, or any other MPEG movie, to send via e-mail.
2. Studio 8 will launch your computer's default e-mail program—Outlook Express, for example—and attach the video to an e-mail, ready to send to whomever you wish.
3. Check the files size of the movie to make sure it is not too large for the person to whom you are sending it, then select the recipient's e-mail address and send the e-mail like you would any other e-mail.

Streaming Video

An important technology for viewing movies online is known as video streaming. Streaming allows your online movie to begin playback before it has completely downloaded. Since a movie can take a while to download, giving your viewers something to watch before download is finished is a great advantage.

There are two types of streaming technology. The most common and least expensive streaming technology allows a viewer to begin watching your movie as soon as a portion has been downloaded. Then, as data is transferred according to the connection quality and modem speed, more video will be displayed. This method is called Web Server-based, or Single-rate streaming. It is also sometimes referred to as HTTP streaming.

More advanced streaming requires the Web host to provide a Streaming server, also known as Multi-rate streaming. The company hosting your Web site may very well offer a streaming server solution if you inquire. With Multi-rate streaming, playback begins as soon as the visitor clicks on the page or clicks the Play button. Streaming servers provide an "intelligent" connection for your movie that not only begins playback as soon as the visitor views the page, but adjusts transmission of video data according to Web traffic. The server will always download your movie as fast as the connection will allow, and it is capable of delivering smooth playback in bad Internet traffic. If you want Multi-rate streaming, you will pay an extra monthly fee to your Web host and follow specific setup instructions.

Pinnacle Studio 8 will format your project as a streaming movie. There are two types: RealNetwork's RealVideo (.RM) movies, and Microsoft's Windows Media Video (.WMV). Both streaming technologies allow you to create Single-rate streaming and Multi-rate streaming.

How will you know which type of streaming movie you are creating? When you choose your streaming movie options, you will be prompted to choose a target audience; for example, 56 Kbps Modem or Dual-ISDN. Now, the dialog boxes allowing you to make this choice will let you choose more than one, and that is when you have crossed the line. If you choose more than one target audience, the program will format your movie for Multi-rate streaming. If this is your intention, you will have to get with your Web host and set up this technology. If not, then just choose one target audience for your streaming movie.

To create a RealVideo or Windows Media movie using Pinnacle Studio 8, do the following:

1. With a video project loaded, click the **Make Movie** button at the top of the Studio 8 screen.
2. Click the **Stream** tab on the left.
3. Click the **Windows Media** or **RealVideo** button (above and to the left of the Settings button), whichever format you'd prefer for your Web movie.
4. After choosing which movie type to use, click the **Settings** tab.
5. Choose playback options for your video. You can choose frame dimensions, target audience, playback and audio quality, and many other options.

6. If you choose Windows Media Player, you can opt to have File Markers that allow viewers to move between clips in your project (Figure 10-30). Your audience can preview segments of your video, rather than sit through the whole thing.

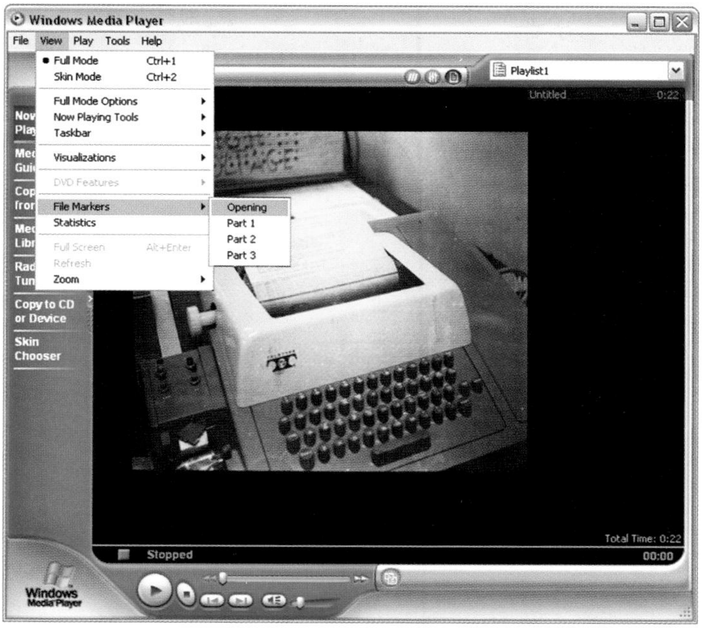
Windows Media Player
File View Play Tools Help
Full Mode Ctrl+1
Skin Mode Ctrl+2
Full Mode Options
Now Playing Tools
Taskbar
Visualizations
DVD Features
File Markers
Statistics
Full Screen Alt+Enter
Refresh
Zoom
Opening
Part 1
Part 2
Part 3
Playlist1
Untitled 0:22
Copy to CD or Device
Skin Chooser
Total Time: 0:22
Stopped
00:00
Windows Media Player

Figure 10-30 In a Windows Media movie, your movie clips can be saved as File Markers.

7. If you choose RealVideo, you can select several target audiences for your movie by selecting the RealServer option. As mentioned above, you will have to work with your Web host to set up the details of how to deploy movies with Multi-rate streaming.
8. After choosing your options, click **OK** to close the Settings dialog box.
9. Click the **Create Web** file button. A Browse dialog box appears, prompting you to choose a file name and location. After doing so, click **OK**. The video will be created.
10. When finished rendering, you can view the movie by browsing to its folder and clicking it.

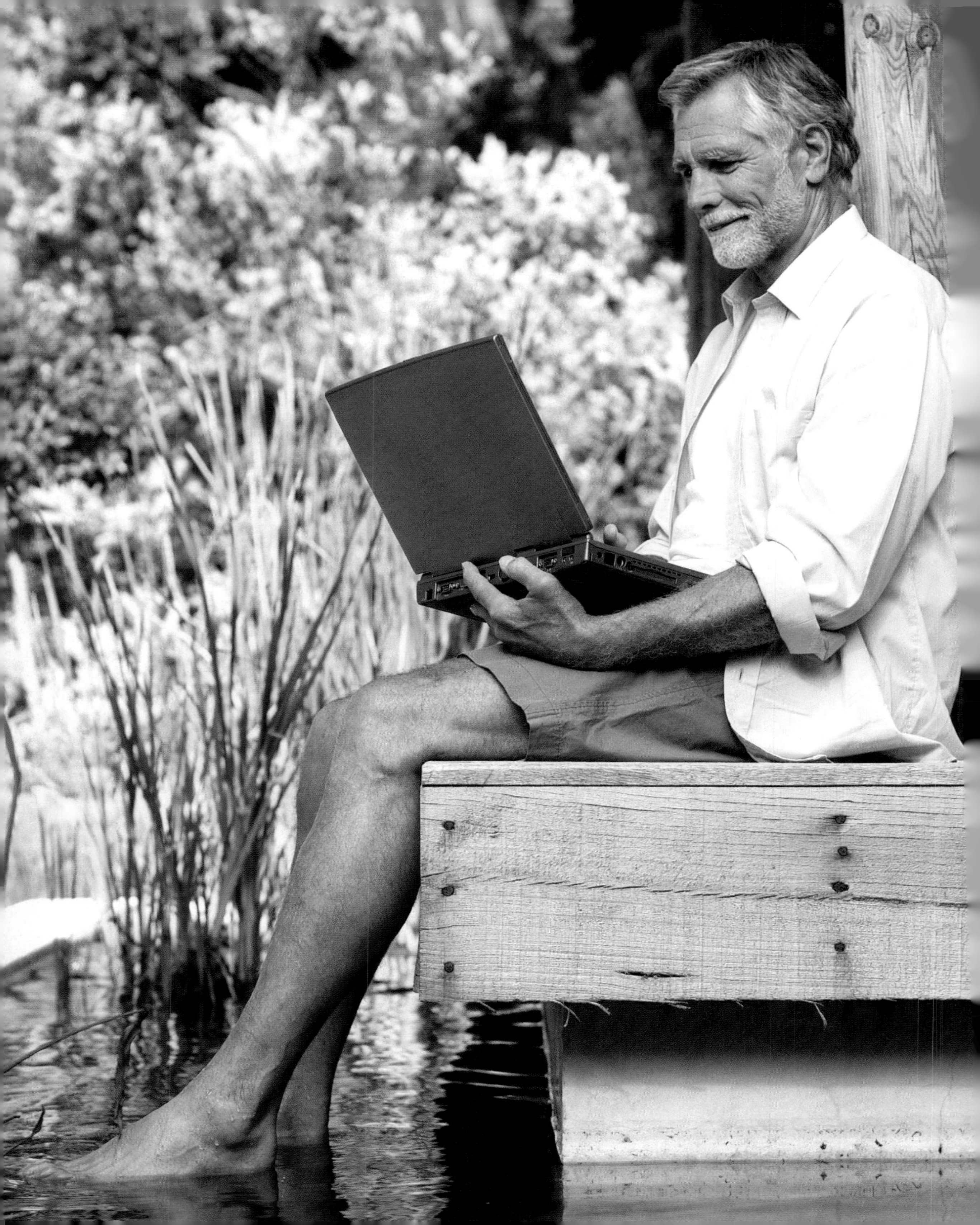

CHAPTER 11

Where Do We Go from Here?

A large portion of our population has experienced the advances in digital technology. But no matter what we have today; tomorrow we want it to do more. On top of that, we want it cheaper, faster, and more powerful. Fortunately, these desires are what fuel the digital revolution.

However, no one can really know what the future holds. Perhaps people will not even want an all-digital future, and the economy is certainly an issue to consider as well. But in spite of the uncertain nature of our technological future, many experts have confidently set out their vision of how life may be different when we are surrounded by integrated digital technologies. Whether or not this vision of the future can be realized depends on a variety of factors, including the desires of the people who will or want to be able to afford it.

The Future of Music

Everywhere you turn, you hear music. You hear music on the radio, you hear it in a restaurant, and you hear it when you're shopping. While it's not yet clear exactly how music will be distributed in the future, the possibilities are boundless. Here are a few examples:

MP3Pro

Despite all the hype that MP3 caused, there remains a significant disadvantage: the user's connection to the Internet. While many users now have a broadband connection to the Internet, for modem and ISDN users, downloading large files of several megabytes is still an exercise in patience.

An MP3 song of decent sound quality and 3 minutes long is roughly 3 megabytes in size, which for an average transfer rate of 3 to 4 kilobytes per second (56K modem) means a download time of 14 to 15 minutes. So what can be done?

Enter MP3Pro. A newer technology with better compression techniques, MP3Pro files are roughly half the size of MP3 files and provide even better sound quality than traditional MP3 files.

MPEG-4

Also known as MP4, MPEG-4 structured audio is the collective name for a set of standards which promises to revolutionize the Internet multimedia experience. The video is DVD-quality, and the audio is near CD-quality. Where an MP3 player is a portable device that plays MP3 audio files, an MP4 player is a portable device that specializes in playing MP4 files. On an MP4 player, you will be able to watch high-quality movies and music videos with awesome sound on a device that can fit in your shirt pocket! You will be able to download the video from the Internet and then transport it to your player and take the movies with you.

Since an MP4 player is essentially a computer peripheral with a hard drive, the display screen can also be used to organize digital audio music files, digital photos, or files such as word processing documents and PowerPoint presentations.

MP4 devices such as the RCA Lyra, seen in Figure 11-1, contain a built-in MPEG-4 encoder and decoder, enabling you to watch up to 80 hours of pre-recorded television shows, feature films, or home videos directly on the LCD screen.

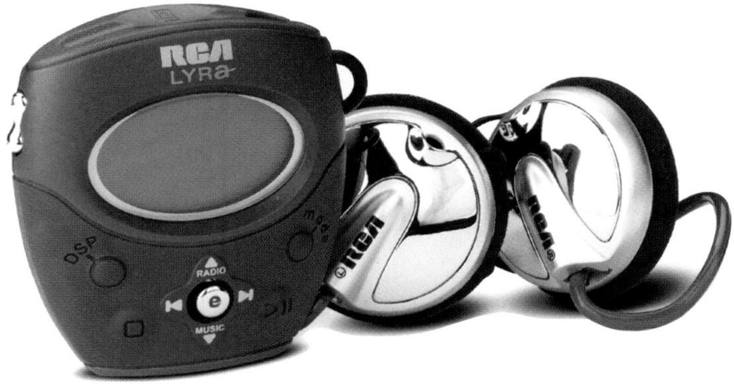
RCA
LYRA
RADIO
MUSIC

Figure 11-1 The main focus of an MP4 player is video.

What's New in Digital Photography

Manufacturers have greatly improved the quality and feature sets available on consumer model digital cameras, especially compared to early models. For starters, the resolution and sharpness of an image produced by the latest digital cameras are comparable to or better than that of a traditional photograph. Today's digital cameras are leaps and bounds beyond first-generation digital cameras of a comparable price. These devices have also become smarter; you just turn the camera on and press the button. The camera has already adjusted to the light conditions, so you'll likely end up with a great-looking picture.

Technology has improved more than just photo quality. With certain models, you can save (or stamp) data to an image, including the date, time, shutter speed, whether the flash was used, and more. Although including the date and time on the actual print is nothing new, the expanded amount of data saved behind the scenes is valuable when it comes time for you or a photo processor to print the image. Some cameras can even use data from a global positioning system to record the exact place you were on the planet when the picture was taken!

Many new high-end digital cameras can save images in a format called RAW, instead of the typical JPEG or TIFF formats. RAW format, which means exactly what it sounds like, provides raw data straight from the camera's image sensors. JPEG or TIFF formats provide the final image in a format that has already been processed by the electronics within the camera, while RAW is all of the data that the camera has collected, with no processing at all. By saving images as RAW data, you can use your PC software to provide the processing instead of the less-powerful camera computer.

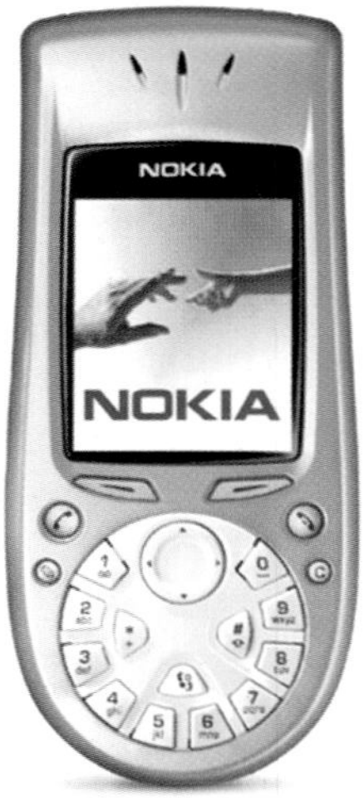
NOKIA
NOKIA
Figure 11-2 Immediately e-mail an image to a friend.

Recently, digital cameras have started showing up as peripherals on portable devices such as PDAs and cellular phones (Figure 11-2). This capability houses tremendous potential. You can take pictures, view them with the device's monitor, and send them to another compatible phone or PDA.

Expect faster, better camera computer chips. Digital cameras have a light-sensitive chip which splits the light coming into your camera into red, green, and blue components. Each color gets forced off to its own sensor, and then when you take a photograph, the camera computer has to integrate the separate color images back into a full-color one. The result can be a less-than-film-crisp image. A new chip, rapidly gaining in popularity, can capture all three bands of light—red, blue, and green—in one single pixel. Basically, the sensors are stacked on top of each other. The new chip design will also require less light and energy, and produce a much, much sharper image. The new chip will generate sharpness and color accuracy about twice that of 35mm film.

If the advancements of recent years are any indication of the future, you can expect to see more amazing breakthroughs soon.

Other Upcoming Digital Items

Living in the digital age means improved, easier-to-use everyday devices that streamline our daily tasks and enhance our lives. Here are a few new and upcoming digital trends:

✦ **Wearable computers.** A wearable computer is a *very* personal computer. Clothing, known as smart clothing, is becoming available and will have built-in mobile phones, digital music players, or even personal computers.

✦ **Emergency clothing.** Does your underwear cry for help? German researchers have developed electronic underwear that not only monitors vital signs but also calls emergency services when help is needed. Sensors woven into the underwear monitor the heartbeat of people with existing heart conditions. A microprocessor unit analyzes the signals to look for signs of dangerous heart rhythms. If it detects trouble, it automatically calls for medical assistance via a Bluetooth-enabled mobile phone.

✦ **Gizmo watches.** A plethora of new watches are becoming available. Look for watches that have built-in digital cameras or watches that provide e-mail access, news, weather, sports, stock market reports, restaurant listings, and much more.

✦ **Electronic jewelry.** Some upcoming jewelry will have a digital photo viewer built in. You can use the infrared port to upload photos directly onto the wearable display.

✦ **Electronic paper.** Electronic, reusable paper is a display material that has many of the properties of paper. It stores an image, is viewed in reflective light, has a wide viewing angle, is flexible, and is relatively inexpensive. Unlike conventional paper, however, it is electrically writeable and erasable.

11

✦ **Smart appliances.** Connectivity will extend beyond the range of devices that we currently use. For example, refrigerators and microwave ovens will have permanent connections to the Internet, making it possible to do your shopping or send and receive emails from your kitchen. Sunbeam® is developing a group of appliances that will modernize your house, including daily essentials such as a coffee maker, electric blanket, smoke detector, stand mixer, bathroom scale, and blood pressure monitor. All of these can be controlled with a kitchen console that can be used to control every applicable appliance in your home.

With all these new devices in our future, isn't this a great time to be alive?

Glossary

Adobe® Photoshop Album® A popular program used to track, store, and manage your digital images. This is a third-party program and must be purchased separately from Windows XP.

Adobe® Photoshop Elements® A popular software application used to edit and manipulate your digital images. This is a third-party program and must be purchased separately from Windows XP.

amplifier A device that increases the amplitude, power, or current of a signal. The resulting signal is a reproduction of the original with this increase.

analog Sounds created continuously, without any breaks used to carry information (such as by modems over telephone lines) or produce audio (such as with some speakers).

anti-virus A program that continually scans your system for any sign of virus infection. These types of programs can also scan each file you download to make sure it's not infected.

aperture The opening of a lens which exposes each frame of film or video. It's also the light-gathering area of a lens.

autorun A program that automatically opens a file or begins an installation routine when a CD is placed in a computer's CD-ROM drive.

AVI (audio-video interleaved) The file format used by Windows for video. AVI is the video format created by Microsoft for digitizing and compressing video and audio signals. AVI movies employ a number of codecs and compression schemes that support the Windows operation system.

bandwidth Measured in MHz, the range of signal frequencies that a video recording or playback device can encode or decode. Also, the amount of information that can be carried by a signal path, such as downloaded content via telephone lines over the Internet.

battery compartment The slot on a camera where the batteries are stored.

binary A system used by computers of representing numbers that uses only two digits: 0 and 1.

bit The smallest unit of data in a computer system.

bit rate A measure of digital file compression. The number of bits (small size of space on your computer) used for each second of music. 128 Kbps is commonly referred to as CD quality. Files compressed at a lower bit rate are smaller in file size and lower in sound quality.

BMP This is the format used for Microsoft Paint. BMP files can be up to 16.8 million colors and are larger than JPEG files.

broadband A type of network connection supporting a wide range of transmission frequencies. In other words, a connection medium that can support multiple simultaneous connections. For example, cable modems and DSL are broadband technologies used to gain Internet access.

buffer A designated area of memory that playback and recording devices use to pre-load material in order to maintain a consistent stream of data to the player or recorder.

burners Burning simply means recording a CD. This term can refer to either the CD recorder drive in your computer or the software program used to collect tracks and initiate the recording process.

burning a CD The process of writing data to a CD-R or CD-RW.

byte A unit of data that is 8 bits long, the most fundamental unit of computer data. A byte usually represents a single text character or the red, green, or blue component of an image pixel.

cable modem A method of delivering broadband Internet access using a cable jack connection.

camcorder A device combining camera, tape, or DVD recorder and playback monitoring screen into one unit.

camera option buttons Buttons on a digital camera that enable the user to move among camera commands or pictures stored in the camera's memory.

cassette tape adapter A device that allows for connection between a portable device, such as a portable digital music player, and a cassette tape player. These adapters are often used to connect a portable device to a car stereo.

CD (compact disc) A medium-capacity optical storage medium; CDs are like DVDs, but store only 650 and 700 MB of data, which may be audio or video, but is likely to be software or other data.

CDDB Powered by Gracenote®, the CDDB is an online database that catalogs album information. It can be used by programs to automatically find and display the album, title, and artist information for the CD you are playing.

CD-R (compact disc-recordable) A CD storage medium that can be recorded only once, but can be played or read many times.

CD-ROM (compact disc-read only memory) A CD storage medium that uses the same type of discs you play in your audio CD player to store computer programs and files; you can read from CD-ROM discs but you cannot write to them.

CD-ROM drive A device that reads CDs. CD-ROM is a read-only medium; the "ROM" in its name stands for Read-Only Memory.

CD-RW (compact disc-rewritable) A CD storage medium on which data can be stored and then erased as needed; thus, CD-RW discs are reusable.

clip A digitized or captured portion of video, sometimes further defined by setting In and Out points.

closed The final stage of recording data to a disc (CD or DVD), which makes a recordable disc readable on an ordinary CD or DVD drive.

codec (Contraction for Compression/ Decompression) Represents the combining of COmpression and DECcompression technologies, allowing compressed video to be played back in real time, rather than waiting for an entire video to decompress before playback can begin.

composition The organization of subject and background in a photograph; the way you compose your image.

compressed The state of a file that has been reduced in size, commonly without noticeable loss in sound quality.

compression The conversion of media data to a more compact form for efficient storage or transmission, requiring less storage space than the original data.

connection port An interface on a computer to which you can connect devices with cables, plugs, and other connectors.

copyright Laws designed to protect the creation of original works and their owners (including artistic, musical, literary, dramatic, and other intellectual works).

CPU (central processing unit) The main processor chip on a computer's motherboard—not the whole system unit. It interprets and carries out instructions, performs computations, and controls the devices connected to the computer.

crop To remove a portion of an image.

cutout A region cropped from an image, usually to be pasted into another image. The boundaries of the cutout area are either drawn manually or selected with an image-editing program's automatic selection tools.

data compression A way to make a file smaller while still retaining much of the original quality. Data compression is used to conserve storage space or improve transmission time.

data rate The amount of data moved through a pathway over a specified period of time, used to describe the efficiency of data transmission in a given situation using a given technology.

depth of field When focusing a camera, the depth of the area in which all objects are in focus, dependent on the distance of the camera to the subject, focal length of the lens, and f-stop.

device driver A special type of software that allows a specific hardware device to communicate with a PC. Without a device driver, hardware devices won't work. Sometimes called a driver.

digital Electronic technology that generates, stores, and processes data in terms of two states: positive and non-positive. Positive is represented by the number 1 and non-positive by the number 0.

digital album Like a conventional photo album, a way to present and arrange pictures in an order you choose.

digital bits An electronic equivalent of a 1 or a 0 representing small bursts of information. A stream of digital bits can be used to represent an audio signal or computer communications over a wire.

digital image Any image that has been created by a source, such as a digital camera, and converted electronically to be viewed on screen. *See also* pixel; scanner.

digital music player A software player program that plays music on a computer. Also, a portable, car, or home stereo component capable of playing digital music.

digital recording The process of measuring, or "sampling," sound waves and converting them to a series of zeros and ones capable of being played back with a digital music player.

digital zoom Magnifying an image by electronically enlarging selected pixels, rather than changing lens focal point and length. Digital zoom introduces distortion into an image, or video, and should be used with caution.

download To acquire digital information from another computer or network of computers (usually over the Internet). Also, files acquired over the Internet and saved to a computer are also often referred to as downloads.

dpi (dots per inch) The standard measurement of resolution used with printed images. Generally, a higher dpi indicates higher resolution. *See also* resolution.

driver A file that tells the Windows operating system the details of a particular hardware component, such as a printer, digital camera, or scanner. When the component is installed on a computer, a driver for it is copied to the computer.

DSL (Digital Subscriber Line) A method of delivering broadband Internet access using a regular phone line connection.

DTV (digital television) A digital television signal providing an extremely sharp picture.

DVD (digital versatile disc) A high-capacity optical storage medium, a DVD looks the same as a CD, but can store between 4.7 and 17 GB of data which may be audio, video (it's a preferred format for movies), or other information.

DVD-R (digital versatile disc-recordable) A DVD storage medium that can be written to only once. DVD recorders and discs use much narrower tracks than those used on CDs, allowing them to store up to seven times more data than CDs.

DVD-RAM (digital versatile disc-random access memory) A storage technology for computers that uses a type of disc similar to those used in a TV's DVD player. DVD-RAM discs can be read and written many times, so they may be used like a computer's hard disk drive.

e-mail Any of a number of messaging systems used on the Internet. E-mail may be plain text, but messages can include pictures, formatting, and animation. You can also attach just about any kind of file to an e-mail message.

encoder A program that changes a file from one format to another. For example, there are encoders that can change a WAV file to an MP3 file.

EXIF (Extended File Format) A format used by digital cameras to store additional information, such as the date, time, or whether the flash was used, along with the image data. This data can be accessed while editing the image.

expansion card A computer component installed inside the computer, usually to an ISA or PCI slot. An internal sound card is an expansion card.

exposure The process of exposing a camera's image sensor or film to light to create an image. Exposure is affected by settings such as focus, aperture, and shutter speed.

file extension A three-letter code following the period on a file name and indicates the type of file. The extension usually refers either to a method of compression (.zip, .mp3, .wma), or its associated program (.doc = Microsoft Word, .xls = Microsoft Excel).

file format The method used to store data in a file. Different types of programs use different file formats. For example, audio programs use audio file formats, and word processors use document file formats.

firewall A software program that blocks certain types of Internet traffic.

FireWire Data transfer technology that facilities high-speed transfer of large data amounts, e.g., video. FireWire data transfer requires devices with FireWire connections, a FireWire cable, and a computer with a FireWire card.

flash A device used to produce a bright flash of light to illuminate the subject of a photograph.

flatbed scanner A scanner that converts text or images into digital files using a moving light source similar to that used by a copier. Flatbed scanners are the most common type of scanner. *See also* scanner.

frequency The number of times per second audio is sampled. CDs use a frequency of 44,100Hz, which means there are 41,100 packets of information used to store each second of music.

GIF A digital image file format used mostly for Web graphics.

gigabyte (GB) A unit of computer memory or data storage capacity equal to 1,024 megabytes.

graphic equalizer Controls that allows you to adjust the volume of specific frequency ranges independently.

hard drive The internal storage device responsible for storing your operating system, programs, documents, and other files. External hard drives, such as those inside some portable digital music players (hard drive players), are capable of storing thousands of songs.

hardware All physical objects or devices attached to a PC, including the monitor, keyboard, mouse, printer, and the system unit itself qualify as hardware.

hue The differentiation between RGB colors. In video editing, the adjusting of video color along the RGB color wheel, usually by use of a slider that moves the entire spectrum of colors used in the video to a new location along the RGB color wheel.

image-editing program A program that enables the user to view, edit, and print digital images.

inkjet printer A printer that produces output by spraying microscopic drops of ink onto the paper as it passes through the printer. Most inkjet printers can print both color and black images.

interlaced Video produced by capturing every other line of an image, or every other frame of the video. Video frames are played back quickly enough to produce the illusion of a complete image per frame.

Internet A physical network of millions of computers around the world. This network allows the computers to communicate back and forth. Also called the information superhighway.

Internet Explorer A Web browser you can use to surf Web sites located on the Internet throughout the world.

Internet radio Live audio broadcasts that can be listened to using a streaming audio player. Also called Webcasting.

ISP (Internet service provider) A company that provides Internet access to subscribers.

KB (kilobyte) In digital video, used when calculating storage or transmission requirements. 1 KB = 1024 bytes.

laser printer A printer that produces output by using lasers to adhere and bond a powdered toner onto paper. Laser printers produce detailed high-quality images.

LCD (liquid crystal display) An LCD screen on a digital camera or camcorder that displays pictures and messages.

Mbps (megabits per second) Stands for one million bits per second, or 125,000 bytes per second. Used to measure data transfer speed.

media Individual items, such as floppy disks, CD-Rs, CD-RWs, DVD-Rs, tapes, or Zip/Jaz cartridges, that you can insert into or remove from a removable storage device.

media card Removable solid-state media storage that can be used in a portable device such as a digital music player or digital camera. Flash and SmartMedia are two popular media card types.

media library The feature available on many software players, including Windows Media Player, that allows you to consolidate music on your computer, create playlists, and perform other organizational tasks.

media slot A slot in a digital camera into which a media card can be inserted. *See also* media card.

megabyte (MB) A unit of computer memory or data storage equal to 1,048,576 bytes. In terms of digital images, 1 megabyte is about the disk space required to store one 5×7 inch print-quality digital image, and in terms of digital music, one minute of music in MP3 format (encoded at 128Kbps) occupies about 1 megabyte of storage space.

megapixel One million pixels. Megapixel is the unit used to measure digital camera quality; there are one-, two- and four-megapixel (and higher) cameras. *See also* pixel.

memory *See* RAM.

menu button A button on a digital camera that enables the user to access camera commands for setting the date, selecting the resolution, and so on.

microphone An instrument for converting sound waves into electrical energy. On your computer's microphone, the electric current is fed from the microphone to the soundcard, where it's converted to digital form. The jack on a sound card that accepts a microphone.

Microsoft® Picture It!® A popular program used to store, manage, edit, and manipulate your digital images. Microsoft Picture It! is included with the Microsoft Works program or can be purchased separately.

mode A setting that affects how a digital camera works. Modes include picture mode, for taking pictures, and playback (review) mode, for reviewing pictures. Mode names vary from camera to camera.

modem A device that allows a PC to communicate with other PCs using a standard phone line. A modem can be an expansion card installed inside the system unit or an external device connected via a USB or serial cable.

MP3 (MPEG 1 Audio Layer 3) A compressed digital audio file format. With their small size and high sound quality, this file format is the most common for storage on a computer and distribution over the Internet.

MP3 player *See* portable digital music player.

MPEG (Motion Pictures Experts Group) A working group of the International Organization for Standardization (ISO) that has defined several video and audio standards for digital technologies. MPEG also refers to an efficient and popular compression scheme developed by the same organization.

open To make an image available to be edited.

operating system (OS) The fundamental software that runs on a PC (or other computer) to create a working computing environment that supports access to the hardware, and permits other programs (word processing, Web browser, e-mail client, and so forth) to run.

optical zoom A lens on a film-based or digital camera that can be used to change the range of space captured by the camera's film or image sensor while keeping the image in focus. *See also* digital zoom.

Outlook Express A Microsoft e-mail program that enables you to read and send e-mail to anyone with an address on the Internet.

overexposing A condition in which too much light reaches the film, resulting in light, undefined images.

passport An electronic identification badge that provides access to sites and services on the Internet through a single log on or account.

PCI slot Connection slot to a type of expansion bus found in most personal computers. Most video capture cards require this connection type.

PDA (Personal Digital Assistant) A portable computer designed to act as an organizer, note taker, communication device, and so forth. PDAs are fast, functional, and include various user-friendly applications to help you organize business and personal activities.

PDF (Portable Document Format) PDF files, which can be viewed with Adobe Acrobat Reader, are often used for Web pages and transfer over the Internet.

Pinnacle Studio A popular video-editing software program used to edit and manage your digital video. This is a third-party program and must be purchased separately from Windows XP.

pixel A tiny dot of light, which is the basic unit of measurement for images on a computer screen or in a digital image.

playlist A custom compilation of music tracks that play in a specified order. You can create, organize, and play playlists using software players on your computer. Many portable digital music players and digital car audio players are also capable of organizing tracks into playlists.

Plug and Play setup A set of specifications developed by Intel for automatic configuration of a computer to work with various devices, such as digital cameras.

port An opening on the back or front of a computer into which a cable can be plugged to connect a printer, digital camera, or other hardware component. Port types include parallel (or LPT) ports, serial ports, and USB (universal serial bus) ports.

portable digital music player A portable device capable of playing digital music. These devices include dual-mode CD/MP3 players, media card players, and hard drive players.

printer A device that prints text or graphical images from a computer. A printer can produce black or color output on paper and typically connects to a PC using a parallel or USB port.

PSD (Photoshop Format) This is the native format of Adobe Photoshop and Adobe Photoshop Elements. Files saved in this format can be opened in Photoshop products. Some other image-editing programs are also capable of opening PSD files.

RAM (Random Access Memory) Temporarily stores data, software, and the operating system while a computer is operating; everything in RAM is temporary.

red-eye A common flaw in photographs in which eyes are displayed and printed as red. Most image-editing programs can correct this problem.

resolution The measure of a digital image's quality. For scanners, resolution is measured in ppi. For printers, resolution is measured in dpi. Generally, a higher dpi indicates higher resolution. For cameras, resolution is measured by megapixel.

RGB (red, green, blue) The three primary colors used to display color on a computer monitor or television screen.

ripping The process of creating a digital audio file on your computer's hard drive from a song on a music CD.

rotate To adjust an image. This can be used to correct images that were scanned at an unsatisfactory angle.

sampling The process of converting analog sound to digital bits.

satellite radio Radio broadcasted digitally using satellites. A central broadcasting station transmits data to satellites, which in turn transmit the broadcast to special receivers, usually located in cars or in home stereos, which descramble the encrypted digital signal and convert it to analog sound. XM Radio, Sirius, and WorldSpace are three existing satellite radio service providers.

save To copy an image to permanent storage. It's a good idea to save your original image and then work from a copy.

scanner A hardware component that can convert documents and pictures into digital files. See also sheet feed scanner, flatbed scanner, film scanner, and handheld scanner.

search The process of searching for something either locally or over the Internet, such as people, songs, or programs.

search engine An Internet program that performs its search against Internet content. It uses automated software tools known as spiders, robots, or crawlers to create and maintain a database of information about the Internet. The spiders, robots, or crawlers download nontrivial content from every single Web page they can find on the Internet.

shutter button A button on a camera that the user presses to take a picture. It is almost always on the top of the camera.

skin A software player interface. A variety of skins can be applied to many software players to adjust the size, appearance, and available controls.

slide shows Presenting pictures where each of the images is displayed full-screen on your computer, one after another.

software player A digital music player program that plays music on a computer. These programs are also sometimes capable of organizing playlists, organizing music, burning CDs, and additional features. Examples are Windows Media Player, MusicMatch Jukebox, and Winamp.

sound card A hardware component that converts data in an audio file to sound. Sound cards can be integrated into a motherboard, installed in a computer's PCI/ISA port, or connected to an external USB or FireWire (IEEE 1394) port.

speakers Devices that produce audio output from a PC. Through speakers or a set of headphones, you can hear operating-system sounds, music, sound effects, and so forth.

spyware Programs that hide in the background while you're connected for file-swapping; they collect information about your surfing habits.

storyboard In video-editing programs, the layout of video clips as thumbnails, facilitating easy re-sequencing of the clips by repositioning the thumbnails.

streaming The process of sending video over the Web or other networks to allow playback on the desktop as the video is received rather than requiring the entire file to be downloaded prior to playback.

streaming audio A delivery means by which a multimedia presentation can be played while it continues to download. This is also called "streaming."

streaming audio player A multimedia player software that can be installed onto your computer. This is a type of computer program that enables you to listen to a sound file even before it has finished being downloaded to your machine or, in the case of Internet radio, to listen to a continuous sound file.

subscription music services Internet sites that enable users to download multimedia files for a fee.

system requirements Refers to the minimum components necessary to run a software program or use a hardware device. Examples are operating system, CPU speed, RAM, and available hard drive space.

tag Information, such as a category or description, assigned to an image that allows you to find it easily using image-management software. When used with audio files, track describes information associated with a track, including artist, album, and song title.

throughput A rating of how much data can be sent or received by a device within a specific amount of time; normally measured in Kbps, Mbps, or Gbps.

TIFF (Tagged Image File Format) A high-quality digital image format often used for pictures appearing in printed publications.

timeline In video-editing programs, the layout of video clips as filmstrips, showing the length of time each video clip is on the screen. Facilitates cutting and pasting video segments by using time markers for making cuts.

track On an audio CD, or in a digital media player, a track is a single section of audio you can jump to immediately.

TWAIN The official technical standard for scanning images. Almost all scanners come with a TWAIN driver.

Ulead VideoStudio A popular video-editing software program used to edit and manage your digital video. This is a third-party program and must be purchased separately from Windows XP.

underexposing A condition in which too little light reaches the film, resulting in dark, undefined images.

URL (Universal Resource Locator) A special kind of Internet address that you must supply to access a Web site.

USB (Universal Serial Bus) A common method of connecting a computer to peripherals, including external storage devices such as portable digital music players, external sound cards, keyboards, digital cameras, and other devices. USB connections deliver power to the external device, eliminating the need for an additional AC adapter power source in many cases.

video capture To transfer video from camcorder to computer, storing the video on hard drive. After capture, the video is available for digital editing.

viewfinder On a camera or video camcorder, a single-eye eyepiece for previewing and monitoring video recording.

virus A program, often mislabeled or automatically launched from another application, that transfers itself typically between e-mail users, with the intention of causing harm to users' computers, such as changing or deleting files on a hard drive, causing the computer to crash, or causing other undesirable results. All viruses are created intentionally, but anti-virus software can be used to guard against computer viruses.

visualizations Cool-looking graphics that may move in time to the music and appear on most media players.

WAV Uncompressed audio format that is extremely high in sound quality but occupies about 10 MB per minute of audio. This is the format generally used for burning to a CD.

WAV file A digital file of sound data. The .WAV format is native to Windows-based PCs and is thus very widespread and popular.

Web browser A software utility used to access the World Wide Web.

Web page A document formatted for viewing over the Internet through a Web browser A Web page often includes links to other Web pages or Web sites.

Web server A computer on the Internet that houses one or more Web sites; Web browsers communicate with Web servers to access Web pages.

Web site A collection of online documents maintained by a group or an individual that addresses one or more topics.

Webcasting *See* Internet radio.

Windows Media Player A utility program included with Windows XP that can play back many types of music and video files, Internet radio, Internet TV, CDs, and DVDs.

Windows Movie Maker A video-editing application included with Microsoft Windows XP. If you have a video input card or a digital video camera with USB or FireWire connections, you can use Windows Movie Maker to create your own customized home videos.

wizard A Windows feature that leads the user through a process step by step. For example, the Add Scanner or Camera Wizard enables the user to install a new scanner or digital camera.

WMA (Windows Media Audio) Developed to compete with MP3, this compressed file format boasts higher sound quality for audio files encoded at lower bit rates.

worm Similar to a virus, a computer program that copies itself to many computers on a network such as the Internet, causing a slowdown in transmission speeds.

zip A file or number of files compressed and packaged into a single file of a smaller file size. In Windows XP, these files usually look like a file with a zipper down the middle and can be decompressed by simply moving them out of the compressed folder.

zoom Magnifying an area of a photo or video scene by centering that area into view and increasing the lens length (or digitally increasing image detail of that area). This is carried out by pressing the camera or camcorder's Zoom button.

Index

A

B

C

W

X

Y

Z

GATEWAY, INC. END-USER LICENSE AGREEMENT

IMPORTANT - READ CAREFULLY: This End-User License Agreement (EULA) is a legal agreement between you (either an individual or an ent the End-User, and Gateway, Inc. ("Gateway") governing your use of any non-Microsoft software you acquired from Gateway collectively, the "SOFTWARE PRODUCT".

The **SOFTWARE PRODUCT** includes computer software, the associated media, any printed materials, and any "online" or electronic documentation. By turning on the system, opening the shrinkwrapped packaging, copying or otherwise using the **SOFTWARE PRODUCT**, you agree to be bound by the terms of this EULA. If you do not agree to the terms of this EULA, Gateway is unwilling to license the **SOFTWARE PRODUCT** to you. In such event, you may not use or copy the **SOFTWARE PRODUCT**, and you should promptly contact Gateway for instructi on returning it.

SOFTWARE PRODUCT LICENSE

The SOFTWARE PRODUCT is protected by copyright laws and international copyright treaties, as well as other intellectual property laws and treaties. The SOFTWARE PRODUC licensed, not sold.

1. **GRANT OF LICENSE.** This EULA grants you the following rights:
   - **Software**. If not already pre-installed, you may install and use one copy of the SOFTWARE PRODUCT on one Gateway COMPUTER, ("COMPUTER").
   - **Storage/Network Use**. You may also store or install a copy of the computer software portion of the SOFTWARE PRODUCT on the COMPUTER to allow your other compu to use the SOFTWARE PRODUCT over an internal network, and distribute the SOFTWARE PRODUCT to your other computers over an internal network. However, you mu acquire and dedicate a license for the SOFTWARE PRODUCT for each computer on which the SOFTWARE PRODUCT is used or to which it is distributed. A license for the SOFTWARE PRODUCT may not be shared or used concurrently on different computers.
   - **Back-up Copy**. If Gateway has not included a back-up copy of the SOFTWARE PRODUCT with the COMPUTER, you may make a single back-up copy of the SOFTWARE PRODUCT. You may use the back-up copy solely for archival purposes.

2. **DESCRIPTION OF OTHER RIGHTS AND LIMITATIONS.**
   - **Limitations on Reverse Engineering, Decompilation and Disassembly**. You may not reverse engineer, decompile, or disassemble the SOFTWARE PRODUCT, except a only to the extent that such activity is expressly permitted by applicable law notwithstanding this limitation.
   - **Separation of Components**. The SOFTWARE PRODUCT is licensed as a single product. Its component parts and any upgrades may not be separated for use on more than one computer.
   - **Single COMPUTER**. The SOFTWARE PRODUCT is licensed with the COMPUTER as a single integrated product. The SOFTWARE PRODUCT may only be used with the COMPUTER.
   - **Rental**. You may not rent or lease the SOFTWARE PRODUCT.
   - **Software Transfer.** You may permanently transfer all of your rights under this EULA only as part of a sale or transfer of the COMPUTER, provided you retain no copies, you transfer all of the SOFTWARE PRODUCT (including all component parts, the media and printed materials, any upgrades, this EULA, and the Certificate(s) of Authenticity), if applicable, and the recipient agrees to the terms of this EULA. If the SOFTWARE PRODUCT is an upgrade, any transfer must include all prior versions of the SOFTWARE PRODUCT.
   - **Termination**. Without prejudice to any other rights, Gateway may terminate this EULA if you fail to comply with the terms and conditions of this EULA. In such event, you mu destroy all copies of the SOFTWARE PRODUCT and all of its component parts.
   - **Language Version Selection.** Gateway may have elected to provide you with a selection of language versions for one or more of the Gateway software products licensed under this EULA. If the SOFTWARE PRODUCT is included in more than one language version, you are licensed to use only one of the language versions provided. As part the setup process for the SOFTWARE PRODUCT you will be given a one-time option to select a language version. Upon selection, the language version selected by you will set up on the COMPUTER, and the language version(s) not selected by you will be automatically and permanently deleted from the hard disk of the COMPUTER.

3. **COPYRIGHT.** All title and copyrights in and to the SOFTWARE PRODUCT (including but not limited to any images, photographs, animations, video, audio, music, text and "applets," incorporated into the SOFTWARE PRODUCT), the accompanying printed materials, and any copies of the SOFTWARE PRODUCT, are owned by Gateway or its licensors or suppliers. You may not copy the printed materials accompanying the SOFTWARE PRODUCT. All rights not specifically granted under this EULA are reserved by Gateway and its licensors or suppliers.

4. **DUAL-MEDIA SOFTWARE.** You may receive the SOFTWARE PRODUCT in more than one medium. Regardless of the type or size of medium you receive, you may use only one medium that is appropriate for the COMPUTER. You may not use or install the other medium on another COMPUTER. You may not loan, rent, lease, or otherwise transfer th other medium to another user, except as part of the permanent transfer (as provided above) of the SOFTWARE PRODUCT.

5. **PRODUCT SUPPORT.** Refer to the particular product's documentation for product support. Should you have any questions concerning this EULA, or if you desire to contact Gateway for any other reason, please refer to the address provided in the documentation for the COMPUTER.

6. **U.S. GOVERNMENT RESTRICTED RIGHTS.** The SOFTWARE PRODUCT and any accompanying documentation are and shall be deemed to be "commercial computer softw and "commercial computer software documentation," respectively, as defined in DFAR 252.227-7013 and as described in FAR 12.212. Any use, modification, reproduction, rele performance, display or disclosure of the SOFTWARE PRODUCT and any accompanying documentation by the United States Government shall be governed solely by the t of this Agreement and shall be prohibited except to the extent expressly permitted by the terms of this Agreement.

7. **LIMITED WARRANTY.** Gateway warrants that the media on which the SOFTWARE PRODUCT is distributed is free from defects in materials and workmanship for a period ninety (90) days from your receipt thereof. Your exclusive remedy in the event of any breach of the foregoing warranty shall be, at Gateway's sole option, either (a) a refund amount you paid for the SOFTWARE PRODUCT or (b) repair or replacement of such media, provided that you return the defective media to Gateway within ninety (90) day your receipt thereof. The foregoing warranty shall be void if any defect in the media is a result of accident, abuse or misapplication. Any replacement media will be warran set forth above for the remainder of the original warranty period or thirty (30) days from your receipt of such replacement media, whichever is longer. EXCEPT AS EXPRE SET FORTH HEREIN, GATEWAY, ITS SUPPLIERS OR LICENSORS HEREBY DISCLAIMS ALL WARRANTIES, EXPRESS, IMPLIED AND STATUTORY, IN CONNECT THE SOFTWARE PRODUCT AND ANY ACCOMPANYING DOCUMENTATION, INCLUDING WITHOUT LIMITATION THE IMPLIED WARRANTIES OF MERCHANTABIL NON-INFRINGEMENT OF THIRD-PARTY RIGHTS, AND FITNESS FOR A PARTICULAR PURPOSE.

8. **LIMITATION OF LIABILITY.** IN NO EVENT WILL GATEWAY, ITS SUPPLIERS OR LICENSORS, BE LIABLE FOR ANY INDIRECT, SPECIAL, INCIDENTAL, COVER O CONSEQUENTIAL DAMAGES ARISING OUT OF THE USE OF OR INABILITY TO USE THE SOFTWARE PRODUCT, USER DOCUMENTATION OR RELATED TECH SUPPORT, INCLUDING WITHOUT LIMITATION, DAMAGES OR COSTS RELATING TO THE LOSS OF PROFITS, BUSINESS, GOODWILL, DATA OR COMPUTER P EVEN IF ADVISED OF THE POSSIBILITY OF SUCH DAMAGES. IN NO EVENT WILL GATEWAY, ITS SUPPLIERS' OR LICENSORS' LIABILITY EXCEED THE AMO BY YOU FOR THE SOFTWARE PRODUCT. BECAUSE SOME JURISDICTIONS DO NOT ALLOW THE EXCLUSION OR LIMITATION OF LIABILITY FOR CONSEQ INCIDENTAL DAMAGES, THE ABOVE LIMITATION MAY NOT APPLY TO YOU.

9. **Miscellaneous.** This Agreement is governed by the laws of the United States and the State of South Dakota, without reference to conflicts of law principles. The ap United Nations Convention on Contracts for the International Sale of Goods is expressly excluded. This Agreement sets forth all rights for the user of the SOFTWAR and is the entire agreement between the parties. This Agreement supersedes any other communications with respect to the SOFTWARE PRODUCT and any assoc documentation. This Agreement may not be modified except by a written addendum issued by a duly authorized representative of Gateway. No provision hereof sh waived unless such waiver shall be in writing and signed by Gateway or a duly authorized representative of Gateway. If any provision of this Agreement is held inv remainder of this Agreement shall continue in full force and effect. The parties confirm that it is their wish that this Agreement has been written in the English langu